POINT, CLICK

& WoW!!

A Quick Guide to Brilliant Laptop Presentations

POINT, CLICK & WoW!!

A Quick Guide to Brilliant Laptop Presentations

Claudyne Wilder and David Fine

Pfeiffer
& COMPANY

Johannesburg · London
San Diego · Sydney · Toronto

Library of Congress Cataloging-in-Publication Data

Wilder, Claudyne
    Point, click, & wow! : a quick guide to brillant laptop presentations / Claudyne Wilder and David Fine
      p.   cm.
    Includes index.
    ISBN 0-88390-484-5 (pbk.)

    1. Business presentations—Graphic methods. 2. Multimedia systems in business presentations.   I. Fine, David, 1954- .
II. Title.   III. Title: Point, click, and wow!
HF5718.22.W55   1996
658.4'52—dc20   96-503
                                              CIP

Published by Pfeiffer & Company
8517 Production Avenue
San Diego, CA 92121-2280
United States of America

Editorial Offices: (619) 578-5900, FAX (619) 578-2042
Orders: USA (606) 647-3030, FAX (606) 647-3034

ISBN: 0-88390-484-5

Printing 10 9 8 7 6 5 4 3 2 1

Dedication

To our partners in life:
Helena who is the joy of my life.
Tad who dances with me through life.

Contents

Acknowledgement

We would like to thank the following people for giving freely of their time and ideas: Bob Amueller, Dennis Belcher, Carole Berkson, Brenda Besdansky, Mike Callahan, Nancy Cappuccio, William Daniels, Bobbi Dobbs, Robert E. Griffin, Steve Gorski, Sally Harrison, Roger Homer, Ann Marie Joyce, John Kelsey, Len Lastuck, Hong Lin, Russ Manthy, Mike Melko, Barry Mirrer, Cheryl Cornell-Powers, Michelle Price, Dana Shultz, Kathy Shiels, Barbara Stennes, Tom Silver, Nick Landholdt, Jim Neigh, Jim and Suzanne Delay, Bob Cooley, Tom Longo, and Bill Sobel. Special appreciation goes to Bob Weaver who encouraged, or rather insisted that Claudyne write this book.

Claudyne thanks Tad Jankowski, who cooked dinners and made her laugh so she could have the energy and enthusiasm for writing. Claudyne also thanks all the participants in her Presentations Kit Seminars for teaching her about the delights and perils of computer-generated presentations.

David thanks his colleagues—Wayne Mang, John Pelton, and Burt Weisner—for the opportunity to develop the knowledge and experience required to write this book. A special thanks goes to Helena, Benjamin, and Ariella Fine for their support, encouragement, and patience.

We also thank Bill Pfeiffer who took the time to discuss the book. JoAnn Padgett, our editor and main Pfeiffer contact has been fantastic. She encouraged us, gave us support, and graciously sent faxes with excellent ideas. She's a dear human being as well as a smart editor. Thanks also to Dawn Kilgore, who did a masterful job of managing the production and electronic preparation of this book, and to Susan Odelson, who created a brilliant cover and graphic design for our book.

INTRODUCTION

Many of my clients are using the laptop computer in all aspects of their sales effort. They want advice on how to effectively incoporate this powerful tool into their presentations.

Cheryl Cornell-Powers,
Powers and Associates

The competition is using multimedia presentations to present to our customers and we want to know how to do it.

Jim Delay,
Syntax-The Word Company

Now that the benchmark is computerized presentations, employees have an excellent opportunity to learn to give computer-generated updates.

Ann Marie Joyce
The Gillette Company

Today more and more businesses are using electronic equipment to make presentations, yet those given the task aren't always sure what to do or how to do it. As companies make greater and greater capital investments in presentation technology, employees often end up struggling to use it properly.

That's why we wrote this book—to enable businesspeople, especially salespeople, to effectively and creatively use this new technology to communicate better.

Three themes run through this book:

❶ *Be judicious with the new presentation technology.* It offers all types of exciting features that can easily do more harm than good if misapplied. In many companies, everyone who makes presentations is expected to create visuals on a computer. It is now a "user made" world, with users having access to a wider range of fancy presentation tools than ever before. It is often fun to apply clip art, builds, colors, and other multimedia features. However, without some basic guidelines and design skills, presenters can end up with a visual feast of pictures and graphics that dazzle the audience but blur the key messages. People will walk out saying "I really liked the graphics and motion—I wonder what software program they used. But what was the point she was trying to make?"

❷ *You are still the message.* People must buy you as well as your fancy presentation. Effective communication skills are one of the most important requirements for job success. If you are relaxed using the new technology, you will come across as a personable, sincere presenter. This book is designed for every person who wants to become comfortable with electronic presenting. That includes sales managers, sales representatives, trainers, department/division heads, consultants, investor relations officers, purchasing managers, and company presidents.

❸ *Learn the technology.* We want to help people who are now comfortable with laptop computers to learn how to marry their computers to display technology. This book provides practical guidelines, tips, and checklists for giving compelling electronic presentations. Even if you have access to an expert at all times you still need to learn some basic skills, and you need to know the key questions to ask your technical people and the audiovisual staff at hotels and conference centers where you present.

When you apply the design and technology suggestions in this book, you will boost the impact of your presentations. For a more complete review of how to develop a successful presentation, we suggest *The Presentations Kit: 10 Steps for Selling Your Ideas!* by Claudyne Wilder (John Wiley & Sons).

The Advantages of Electronic Presentations

Sales of electronic presentation equipment are soaring, with annual growth rates of 25 to 50 percent. The reason is clear. Electronic presentations offer a number of advantages:

➤ The ease of making changes lets a presenter tailor a presentation to the audience.

➤ Visual effects such as text builds, sequences that simulate motion, video clips, and sound effects maintain audience attention. The results can be a more lasting impression and a greater retention of the message.

➤ Flexibility to alter the sequencing introduces a nonlinear, interactive element. The presenter can get the audience actively involved in the presentation.

➤ The sophistication of the presentation gives the presenter an image of being technologically advanced.

➤ Smooth transitions from one slide to the next maintain continuity and increase audience comprehension.

➤ The presenter can take the audience on tours of on-line catalogs, Internet sites, or databases.

With these potential advantages also come risks. The temptation is to use many of these new tools and features simply because they are there. The history of personal computers is filled with technology eagerly misapplied! For this reason, a strong theme running throughout this book is to *use the new presentation tools only when they genuinely enhance the messages you are conveying.*

People Respond to Information, Not Data

Imagine that your 10-year-old son comes home from school and tells you he scored 82 percent on his math test. How do you react? Do you congratulate him enthusiastically? Or do you express some other view?

Although your son has shared some raw data, it is not useful information on which to base a decision. If he goes on to tell you that the class average was 89 percent and that only three kids got less than 85 percent, the information starts to become useful. If he adds that he studied extensively for the test but was feeling ill on the day it was given, this information adds a whole new perspective to the situation. You are now emotionally involved and even moved by his story. The additional data provide a perspective that is dimensions above the initial 82 percent data point he provided. If he had told his story with visuals, such as charts and pictures, he could have made a highly effective presentation.

Quite frequently, however, we see presentations with fancy screens used to glorify the communication of raw data, such as the 82 percent math score. After seeing tables filled with numbers, people walk out of such presentations asking, "What did all that mean?"

The world around us is awash in raw data; people don't know what to do with it. They want information that enables them to make decisions. The visual framework in Figure Intro.1 depicts four levels of communication, from the most basic form of conveying data to the higher level of achieving understanding. This framework highlights the communication challenge: to use these powerful new presentation tools not merely to regurgitate raw data in fancy visuals, but to convert data into higher-level communication that will stir your audience and trigger a response.

When you stir viewers' emotions and entertain them in the process, their retention will be higher and your presentation's impact much greater. Your audience will be more willing to commit to action and support you and your presentation recommendation.

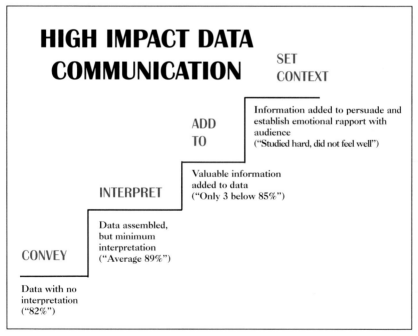

Figure Intro.1 High Impact Data Communication

POINT, CLICK & *WoW!!*

1

REMEMBER, YOUR AUDIENCE IS HUMAN

"Don't act like a machine even if you use one!"

You or your company may have spent a fortune on buying fancy electronic equipment and on creating exciting presentation screens. But it is not the equipment that counts—it is your audience and your relationship with them. Don't give a mechanical, robotlike presentation. Relax! You need to be a living and breathing person up there in front of everyone. Show your humanness, and your audience will like you. When you think of your audience first, your preparation and delivery will be authentic. Your audience will react favorably if they sense you have put some thought into caring about their interests. Keep this in mind as you present: "First and always I must establish and keep rapport with the audience. It is me they have come to see and hear, not my fancy computer presentation."

In this chapter you will begin to put yourself in your audience's shoes and create a presentation for them. You will also consider how to personalize a talk.

Think About Your Audience

Many people are afraid to present. They stand in front of an audience truly believing that the audience dislikes them and wants them to do poorly. They are uncomfortable thinking of themselves as the center of attention. They give the impression of wanting to get the talk done as fast as possible. Such people liked to do slide shows because the room was dark and they thought (incorrectly) that how they talked and acted didn't really count, since the focus was on the slides. With the advent of overheads, presenters actually had to look at the audience and realize that people were paying attention to them. This was difficult for many people. One reason is that very few presenters rehearse their talk out loud before the actual presentation. Because they have no idea how they will sound or what specifically they will say about the visuals, they have a right to be nervous.

Now that electronic presentations are being given in dark rooms again, nervous presenters are happy. They think nothing counts but their creative laptop slide show. They believe that fancy laptop presentations preclude a need to connect with the audience personally. They believe the visuals will convince the audience of their sincerity, true interest, and desire to know each of them as individuals. They also think that the sophisticated graphics, gorgeous colors, and incredible effects will convince the audience that their products or ideas are the best in the business. Not true.

Nothing takes the place of a sincere, compassionate presenter who really cares about the audience and their response to the presentation. *The computer is only a tool to enable communication.* You, as the presenter still have to communicate using your voice, your body, and the positive energy that you send to your audience. Yes, it is great to have a creative laptop presentation. But if you show no true interest in your audience, you won't get far. This interest comes from your heart and your desire to truly meet your audience's needs. Because the visuals can sometimes be overpowering, you have to work harder to let your audience members know you care about them and about your subject. In particular, you have to work on your voice. Your voice must sound confident and enthusiastic, and you must pause at the end of your sentences so your audience can digest what you have just said. Also, if you are in a dark room, you need to spend some time with the lights on. Your audience must see you and your gestures, or else all they will remember about you is your voice.

Following are three major keys to giving a sincere talk that will maintain your audience's interest.

Care About Your Audience

No one can make you act gracious and pleasant toward your audience. This is your job and your job alone. Your audience needs to feel that you care about them. When you focus more on the audience than yourself, you will find that you are also less nervous. You are no longer the focus. When you make your audience center stage and work on keeping them happy and comfortable listening to you, they will respond in kind. Audiences can feel your positive energy.

Here are some behaviors to avoid and preferable ones to use instead.

❶ *Don't read the information and be done with it.* When all you do is read your visuals word for word, you're not adding anything. If you believe that the most important thing is to give all this information to your audience, if you are convinced they don't need to hear an interested vocal tone or a well-modulated voice, if you think they don't need to know that you are excited about the topic, you will be disappointed in your results.

      Do say more than the few words on the screen. Display just a few words at a time so you can look at your audience and use your voice and passion to convey information not listed on the screen. You want people to focus on what you are saying as you add valuable information to what is being shown.

❷ *Don't stick to your standard, off-the-shelf presentation.* A recent incident highlights this pitfall. One of the authors went with a colleague to give a two-day course to a nonprofit agency. On arrival, we were told that the course could only be one day. I suggested we cover the key elements of the course. My colleague thought we should just do the material for the first day. She didn't think about modifying it to meet the needs of the audience. In her mind we had created the seminar one way and it would be given that way no matter what the situation. Many presenters do this; they never stop to modify the talk based on their audience's needs. In theory, the whole point of giving a laptop presentation is that it is easy to customize even until the last moment. Yet many presenters simply don't bother.

Do tailor your presentations to your audience. The talk you give to the executive committee won't be the same as the one to peers in your department. Each audience is looking for a different type of information and level of detail. Put people's and companies' names on the screens. This shows you care enough to include them in your talk. Include the names on multiple screens, not just one. Take time during the talk to find out about your audience's expertise and interests. Put questions for your audience on a screen so you won't forget to ask them. This is especially important if you weren't able to learn much about your audience before the presentation.

❸ *Don't talk about what interests you and ignore what interests the audience.* One group of technical specialists were asked to make a presentation to top management. They included all the interesting (to them) technical data. They overwhelmed these executives with their world of details. Not only did the executives not have time to listen to all the details, they were frustrated because they could not fully grasp ramifications of these details for the company.

Do consider your audience and what they would like to know. In the above example the executives wanted to know such things as whether the trends in manufacturing goods were going up or down, how the proposed project would help with cost reduction, and so on, rather than the minutia about the project. You can find people who know about your audience's interests. Ask them. Force yourself to leave out the details that are not high priority for that particular audience.

❹ *Don't consider every question as being from an adversary.* Suppose that as you start off your presentation, someone asks you a simple question. You realize that you should have included that information in your screens, but didn't. You decide the person is hostile and out to make you look incompetent. You are gruff with your answers for the rest of the presentation. You could have enjoyed the talk, but you made it unpleasant for everyone.

Do think that people who ask you questions are genuinely interested. People who ask questions are usually the most keen and attentive participants. And keep in mind, someone can question your ideas and still think you have done a fine presentation.

❺ *Don't believe you will get all the time you want or were told you will have.* Suppose your audience has been sitting all day, and now you are the last speaker. You go on too long. You never rehearsed the talk out loud to test how long it would really take. If you keep going, you show lack of consideration for your audience. Being last in a day's program, you should have known you would not get your full time. For your allotted hour, you should have made your talk only 45 minutes and then planned how to cut it to 25 minutes if needed.

Do find out if you will really get all the time you are told you will have. Think more about your audience than yourself. If they are tired, cut down your talk. If they need a stretch, cut down your talk by 5 minutes and let them stretch. They will appreciate it.

Make the Graphics Friendly

Presenters like to take pride in the fancy, colored, bells-and-whistles presentations they've put together. This is especially the case if they've spent days making it. They want to show off their "baby." To some extent this is acceptable, but keep in mind that whether or not you have a fancy presentation, you still have to talk. And you have to talk to your audience. Your audience is first. Keep your attention and enthusiasm directed toward them.

To keep yourself mindful of the audience's reaction to your talk, here are some don'ts and dos.

❶ *Don't use the wildest template you can find.* Suppose you are bored with the templates you have been using. So you pick a lavender background with circular shapes on it for your presentation to convince the management committee to give you $50,000 more for your project. The management committee members can't figure out how your subject fits with the bizarre template they see on the screen. There is dissonance among your project, the money you want, and the lavender and circular designs they are seeing. Maybe they can't tie their resistance to the template, but they are becoming concerned about giving you the money.

  Do remember the best screen is sometimes the simplest. Use a template that will appeal to your audience and that is appropriate for your subject. Think about what style appeals to them. You may need to change your templates, not the presentation content, depending on the audience.

❷ *Don't get so enthralled with the beautiful graphics and special effects that you lose sight of your message.* You have made the slickest, most up-to-date presentation. You even paid someone to include video clips, and you've added fancy arrows moving all kinds of ways on the screen. It looks fantastic. You know no one will be bored with your talk. They will really have to keep their eyes open to see everything you have included. There is only one problem. The audience becomes so entranced with the graphics and special effects that they don't get the message. They walk away saying to each other, "Wasn't that exciting? I've got to get that graphics package." Not only has the message of your talk been lost, but the audience never got an opportunity to experience you as a person. You took no time to let the audience get a sense of you as the presenter. You hardly introduced yourself before the talk and you closed with a dark room showing an animated visual. The audience will remember the graphics, but you as a sincere presenter, focused on a key objective, never got across.

Do keep your message center stage, not the graphics. Keep reminding yourself to create the screens around your central objective. And, at least at the beginning and end of your talk, you should be center stage, with the lights on high.

❸ *Don't organize the data in a haphazard manner.* You may have beautiful visuals, but they won't have much meaning without structure. If the material is presented in a stream-of-consciousness style, if you have not organized the data in any logical sequence, your audience will feel frustrated that you did not take the time to present the information in such a way that they could easily follow it.

Do organize the data! All forms of communication need to have some kind of structure to be effective. Over three-fourths of the presentations that we see are not organized, and even more are not organized to appeal to the audience—they are organized to appeal to the presenter! Claudyne Wilder's book, *The Presentations Kit,* offers 10 formats to use to organize data.

Become Familiar with the Technology

You need to spend time (usually your own time) learning everything you can to give a competent presentation without technical delays or mishaps. Your audience will wonder how sincere and interested you are in their well-being if you make them wait for half an hour because you didn't take the time to learn what you really should know. And they don't care if your company didn't give you the time.

❶ *Don't use software programs you are unfamiliar with.* You may be in front of your audience and know that the program is not working, but not know what to do to fix the problem. It may be that someone else produced the presentation or that you have minimal experience with this software program. Finally, you're saved. Someone in the audience gets up and shows you what to do. It's hard for people to take you and your topic seriously if you can't even run the software package.

Do learn the software program. Take a class. See a video. Read a book. Practice on your own. Some software training numbers are listed in the back of this book in the Resources Section. Learn the program now!

❷ *Don't use unfamiliar equipment.* Here you are trying to sell people a product and you can't even get the equipment to work. How good can you be? How good can your company's customer service be if they send out people who can't run some simple equipment? These are some of the thoughts that run through your viewers minds. Is that the kind of impression you want to make?

Do make someone teach you how to run the equipment. Find out about some of the trouble spots that can occur with the equipment and know what to do. Find someone who has been using the equipment for a while and ask what has gone wrong. You owe it to yourself and your audience to be able to make it work.

Personalize the Talk

Audiences love to feel part of the presentation. They become more involved and retain more of what you say. They also realize that you spent some time thinking about them before the presentation.

Here is an idea on how to personalize a talk. Claudyne was asked to give a talk on values and goals to a team of about 15 people. Before the talk, she called 10 people to find out about everyone on the team. She gathered comments about each person. First, she put the team name on every screen. Then she put everyone's name on different screens during the talk. They loved seeing their names come up on the screen. This approach was especially effective, since the concepts and ideas were not especially new but were being reemphasized. Having people's names on the visuals added some excitement and interest to the concepts.

To maintain the magic of people seeing their names come on the screen, participants received handouts of the screens after the talk. Figures 1.1 and 1.2 show examples of the screens. For the "My Values and Goals" screen, Claudyne showed both the boat and Bill's name at the same time. This got a good laugh from people who knew how much Bill liked to fish.

Some other ways people personalize their talks include: 1) Using up-to-the-minute data. Top management likes to know the very latest information and trends. 2) Putting the customer's name in the presentation in more than one place. 3) Speaking only to the needs of the audience. The focus would change from one presentation to another, even though the basic information stays the same. For example, the management committee wants to hear what is being done to reverse a negative trend whereas the technical people want to hear the details and process issues surrounding the negative trend. 4) Showing photos and giving examples that directly relate to those companies represented in the audience.

My Values & Goals

The Best Team

- Family, health, financial, security, helping, compassion, travel
  - David: Stay in one place
  - Beth: Getting the job done with style
  - Bill: Fish as much as possible

Figure 1.1 My Values & Goals

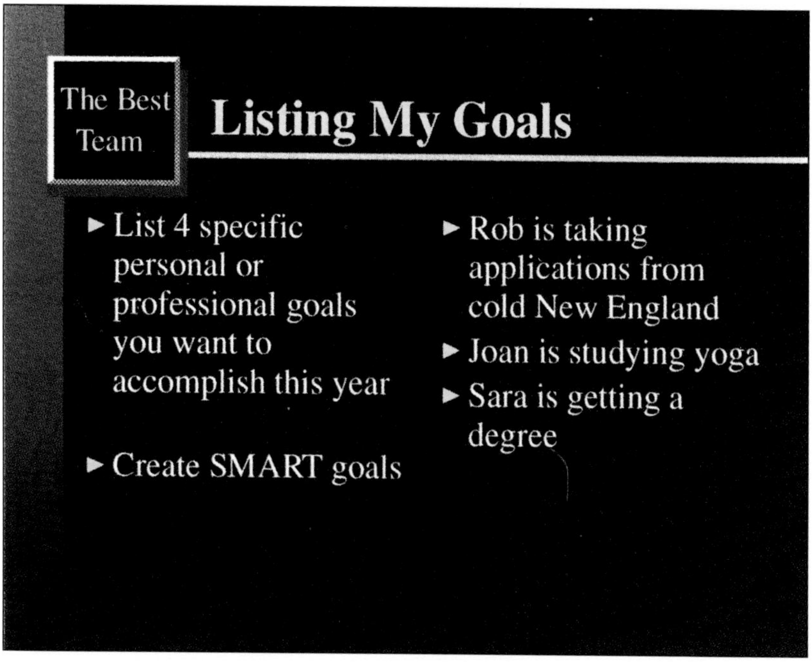

Listing My Goals

The Best Team

- ► List 4 specific personal or professional goals you want to accomplish this year

- ► Create SMART goals

- ► Rob is taking applications from cold New England
- ► Joan is studying yoga
- ► Sara is getting a degree

Figure 1.2 Listing My Goals

Here are some additional ideas for how to personalize talks:

*People don't want canned presentations anymore.
Now we do our homework. We ask our potential
customers these types of questions. What do you want
to hear about the equipment? What level of detail
about the system do you want to hear? Then we
either add in or take out some of the information.*

Len Lastuck, Rainmaster

*I spontaneously share personal experiences to illustrate
key points, and invite participants to do the same.
They usually do.*

Russ Manthy, King's View Consulting

*I personalize my presentations through the use of a
preprogram questionnaire of one-on-one interviews.
To get the audience's attention, I open with a
well-known song—but I change the lyrics to fit the
audience's background and the presentation topic.*

Dana H. Schultz, Dana Shultz & Associates

*I teach people to immediately establish a personal
relationship with the audience. They can do this
by interacting with the audience by opening
with a personal story and through the use of
eye contact and open gestures.*

Brenda Besdansky, Speaker's World

13

Design
the
Flow

Can't we go all these places at once?

An effective presentation has a flow to it. Regardless of content, the audience connects to the information at the beginning, processes the content through the middle of the talk, and feels ready to hear the conclusion at the end. To create this flow, a presenter must organize material around a central idea, make the presentation lively and vital, and keep the technology running. In this chapter we give you ideas on how to do those things, as well as how to set up the flow for a customer conference and how to launch a company initiative.

Organize Around an Objective

Although the focus of this book is not on organizing a presentation, we are including a small section because so few presenters organize their material around one key objective. A logical flow is invaluable for audience comprehension. If you skip from one unrelated point to another, the audience will wonder in frustration, "How does this fit together?" Sophisticated technology loses its value when the presentation screens don't point toward the objective.

You should have only one clear, concise objective for a presentation. You may have other underlying goals you wish to accomplish, but you need to specify one overall objective *before* you start making the presentation. This objective comes from the answers to these two questions: What does my audience want from my talk? What do I want to give my audience? By discussing the answers to these questions with knowledgeable people, you can arrive at the main point of the talk.

Here's an example that highlights the need to focus on only one objective. Tan is an expert in water filtration. He has studied it for years. He has been asked by a salesperson to give a technical talk to a customer. Tan starts to prepare his talk. He makes fancy graphs and charts to show the filtration system. He has worked on this system for years and prides himself in being a technical expert. He builds a water filtration system on the screen, and the visuals are impressive. He has included all the small technical details he personally considers important.

His objective, by looking at all his visuals, *is to share all the nitty-gritty details of the water filtration system.* Unfortunately, that is not the objective the salesperson has in mind. The salesperson's objective for Tan's talk is *to sell the benefits with a little bit of technical information included to support the benefits.* Tan would have made a very different presentation if he had spent some time discussing the objective with the salesperson. This type of situation happens all the time between salespeople and technical experts. It is solvable when they agree on the objective and the presentation is then created around that objective.

Another situation in which this sharing of too much technical information occurs is when salespeople are brought in from the field to learn about new products. They usually hear all the technical information about the product, with very little emphasis on benefits for the customer. The real objective of a product update or release presentation to salespeople should be *to prepare them to sell the product and not to give them every bit of product knowledge that exists.* The presentations and presentation handouts should be created and built around that objective.

The presentation objective gets even more lost within all the incredible and exciting technology. Let's examine a company that is selling its mutual funds to clients. The presentation is stunning, with lots of colors flowing on the screen. The talk is full of key information to these potential clients. But the agenda points are lost in the quick transitions and fancy graphics. These are clients who are not familiar with mutual funds. They might want to invest but wonder whether the process is too complicated. So what are they shown? A complicated, colorful, detailed presentation. The message is not one of simplicity or ease of buying.

If the presentation is supposed to motivate people to buy, the objective needs *to be to show how simple it is to invest.* This objective now determines the way the presentation will be designed. It is too bad the person who made the gorgeous presentation never had to stand up and experience its effect on the audience. If the person had to do so a few times, he or she might make it easier to look at, easier to give, and easier to understand.

The Solution Format

The Presentations Kit by Claudyne Wilder provides 10 formats for organizing. We've adapted one of these formats, which we call the Solution Format. In this instance we're using the Solution Format to sell upper management on the idea of investing in effective presentation equipment. (We'd like to thank Bill Sobel of Whirlpool for the subject idea of this presentation.)

First you see the solution format overview (Figure 2.1). Next you see the colored overheads that follow this format (Figures 2.2 through 2.9). Imagine how to use builds to display the information. Of course, you don't use builds on every screen. For example, you could show all the requirements at the same time.

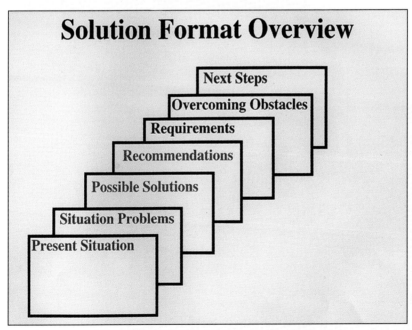

Figure 2.1 Solution Format Overview

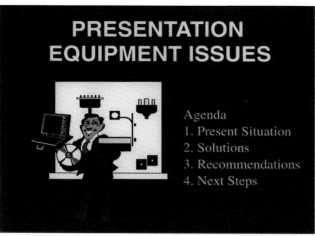

Figure 2.2 Presentation Equipment Issues

PRESENT SITUATION

1. **Use hotel presentation equipment**
   - Request equipment by phone
   - Send follow-up request fax
   - Test equipment a few hours before
2. **Take our laptops**
3. **Carry cables just-in-case**
4. **Make presentation**

Figure 2.3 Present Situation

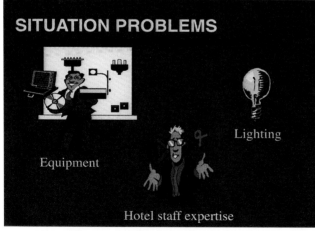

Figure 2.4 Situation Problems

POSSIBLE SOLUTIONS

Options	Implications
1. Keep doing what doing	→ Unreliable equipment
2. Use only key hotels	→ Impossible
3. Order equipment from AV company	→ Cost, logistics, trust factor
4. Acquire own equipment	→ Flexibility & reliability

Figure 2.5 Possible Solutions

RECOMMENDATIONS

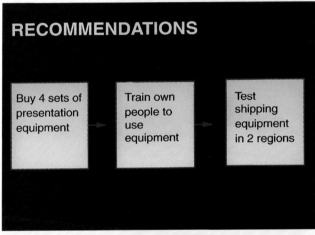

Figure 2.6 Recommendations

REQUIREMENTS

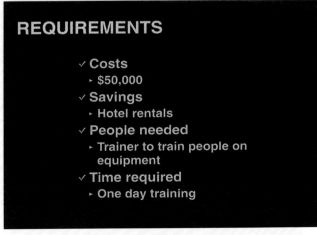

Figure 2.7 Requirements

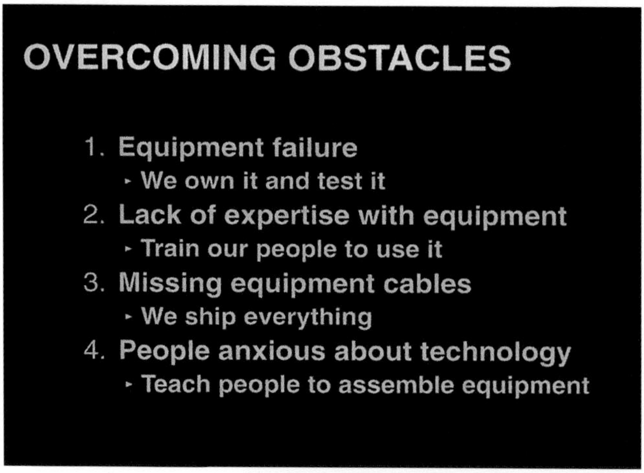

OVERCOMING OBSTACLES
1. Equipment failure
We own it and test it
2. Lack of expertise with equipment
Train our people to use it
3. Missing equipment cables
We ship everything
4. People anxious about technology
Teach people to assemble equipment

Figure 2.8 Overcoming Obstacles

NEXT STEPS
1. Choose vendor for equipment
2. Buy equipment
3. Set up equipment training days
4. Assign expert to be on call
5. Monitor costs

Figure 2.9 Next Steps

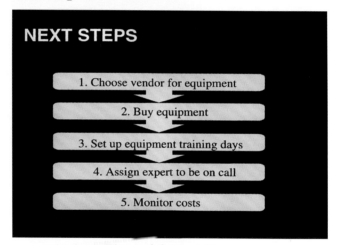

The Presentation Flow

You need to integrate your electronic presentation into the total presentation you are giving. The electronic presentation is part of your "presentation," not all of it. You can't just push the buttons, thank the audience, and leave. Figure 2.10 shows a flow chart for almost any presentation.

This is how you would use the flow chart to give a sales presentation to a small group of 20 people. You would start without the laptop on, asking your audience some questions to hear their concerns and interests. Before starting your electronic presentation, you would tell your audience when to ask questions. If it is a 10-minute talk, you would probably go straight through it. If it is 30 minutes you may stop partway through to ask some questions that assess your audience's reaction to the information. At this point, you can turn the lights up so people can see you. The lights help wake people up if they've gotten sleepy.

You would end the electronic presentation with the lights on high. You, not the electronic media, end at center stage. You should have saved enough time to encourage your audience to discuss their reactions and to discuss the next steps you or they will be taking.

When you are doing almost any presentation, the same dynamics apply. Don't just turn on your media and start. Establish rapport with your audience first. End with enough time left to establish rapport with your audience again. Let them see you, hear you, and feel your energy and sincerity.

Hint: If you are afraid you will forget your opening and closing lines, put them on a sheet of paper with large bullets. You can look down to remind yourself of what you want to say next. The key is to have the points very large so you only have to glance down briefly.

YOU AND ELECTRONIC MEDIA

Open without electronic media

You always want to be center stage before you start showing your visuals. Just make sure the screen is blank as you open the talk. People should only be looking at you as you begin the presentation.

Stop media in the middle to break up presentation

Give the presentation.
If possible part way through the presentation stop the visuals, turn up the lights and take questions. This changes the pace and wakes people up.

Close without electronic media

You always want to close without a visual. You need to be center stage at the end of the talk.

Figure 2.10 You and Electronic Media

Finally, take heed of advice from Carole Berkson, the vice-president of Luminare: "You are there for the audience. You have something they want. Make sure your prepared presentation doesn't prevail over the needs of the audience."

Keep focused on saying what's important for the audience to walk away with. If partway through your talk you realize that the flow you created before your talk is not going to work, change it. Humanness and honesty should prevail over continuing a presentation that is not made for your audience. Be flexible. Change the flow, the order, the dynamics if you sense that would meet your audience's needs.

The Plot-Point Theory of Organizing

Claudyne watched a colleague give a beautiful one-hour presentation that included gorgeous pictures from around the world. After about 30 minutes, she started to get tired. When it was over, she talked about her tiredness to a colleague who writes movies for television. The colleague explained what the plot points are in a movie and suggested that the presenter needed to include some plot points.

What are plot points? They are the two pivotal moments in a television film script. Plot Point One always occurs 20 to 30 minutes into the film and starts the major action of the movie. Something unexpected occurs to the hero and galvanizes him or her toward a goal. Plot Point Two occurs about 70 minutes into the film when it appears that the hero is beaten. At this point an event occurs that causes everything to change with the hero. The hero's goal becomes reachable. These plot points keep the audience awake with eyes glued to the screen.

How can you apply this idea of plot points to a presentation? Let's start first with your graphics. Don't use all your fancy bells and whistles during the first few minutes. You may have the capability to use wonderful graphics with sound and even some video clips, but you don't need to hit the audience with everything at the beginning of your talk. Hold off until about 15 minutes into the presentation. Then add sound for Plot Point One. Or change the way you are presenting the information from builds to showing all the data at once. Save the video clips to use for Plot Point Two, or change the color of the screen to match a change in topics or products (this might be after 30 minutes of talking).

Your talk is unlikely to be as long as a movie. But if it is, you really need to include some changes. Don't change every screen. Do consider how to maintain your audience's interest by varying the pace and design of the presentation screens. Take advantage of presentation variety: color, sound, movement, pictures, style, and design.

What other types of plot points can you create? Even the act of turning up the lights and taking questions during the talk will change the dynamics in the room.

Movies also offer the concept of a tag line. This is a single line repeated again and again in a variety of ways. If you have some type of theme throughout your talk, at each of your plot-point changes you can do a visual or sound "tag line." You could show a visual image slightly different each time, use words in some creative manner, or do something yourself instead of showing a visual.

Consider these four points as you design
your presentation's flow:

➤ Finally, you're it. How will you establish rapport with your audience? How do you want to end so your audience is motivated to take action?

➤ First, be clear and agree with everyone on your one objective.

➤ Second, use a format to organize the talk. This saves you time and it also makes it easier for your audience to follow your talk.

➤ Third, apply the plot point theory from the movies. Create the presentation in such a way that after a certain amount of time it varies and changes by look, shape, sound, feel etc. This keeps the audience engaged.

Technology Issues

The technological aspect of electronic presentations need not be intimidating. A computer presentation in its simplest form is a series of overheads or slides that introduce a sense of movement not possible in a "static" overhead presentation. All the dos and don'ts for designing, organizing, and delivering effective overhead or 35mm slide presentations apply equally to computer slide shows.

In this section we will start by looking at the unique aspects of a computer presentation compared with an overhead or slide presentation. We will then review the equipment options so you can consider your needs.

What Is Different About Electronic Presentations?

When we cut through the mystique that in some people's minds surrounds computer presentations, they are really quite simple. A computer-driven presentation is different from a static overhead or slide presentation in only three ways:

❶ *You now need a computer in order to make the presentation.* A laptop is preferable but not essential. You also need a presentation software program. The more popular programs are Microsoft PowerPoint, Freelance Graphics from Lotus, Harvard Graphics from Software Publishing, and the higher-level multimedia programs such as Gold Disk's Astound.

❷ *You need to learn how to use the "movement" features.* Transitions between slides, builds, and moving charts are all entertainment features that help hold the attention of the audience. More advanced computer presentations can include video clips and sound. A dynamic computer presentation can significantly boost the retention level of the audience. *A word of caution:* Many novice computer presenters are tempted to include all types of transitions, builds, and other special effects into presentations just as soon as they learn them. The result is predictable: a colorful, dynamic presentation that is poorly choreographed and that detracts from the core messages. The audience leaves confused about the objective or so excited about the graphics that they have missed the messages.

❸ *You need to do more equipment planning.* The third difference becomes an issue for audiences bigger than about three to five people. For small audiences up to five, the easiest approach is to either use your laptop screen (for one to two people) or to connect your PC to a color monitor, which can be borrowed from a nearby workstation. For larger audiences the equipment options are greater and depend on the size of the audience, the importance of the presentation, and the budget.

Equipment planning includes compatibility planning. If you are using someone else's equipment, be sure it is compatible with yours. For example, you may bring your presentation on disk only to find that the software program on site is the wrong version or that the equipment doesn't have enough memory to run your presentation. You may have to save your presentation in several different formats. Ask very specific questions to be sure you can use the other person's equipment. Leave yourself adequate time for rehearsing, to be sure all of the versions and equipment work together. For example, a PowerPoint presentation built with Windows 95 may not work with Windows 3.1.

POINT, CLICK & *WOW!!*

Questions for Choosing the Best Equipment for You

Gary Vicari, Vice-President of Computer, Video Projection Products and Presentation Products at Apollo says that here are some general questions you need to answer as you consider what type of equipment to buy.

❶ Will you be doing mobile or stationary presentations?

❷ What will be the size of most audiences?

❸ How often will you be presenting?

❹ What are your technical resources within the company? Are there presentation equipment experts?

❺ Will the same person giving the presentation be creating the visuals?

❻ In what format(s) are the electronic output?

What Is the Best Equipment to Use in Each Situation?

Three factors determine the best equipment for a particular situation:

❶ Size of audience—Is it small, medium, or large?

❷ Darkness of room—If the room cannot be substantially darkened, as the older models of LCD panels must be ruled out.

❸ Budget—The best setup for big audiences is the popular three-gun color projection unit, but it is also the most costly to rent.

Following is a set of six guidelines for equipment options. They show the best setup arrangements for various audience sizes, gradation of room darkness, and budget sizes.

Audiences are grouped in three categories:

Options 1 & 2: Small (1-10 people): One-on-one or small-group meetings with employees, customers, investors, bankers, potential customers

Options 3, 4 & 5: Medium (10-50 people): Presentations to groups of customers or potential customers, suppliers, employees, investors; training presentations; presentations to groups of in-company people on project status or proposals for capital expenditures and new initiatives

Options 6: Large (50-500 people): Customers, shareholders at annual meetings, investors at conferences, road shows, supplier gatherings, employee meetings

Don't get frustrated.

"Where's that @*!?* Cable?"

Follow these equipment guidelines.

Option 1: Laptop Screen
Small Audience (1-2 People)

Presentation Equipment Needed and Equipment Warnings	General Tips and Comments
WHAT YOU NEED: • Laptop with presentation loaded on it • Mouse you are comfortable using **WARNINGS:** • Sit next to person viewing screen, not opposite • Make sure viewer can see screen clearly. Some screens are not clear if viewed from an angle	• Have viewers directly in front of screen • Use arrow in program to highlight points

Option 2: Desktop or TV Monitor
Small Audience (2-10 People)

Presentation Equipment Needed and Equipment Warnings	General Tips and Comments
WHAT YOU NEED: • Color desktop or TV monitor connected to laptop set on meeting table • Mouse you are comfortable using **WARNINGS:** • Make sure someone knows how to set up the equipment and it's compatible with your equipment	• Provide a hard copy to allow the audience to take notes on it • Use arrow in program to highlight points • Make sure everyone can really see the screen • If the TV monitor is very large, could have audience of 20

Figure 2.11 shows a presentation using the laptop screen to display the visuals. Key points to note are:

➤ Both individuals are seated next to each other and share the screen. This is more effective than sitting across from each other.

➤ This approach is more of a dialogue than a presentation. It encourages interaction.

➤ It is important to check ahead of time that the visuals (especially the type size) are large enough to see clearly on a laptop screen. You may need to enlarge them.

➤ This setup is ideal for one-on-one dialogues.

➤ The presenter can sit off to the side. The "audience" of one sits directly in front of the screen.

Figure 2.11 One-on-One Laptop Presentations

POINT, CLICK & WOW!!

Option 3: LCD Panel
Medium Audience (10-50 People)

Presentation Equipment Needed and Equipment Warnings	General Tips and Comments

WHAT YOU NEED:
 	
• Laptop with presentation loaded on it
 	
• LCD panel, screen 4" x 6" or bigger, overhead projector; this overhead projector must be lit from the bottom
 	
• Lavaliere wireless microphone for large group
 	
• Table next to LCD for PC or laptop to sit on
 	
• Powerstrip and extension cord to accommodate overhead, LCD, and PC
 	
• Pointer and remote mouse
 	
WARNINGS:
 	
• Room must be very dark when using older LCD panels.
 	
• Use 400-watt (4,000 to 6,000 lumens) or superpowerful overhead projector. Be sure you have a spare light bulb.
 	
• Tell audio-visual people you need overhead for an LCD panel. Be specific. Make them check the light bulb ahead of time. Personally check it when you arrive.
	• Provide handouts for the audience to take notes (if appropriate).
	
	• LCD panels can easily be rented. These used to be the most common way of delivering computer presentations.
	
	• Two biggest risks with LCD panels:
	  1. Room cannot be darkened sufficiently — check ahead.
	  2. Overhead not sufficiently powerful — insist on powerful one and check ahead.
	  —need 4,000 to 6,000 lumens.
	
	• If speaker needs notes, use podium. Make sure it has separate small light for reading. Ensure light does not reflect onto screen.
	
	• Portable, clip-on microphones are the best, even if using podium.
	
	• LCD panels can be used for audiences as large as 100 people, but clarity of visuals diminishes with bigger screens and bigger audiences.
	
	• Begin with the lights raised and screen blank; end with the lights raised for question period.

Option 4: Portable Projection System
Medium Audience (10-50 People)

Presentation Equipment Needed and Equipment Warnings	General Tips and Comments
WHAT YOU NEED: • Laptop with presentation loaded on it • Projection unit, screen 4" x 6" or bigger • Lavaliere wireless microphone for large group • Table next to projection system for PC or laptop to sit on • Powerstrip and extension cord to accommodate projection system and PC • Pointer and remote mouse **WARNINGS:** • Room must be dark, but with newer models not as dark • No commercial. Check to be sure that the name of the company that made the unit does not appear on screen when presentation ends. • Be sure you have spare bulb for projection system	• This new generation of projectors are alternatives to the LCD panel. • Substantially brighter than an LCD panel, do not need as dark a room. • May cost more to rent than an LCD panel. • Provide handouts for the audience to take notes (if appropriate). • If speaker needs notes, use podium, make sure it has separate small light for reading. • If no podium, place a box on top of table for speaker's notes so speaker doesn't have to look down at notes. • Ensure one of the room lights does not reflect on to the screen. • Portable, clip-on microphones are the best, even if using podium • Begin with the lights raised and screen blank; end with the lights raised for question period.

Figure 2.12 shows a presenter using a portable projection system in a hotel conference room. The audience (not shown) is comprised of 50 people seated at round tables. Like most presentations, compromises and accommodations are required. For example, the ideal setup would be rear projection onto the screen—but the room was not large enough. Key points are:

➤ The presenter faces the audience, not the screen. He uses a remote mouse, which provides freedom to move around.

➤ He looks at the laptop screen, which is set up on a table in front of him. This allows him to face the audience rather than look at the screen.

➤ The speaker uses a portable microphone connected to his lapel.

➤ He stands to the left of the screen, which makes it easier on the eye to look from him to the screen and then read the visuals from left to right.

Figure 2.12 Portable Projection System

Option 5: Color Monitor
Medium Audience (10-50 People)

Presentation Equipment Needed and Equipment Warnings	General Tips and Comments
WHAT YOU NEED: • Laptop with presentation loaded on it and monitor from 26" to 37" in size • Interface to connect PC to TV monitor • Lavaliere wireless microphone for a larger group • Table next to monitor for PC or laptop to sit on • Powerstrip and extension cord to accommodate monitor and PC • Pointer and remote mouse **WARNINGS:** • You may need to modify presentation inserting bigger font size. Arrive early to test equipment and you must be able to fix presentation yourself • Check for reflection of light through windows at certain viewing angles. Close blinds or curtains • Screen colors and size always need fine-tuning. Ensure technician delivering rented monitor connects it to PC and tests it.	• Large monitors can be rented. • Offer a number of advantages over the LCD panel: Fine level of detail, bright colors, less need for dark room. • Main disadvantage: If the audience is spread out, the visuals may be hard to read, even on a 37" screen. • Portable, clip-on microphones are the best, even if using podium. • Start off with the screen blank to keep attention on the speaker. • Provide handouts for the audience to take notes (if appropriate).

Figure 2.13 shows the presenter using a 37" color monitor to display the presentation. Key points to note are:

➤ The presenter faces the audience, not the monitor. He is able to do this by looking at the laptop screen that is set up on a table in front of him. This is an important way of maintaining eye contact with the audience. Occasionally he may turn and point to the screen to highlight a key point.

➤ He uses a remote mouse that provides freedom to move around.

➤ He stands to the left of the monitor, which makes it easier on the eye to look from him to the screen and to read the points from left to right.

Figure 2.13 Color Monitor Presentations

Option 6: Three-Gun Projection Unit
Large Audience (50-500 People)

Presentation Equipment Needed and Equipment Warnings	General Tips and Comments
WHAT YOU NEED: • Three-color projection unit • 8" x 6" or 9" x 12" screen or bigger • Laptop with presentation loaded on it • Lavaliere wireless microphone • Powerstrip and extension cord to accommodate PC • Pointer and remote mouse **WARNINGS:** • Needs to be set up by technician. Takes at least one hour. Colors must be fine-tuned for each PC. • Arrive at location with adequate time to correct worst imaginable problem: projection unit could malfuntion and need to be replaced. Ideally set up the day before to avoid surprises.	• This is the most professional way of presenting for larger audiences. • Rear projection onto screen is better if room layout permits. • Portable, clip-on microphones are the best, even if using podium. • Start off with the screen blank —to keep attention on the speaker. • Provide handouts for the audience to take notes (if appropriate). • Begin with the lights raised and screen blank; end with the lights raised for question period. • If speaker needs notes, use podium; make sure it has separate small light for reading.

A Company Road Show

One key to the success of any presentation is to ensure that the presenter is totally comfortable with the material. Unfortunately, communication often breaks down or doesn't even occur between the people who are preparing the laptop presentations and the people who are supposed to take the show on the road. Far too many companies fall into the scenario we are about to describe.

The Situation: Top-Down Design and Creation

The graphics department in our example company designed a multimedia presentation for salespeople to give on the road. It was created in a sophisticated graphics program, without input from anyone who would actually be giving the presentation. No one thought that the salespeople, who are on the road dealing with customers every day, would have any good ideas.

The vice-president of sales decided he didn't want the presenters to be able to make changes, so the graphics department gave the salespeople only the viewer version of the program. Of course, the whole point of using live electronic presentations is to be able to customize them and change them for the audience. Consequently, the poor salespeople were stuck with a program that could not be tailored to their customers.

The Result: Wasted Time and Effort

Given only the viewer program, many of the salespeople had to start from scratch and make up the whole presentation. They knew they couldn't present to their customers using the version sent from headquarters. This work consumed a great deal of time and effort, considering some 50 salespeople were all modifying the same presentation.

The Problem: Lack of Involvement by All Participants

The vice-president refused to encourage people to work across functions and manage the project together. The graphics people worked in a vacuum and were not usually encouraged to work side by side with the real people who would be giving the presentations. They were told there wasn't time. Everyone had his or her own area of expertise that was off limits to others' new thoughts. The wasted time and productivity was aided and abetted by the advent of laptop presentation systems. Why? Enough salespeople knew that they could make a better presentation, so they just did it. All these people out in the field were spending hours making up their own "better" presentation than the one sent from headquarters. And none of the presentations were shared, as no one wanted to admit to not using the corporate presentation.

The Solution: True Veto Power

A company presentation that many people will need to use should be created by people from many functions. When it is done, the presentation should be tested by a focus group that includes all levels of the company, as well as potential customers who might have to listen to the presentation. Now, at least, the right audiences have been consulted before the program is finished.

The "real" presenters should have veto power. When the salespeople say that the screen headings or flow of the talk don't really work, they should have veto power over those who are preparing it. The people who have to give the talk should have final say.

One other requirement of doing a company road show is to ensure that presenters receive training on the software program itself. Some graphics programs are fairly simple, but the more complicated ones take some time to learn. At the very least, someone should give the presenter a two- to four-page helpful hints sheet on the key things to know in order to make some simple changes, add a screen, or remove a screen. Presenters should also be told about common problems and how to solve them. Finally, the presentation screens should be constructed so that the people who give the presentation the least often will have an easy time speaking from the screens. They should not be designed for the handful of people who can do the talk blindfolded.

The Customer Conference

Many companies organize customer conferences to display and tell about their products, services, and unique capabilities. The key to a successful conference is a well-developed process for creating, producing, and rehearsing the presentations. This approach avoids surprises and leaves the customers with a positive impression.

To give you an idea of what it takes to prepare and organize a customer conference, here is a basic overview of the steps for creating the visuals.

❶ *Topic.* Presenters are given a topic for their presentation.

❷ *Color template.* The graphic designer creates a special color scheme and design for everyone to use in creating screens.

❸ *Format.* A format for organizing and chunking the data in the presentation is created. This format organizes the flow of all the talks and forces all the presenters to focus on what the customers want to hear.

❹ *Training.* A session is held to explain the organizational format as well as some hints on presentation skills. A completed format is handed out as an example to follow.

❺ *Research.* Presenters call three to five customers who have signed up for their session to find out why they signed up and what they want to learn from the meeting.

⑥ *First draft.* A date is set for everyone to turn in a hard copy of their presentations to a manager and graphic designer for review. The purpose of the review meeting is to ensure accuracy and consistency of information. Before the presentations are turned in, the presenters must (a) use a visual assessment checklist to be sure they followed the rules for making effective visuals, and (b) practice their presentation out loud so they can verify that the flow and words on the visuals make sense. If they wait to rehearse until the customer conference handouts are made up, it will be too late to modify the visuals.

⑦ *Changes.* After the review and another rehearsal, the final edits are made.

⑧ *Final presentations.* The presenter turns in one clean hard copy (six slides per page without builds), and two electronic copies (on diskette).

⑨ *Rehearsal.* Presenters meet in small groups of three or four to rehearse the entire presentation. The groups have critique forms. People practice with the equipment, especially to become comfortable with using a remote mouse.

⑩ *Extra disk.* When leaving for the conference, presenters are to take a disk of their presentation.

⑪ *Clothes to wear.* Everyone is reminded to wear something that the microphone can be clipped to. One-piece dresses are not recommended. The presenter needs a place to clip the mike and a place to put the small box for the mike.

⑫ *Partner system.* Presenters designate a partner who will be with them from 15 minutes before to 10 minutes after the presentation. This partner will be available to go for help in case of technical difficulties. The partner will sit in the audience and help field questions. The partner also deals with people who have questions the presenter does not have the time to answer. The partner collects the evaluation forms after the session.

⓯ *The presentation itself.* Everyone has a lavaliere microphone that can be worn. No one has to stand behind a podium and talk into a stationary mike.

Case Study: Company Initiative Launch

Russel Metals Inc., a distributor and processor of metal products with over 57 locations in North America, recently embarked on a new initiative to fundamentally change the cost structure of the business. To launch the initiative, the president decided to travel to all the 25 larger branches in Canada and the United States to present the initiative to the management teams. It was felt that it would be more effective to visit the management in their locations and customize the presentation to reflect the local circumstances of each operation.

This was the first time the company had used a computer-driven presentation for a communications program of this scale. The approach was novel in another respect. The actual presentations were to be made not in the operating units where the environment was predictable, but in the evening over dinner at local restaurants, clubs, and hotels. In addition, the plan was to organize the entire program in-house without using consultants.

The challenge was to organize the logistics: 25 customized presentations in five weeks for groups of 10 to 30 people at different hotels, restaurants, and clubs, each with its own layout, lighting, and technical challenges. The locations were spread out and included Vancouver, Edmonton, Milwaukee, Halifax, Toronto, and Montreal (in French).

Developing and Customizing the Presentation

First, the company developed a core presentation. Considerable discussion went into the objective and key messages which were continuously refined along the way. The designer used a standard blue background, with white letters and yellow bullets, plus lots of visuals and charts. The presentation was developed in PowerPoint. (Astound was used for more intricate presentations.)

Second the presentation was customized for each of the operating units. En route from city to city, the presenters added specific elements to the presentation that made it unique in some way for the local operation. For example, the Edmonton Oilers logo was added en route to Edmonton. A five-year history of each operation's sales and earnings was inserted for each presentation. The opening slide (which stayed on the screen throughout dinner) was always unique, saying "A Dinner Dialogue In [City]" with a picture of the city in the background. The presenters also added points highlighting the recent accomplishments of each unit. The audiences identified more closely with a presentation that was clearly not off the shelf but customized especially for them. (A few of the visuals used are shown in Figures 2.14 through 2.16.)

Figure 2.14 An Evening in Calgary

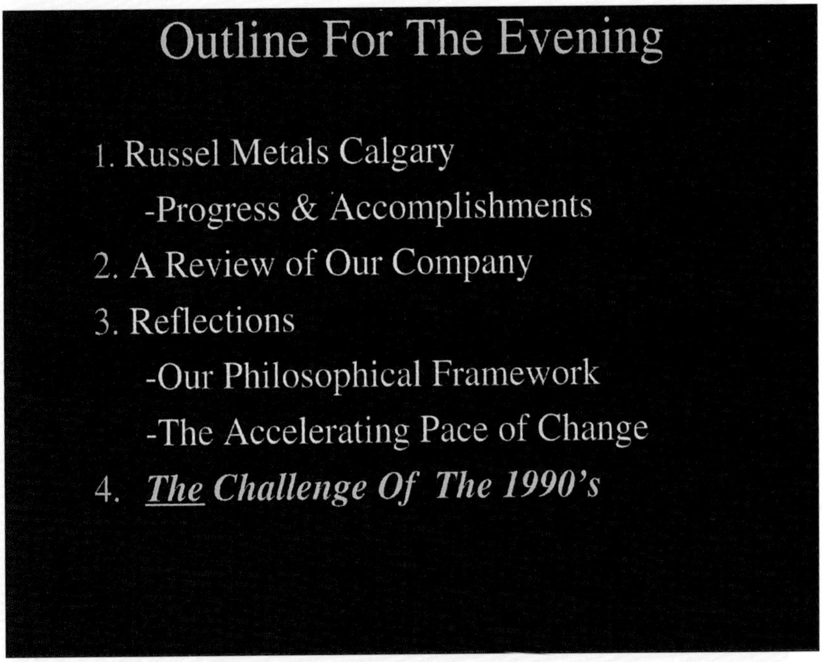

Figure 2.15 Outline for the Evening

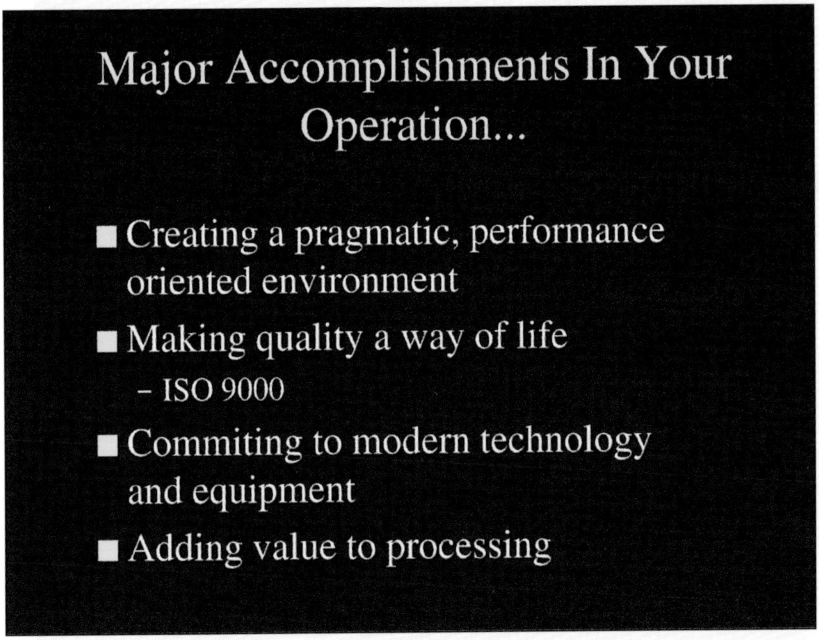

Figure 2.16 Major Accomplishments

Traveling Equipment

The traveling equipment consisted of a Compaq 486 laptop and a LCD panel in a canvas, oversized "lawyer" bag with wheels. The bag also contained a powerstrip, an extension cord, tape to hold the cables on the floor, a steel pointer, an extra overhead light bulb, and an extra laptop battery just to be safe. The PC was always removed from the bag at airport security to prevent it from passing through the X-ray machine.

Planning the Equipment Requirements in Each Location

The biggest challenge was to ensure that the equipment setup and room layout in each location was suitable. Two steps were taken in this regard:

❶ A checklist (see Figure 2.17) was sent to the manager of each operating unit. A detailed conversation about the checklist took place with him or her a month ahead of time. The presenter stressed the importance of a room capable of darkening and the absolute need for a 400-watt or equivalent bulb in the overhead projector.

❷ On arrival in the city, usually around mid-day the presenter proceeded directly to the room where the dinner was planned. *This was the most important step. There is no substitute for checking everything yourself. Do it far enough ahead of time so that any problem can be corrected.* Typically, the room layout needed adjustment, lights above the screen sometimes needed removing, and occasionally special arrangements were needed to cover the windows. In Montreal the presenter taped flip chart pages over the windows to darken the room. (It was midsummer and light until after 9:00 P.M.) Who would have ever thought of that problem?

Backup

Three vital pieces of equipment needed a backup plan: the overhead projector, the LCD panel, and the laptop. The backup plan consisted of two steps:

❶ The presenters did a practice run of the presentation on site at least 4 to 6 hours before the actual time. This provided adequate time to rent or locate a replacement for any of the three pieces of equipment.

❷ If the laptop crashed or did not work properly, the presenters had a copy of the presentation on disk. They also carried a copy of the PowerPoint viewer program. This would allow them to quickly load the presentation onto another PC. It also protected them in the event that PowerPoint was not loaded on the replacement PC.

The result? The 25 presentations were completed without a major glitch. The success was attributable to the detailed planning that took place ahead of time—particularly the on site visits to each location with adequate time still available to correct any problem. The only thing the presenters would do differently the next time around: use a self-contained projector unit instead of the LCD/overhead projector combination, as it generally provides a brighter image and it is easier to travel with only one piece of equipment.

THIS IS ACTUAL CHECKLIST WE SEND

Presentation Checklist

Date of Presentation: _____   Contact: _____

Location: _____   Audience Size: _____

Item	Required
1. Overhead projector with 400-watt (4,000 to 6,000 lumens) or stronger light bulb (for LCD)	
2. Room that can be made very dark	
3. Flip chart(s), markers	
4. Small screen: 6' x 8'	
5. Large screen: 8' x 10'	
6. Powerstrip for PC next to overhead projector	
7. 37" Mitsubishi TV monitor or equivalent (as large as possible)	
8. VCR connected to TV monitor	
9. Interface to connect PC to TV monitor (RGB Extron)	
10. Speakers podium with light	
11. Wireless microphone	
12. Pointer	
13. Table next to overhead projector for PC	
14. Three-color high-powered projector for front or rear-view projection on large screen—for large audiences	
15. Bose 802 speakers, amplifier to link to PC, and mixer	
16. Other	

For audio visual support in the Toronto/Hamilton area, or for the name of a local reliable supplier anywhere in Canada or the U.S. call:
> Flipchart Audio Visual Services, Mississauga, Ontario
> Contact is: Richard Mason
> Phone: (905) 625-5543   Fax: (905) 625-5576

Russel Metals has a corporate supply arrangement and preferred pricing with this company and their affiliated firms in Canada and the U.S.

Figure 2.17 Presentation Checklist

3

CREATE HIGH-IMPACT VISUALS

"Wonderful graphics and special effects.
What do you think was the point?"

The visuals are a key ingredient of any presentation. The role of visuals, however, is one of the most misunderstood aspects of presentations. Visuals are not intended to display the presenter's entire script, or even most of it. Visuals are also not intended to display every specific issue, highlight the key messages. Word visuals should not dominate the presentation. They focus the eyes and minds of the audience on the main point while the presenter is talking about it. Think of them as eye-catching billboard advertisements, not as full-page text ads.

We know of a company that gives talks on its products all around the world. They also train people inside other companies to give their talk. They hired a graphic designer to produce the multimedia presentations. The screens he created were gorgeous. The colors were great. But the show had one major problem. It was not audience friendly in terms of the audience being able to logically follow it.

What happened? The graphic designer did what he was supposed to do—but he was not the presenter. What looks pretty is not always easy to talk from. The screens can pop in and out, but that doesn't necessarily make the talk clear and well thought out. The design may be stunning, but it is of little use if a speaker can't speak from it. Every graphic designer should have to take at least a two-day presentation seminar. At a minimum, every person who creates screens should have to run through the presentation out loud and consider the reaction of the audience. Otherwise, the result may just be a talk accompanied by pretty graphics.

Key Steps for Designing Visuals

There are three key steps for designing effective visuals:

❶ Keep the text simple.

❷ Keep the visual uncluttered.

❸ Guide the eyes to the main point, especially with charts.

Keep the Text Simple

The most common pitfall is to fill the visual with type in a very small size. The audience is not motivated to look at such a visual. Why do people make this mistake? Presenters feel nervous and deal with their anxiety by using the screen as a crutch. They put every possible issue on the screen. If a speaker needs a full script, or many, many bullet points to jog the memory, by all means develop them. But don't put everything on the screen!

Keep the text simple by following these guidelines:

➤ Keep to one thought, concept, or idea per screen.

➤ Have no more than six lines and six words per line.

- Use upper and lower case. All caps are hard to read.

- Capitalize only the first word in a line. People aren't used to seeing phrases written with every word capitalized.

- Use one—or at most two—readable, consistent typefaces.

- Highlight with bold or italics. Don't use italics throughout—they are hard to read.

- Highlight key numbers in charts.

Figures 3.1 and 3.2 show how text can be simplified. Both visuals contain the same information. But in Figure 3.1, the eye wanders looking for meaning, while in Figure 3.2 the eye is guided to read each of the horizontal rows in sequence. The second slide is also more interesting and uses a larger font, with fewer words on it.

Keep the Visual Uncluttered

A picture is worth a thousand words. This old principle still holds true. It is based on the fact that most people absorb and process information more effectively when it is conveyed visually. Many thoughts and ideas can be converted into a visual. The creative challenge is to find ways to represent messages in clear pictures.

For instance, cluttering a slide with numbers is common in many business presentations. To get around this, ask yourself, "What is the main point I want to convey?" Then design the visual around that key point. This approach will help the audience grasp and retain the important point, rather than walk out with a cluttered impression of endless numbers and tables.

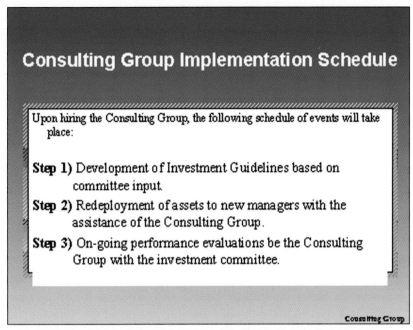

Figure 3.1 Consulting Group Implementation Schedule

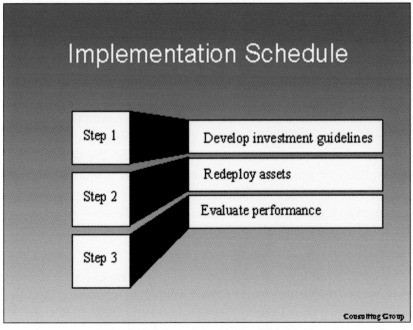

Figure 3.2 Implementation Schedule

Keep the visuals uncluttered by following these guidelines:

➤ Show only key numbers on a chart. If people need to see just the trends and not the numbers, just show the trend line.

➤ Don't repeat the same word five times on a screen. Find a way to use it only once.

➤ Use graphic designs for variety. Use boxes of various shapes and put your key points in them.

➤ Have white space on the visual. Don't cover every inch of the screen with something.

The color visuals in Figures 3.3 and 3.4 highlight the effective use of a chart instead of a table of numbers. The key point is the improvement in earnings per share of the company. So why not make that the main point of the visual as shown in Figure 3.4?

Guide the Eyes to the Main Point

An overlooked, but important consideration in designing visuals is the need for the audience to absorb information in a short period of time. Guiding the eyes to the main point, as depicted in Figure 3.4 and 3.5, reduces the time and effort required by the viewer to interpret, analyze, and focus his or her thoughts. Where does the eye travel when it sees the visual? What does the eye focus on first? Is the eye guided to the main point? If it takes your audience two minutes to figure out your chart, that is too long! In many cases the audience has just figured out the chart and is ready to look at the details just when the screen goes away.

The simplest and most effective way to guide the eye is to use large type for the main point of the visual. Use an arrow that directs the eye toward the information on the slide that supports that point. In Figures 3.6 and 3.7, both charts contain the same data, but Figure 3.7 shows the main point of the

Financial Results
($ Millions)

	1996	1995
Gross sales	438.1	413.1
Net income (loss)	30.1	(26.6)
Earnings Per Share	(1.03)	1.12

Figure 3.3 Financial Results

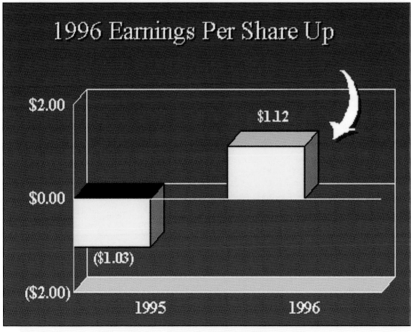

Figure 3.4 Earnings Per Share Up

visual in large letters and guides the eye to focus on the number that supports the point.

When you design charts with builds, first show an empty chart, explain it, and make some general comments. Then, add in your data and, finally, add an arrow focused on the key point or put in a key number that highlights the main point.

Additional tips for designing screens are listed in Figure 3.8.

Further Considerations

Here are some other things to keep in mind as you design visuals.

➤ *You are not selling technology.* The technology is only a tool to enable you to get your message across. You are not selling it.

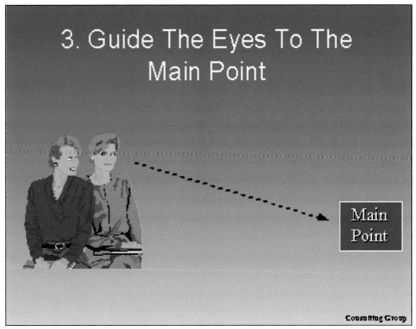

Figure 3.5 Guide the Eyes to the Main Point

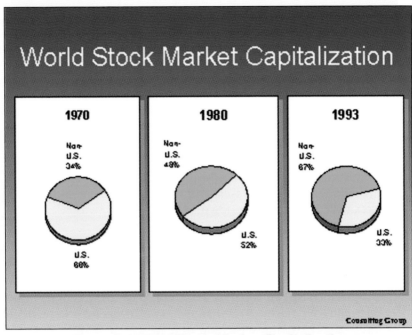

Figure 3.6 World Stock Market Capitalization

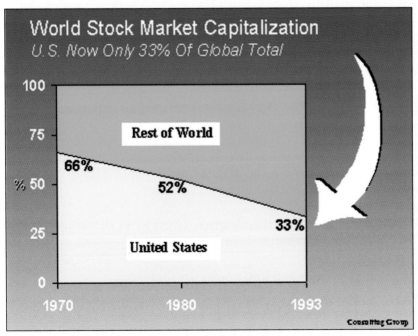

Figure 3.7 World Stock Market Capitalization

Design Tips

Software classes. Take classes on the software you will be using. You will save time, and you will make better-looking presentations. Or buy a video that teaches you the software.

Landscape style. Use a landscape, not portrait style. You can make longer bullet phrases, and it is easier for the audience's eyes to read across than down.

Type size. Use no smaller than 24-point type. Test the size on site to assure readability.

Typefaces. Use the typefaces that come with the program. Don't mix many typefaces. Also, use simple typefaces; those with curled letters and extra lines are hard to read.

Parallel structure. Use parallel structure on each screen. Start each bullet with a verb or noun. This structure makes it easier to present.

Proofing. Have someone who doesn't know very much about your subject proof your text. Don't count on spellcheck.

Numbers versus bullets. Use numbers rather than bullets on a couple of your visuals. This changes the style and gives you a different way to talk. You can say, "Here are the major points about this project. I want to discuss only numbers 4 and 6. If you have questions about the other points, I will be glad to answer them."

Blank space. Leave some blank space. Don't cover the whole visual with words or charts.

Phrases. Use phrases and key words, not sentences.

Figure 3.8 Design Tips

➤ *Covering less is better.* It is better if you cover less information in a relaxed and energized style than to cover so much information that you feel harried and out of time before you start. No one likes to listen to someone in a hurry who keeps saying, "I just don't have enough time."

There are many devices on the market to help you stay on time. For example, a small device called a Pacesetter lights up or vibrates to let you know how much time has passed. You can set it three times. For example, for a 40-minute talk you can have it go off to remind you that you have 25 minutes left, then 15 minutes left and then 5 minutes left. We know someone who always ran 15 to 25 minutes over the time allotted. Once he started using a Pacesetter, he always ended on time. (See Resources "Time Devices.")

➤ *Determining length takes some work.* There used to be guidelines about how many visuals to use in a presentation. Generally, you could plan on about 3 minutes per visual. Now in the world of electronic presentations it is different. When you do builds and show diagrams that are created in front of the audience's eyes, it is harder to judge how many screens you need for a 30-minute talk. Talking the whole presentation out loud is the only way to know how long it will take. (Talking it in your mind isn't the same.)

Also, if you are a technical specialist and you tend to ramble, you should add some time for your rambling. Even better, learn to be concise and stick to the point, but budget in some time for detouring off the presentation.

➤ *The rules are changing for video conferencing.* With most of the equipment available today, you can't do an animated presentation in video conferencing and expect it to look good at the other end. The camera can't pick up the movement. Some presenters send a disk ahead of time and have the program set up on the other end. That way the audience sees it live, not through a camera. Ask about what the equipment can do. Every day something new and more sophisticated comes on the market.

➤ *Make the best use of handouts.* Think about what you want to give out as handouts and when you want to give them out. If you hand out your presentation visuals ahead of time, you take away the element of surprise. Wherever possible, it is preferable to distribute handouts after the presentation. This keeps the audience's attention focused on you.

➤ *Use a reviewer.* Ask someone to review your presentation, preferably someone who knows as much about the subject as your audience. You will be pleasantly surprised at the useful comments you receive.

Templates and Colors

Earlier this year one of the authors (David) attended an investor conference where the CEOs or CFOs of 40 companies each presented their company's story. The audience consisted of 100 financial analysts and portfolio managers from major institutions in the United States and Canada. The presentation that caught David's attention was for a medium-sized forest products company. It was one of the few electronic presentations at the conference.

The designer of the screens must have decided to demonstrate all the visual features offered by the presentation software. The backgrounds changed three times during the 20-minute presentation, from an opening mauve to a closing turquoise.

The colors of the type varied from a conservative white to an occasional hot red. Almost the complete script was shown on the screen in small type. The CEO was an articulate speaker and fortunately diverted the attention of the audience from the slides. His enthusiasm saved the presentation from being a complete disaster.

This near-disastrous presentation sends a clear message. Templates and color schemes are tools to support the overall objectives of the presentation. Improperly used, they can distract the audience and even hurt the image of the presenter and the company. Properly used, templates and color can enhance a presentation, making it more interesting and easier to understand.

Selecting Templates to Fit the Situation

All the major presentation programs come with a variety of ready templates. In fact, the software companies promote the large number of templates offered. The message seems to be that the bigger the selection, the better the product. The reality is that most of these templates should never be used in business. The ones with colored balloons or dots are perhaps intended for children's birthday parties! Also, a template with blocks and lines may look pretty until you put your chart on top of it. Then too much design is competing on the screen.

Here are some key considerations in selecting a template:

➤ *Corporate image.* What type of image do you want to project—conservative, aggressive, or futuristic?

➤ *Audience.* What type of audience will you have serious investors, board of directors, training class, customers, company employees?

➤ *Objective of the presentation.* What is your objective—motivational, informative, project update, good news, bad news?

Selecting Appropriate Colors

When selecting a template, keep in mind that colors cause emotional responses. Table 3.1 lists some common emotional responses associated with popular colors and the best uses of these colors for screens.

Here are a few additional hints for selecting colors:

➤ *Color blindness.* About 10 percent of the male population and 5 percent of the female population is red/green color blind, meaning they won't be able to see the difference between red and green. If you create a visual with red and green elements next to each other, they might see only one element and not the two separately. The safest course is to avoid using red and green together. It is not a popular combination anyway.

➤ *Color variety.* Be careful about using unusual colors. Many people don't think purple, pink, or light greens have a place in presentations. Know your audience.

➤ *Solemn black.* Keep in mind that black as a background gives a solemn feel to a presentation.

Keeping Templates and Color Schemes Simple

Just because you can change the template and background colors in your graphics program does not mean you should. The most important principle is to apply a template consistently throughout a presentation. You could change the background color when introducing certain information or when talking about a different product or concept. But using too many different colors and backgrounds is a distraction for the eye and the mind.

Readability is critical, so high-contrast templates are always preferred. The colors most often used for headlines are white or yellow against dark blue backgrounds.

Table 3.1 Color and Emotional Associations

Color	Emotional Associations	Best Use
Blue	Peaceful, soothing, tranquil, cool, trusting	Used as a background (usually dark blue) in over 90% of business presentations; safe and conservative
White	Neutral, innocence, purity, wisdom	Used as the font color of choice in most business presentations with a dark background
Yellow	Warm, bright, cheerful, enthusiasm	Used in text bullets and subheadings with a dark background
Red	Losses in business, passion, danger, action, pain	Used to promote action or stimulate the audience; seldom as a background; don't use in a financial presentation unless "in the red"
Green	Money, growth, assertive, prosperity, envy, relaxation	Occasionally used as a background, but more often as a highlight color (*Note:* The greens do not always turn out well as backgrounds when projected onto a screen.)

Choose your colors based on the equipment quality. For low light equipment use a light background with dark letters. Reverse for bright light equipment.

When using an LCD panel, high-contrast colors are a must. A dark, dark background with light letters shows up best. Keep in mind that certain LCD panels will not show off colors as well as other types of LCD panels.

If you will be mixing and matching your presentations, use the same template and colors throughout so it will be easy for you to cut and paste without having to fix the screen colors each time.

Transitions, Builds, and Interactivity

Transitions, builds and interactivity are some of the key features that distinguish an electronic presentation from the traditional 35mm slide show or overhead presentation. In electronic presentations, it is the transitions and builds that lead your audience from one scene to the next. They control the viewer's attention span between messages. They also influence the pace of the presentation. For instance, a presentation with many "fade through black" transitions will seem slow, while one with many "wipe right" transitions will feel snappier.

The question you face is: "How do I use the transitions and builds to enhance the effectiveness of my presentation without overloading it with too many effects that distract my audience?"

The trend by software companies is clearly to offer users more and more transition and build options. These features can add interesting movement to the messages or create such a blur of special effects that the audience leaves impressed with the technology but confused about the messages. In short, just because the software company includes a certain feature does not mean it must be used in every presentation.

Note: If you have a slow computer, you won't be able to do transitions and builds. They will take too long to come up on the screen.

The Transition and Build Checklist

In deciding which transition and build tools to include in your presentation, answer the following questions (you can apply similar questions to clip art, pictures, and video):

❶ Is an electronic presentation that includes movement appropriate for this audience? How will they react? You could use your laptop but not do transitions and builds.

❷ Has the audience been previously exposed to electronic presentations? If not you should be cautious with the features you include. The novelty of the motion may distract viewers from your messages.

❸ What type of audience are you facing? What type of atmosphere do you want to create—conservative, informal, upbeat? Each calls for a different transition and build combination (see Table 3.2 on page 67).

❹ Will the movement or picture contribute to the communicating power of your visual? Or are you adding decorative pictures and motions that will create a distraction?

❺ Have you included no more than three different transition effects throughout the presentation? Too many types of transitions distract the audience.

❻ Have you included no more than three different build effects throughout the presentation?

❼ Have you varied your screens? Don't do a build on every screen. That's boring. Show some information all at once.

Selecting the Right Transition / Build Combinations

The selection of slide transitions and build effects provides a unique feel to a presentation—just as the color scheme does. For instance, imagine two presentations, one to a conservative group of bankers and another to a gathering of employees during their lunch hour (most of whom would rather be spending their lunch hour somewhere else). Does the presentation to the group of conservative investors call for a different tone, color scheme, and set of transitions and build effects than the training session on workplace safety? Yes!

For the employee meeting, a lively wipe up transition combined with the text flying in from the top may help keep everyone's attention. This same effect would likely jar the conservative sensibilities of a financial audience.

The most common forms of transitions are wipes, box-in/out, dissolves, fades and cuts:

➤ *Wipes* and *box ins/outs* provide standard transitions for all occasions and draw little attention to the transition itself.

➤ With a *dissolve,* the image incrementally changes into some unclear form and then back into a new, clear image. Dissolves create the impression of time passing and are used between messages or main points. A dissolve may coincide with the speaker taking a sip of water.

➤ An alternative to a dissolve is *a fade through black* transition. Fading to black and returning with a new image provides for a complete change of scene. Fade through black transitions are ideal for introducing pauses between major messages, or prior to the summary.

➤ A *cut* is an immediate change to a new visual that is usually related to the previous one. The new visual may be a more detailed look at one part of the previous visual. For instance, you may have a map of the United States cut to a specific geographic area on which you want the viewers to focus.

POINT, CLICK & *WoW!!*

The transitions and builds are really movie-making techniques. Use them to enhance your story.

Table 3.2 offers help for selecting appropriate combinations.

Table 3.2 Transition and Build Considerations for Various Audiences

Style and Type of Audience	Suggested Transition (maximum of 2-3 different per presentation)	Suggested Builds (maximum of 2-3 different per presentation)	Comments
1. Conservative • customers • potential customers • senior executives • bankers • shareholders • conference attendees	Dissolve, wipe right, box in/out, cut	Fly from left, dissolve, box out	• Use wipe right as a safe transition. • Use cuts to highlight submessages. • Dissolve is always a safe transition between main messages.
2. Informal • employee training session • peer group • department communications • project update	Same as above, plus blinds, checkerboard	Same as above, plus blinds, checkerboard	• Same as above, plus uncover, cover can be used for emphasis of a slide. • Split vertical out (curtain opening) is an interesting opening combined with split vertical in (curtain closing) to end.
3. Special Events • sales conference • convention speech • awards dinner	Fade through black is a useful pause between major sections and prior to conclusion	Fly from top is strong effect, useful when emphasizing a phrase or point	• Change your special effects at different points in the talk.* *Consult the section (in Chapter 2) on the plot-point theory of organizing.

Altering Slide Sequences

Electronic presentations, unlike most 35mm slide shows, provide the important feature of flexibility in sequencing visuals. The presenter is not locked into a fixed sequence. The ability to show a visual at any time or to alter the sequence allows the presenter to adapt to the audience and the situation.

Some programs, such as Freelance Graphics and Astound, offer a branching feature that allows the developer to create screen buttons. When selected, these buttons jump to a specified visual. These buttons can also be used to play video clips or sounds.

Most presenters do not use the buttons to navigate around their presentation because they don't give themselves enough time or don't make the effort. If you plan to do your presentation many times, putting in buttons is worth the effort. It provides tremendous flexibility and your audience will be impressed.

Other programs, such as PowerPoint, offer the ability to jump to any slide at any point in the presentation. The presenter types the number of the selected slide and presses Enter. To make use of this feature, you number the slides in one corner and print out a hard copy set for your own use. (If you prefer not to show the numbers on the screen, you can remove them just before the presentation.)

Following are some uses for this feature:

➤ *Responding to questions.* In preparation for questions, create a set of "back pocket" slides to bring up on the screen when answering specific questions. You will leave an impression with the audience of a well-prepared presenter.

➤ *Skipping slides while presenting.* You will want to skip slides if the audience is getting restless or if you decide at the last minute to cut back on a topic.

➤ *Moving to products your audience wants to discuss.* Salespeople create presentations with buttons so they can quickly move to the products their customers are particularly interested in.

Of course, a fast-growing use of these jumping features is to create interactive presentations, our next topic.

Introducing Interactivity

People's level of interest and retention is heightened when they are actively involved in a presentation, rather than just watching it. Interactivity can be an effective approach to creating such involvement.

A presentation can be designed in a number of ways to encourage audience interaction. The most common way is to set up a main menu with hot buttons next to each subject. The presenter uses the main menu to trigger interaction with the audience, asking them to choose the subjects of interest.

Figures 3.9 to 3.14 show an interactive presentation used to discuss four main presentation tools available to employees at Russel Metals. It is a simple but effective presentation that encourages the involvement of the audience by asking, "Which presentation tools would you like to talk about now?" The hot buttons at the bottom right corner of each slide of the subsections return the presenter to the main menu.

Making Creative Use of Transitions

A 20-minute presentation with 10 overheads can be delivered with 30 electronic screens in the same time frame. In short, you can use more screens, with each containing a specific focused point. By revealing the information in stages, the audience can more easily absorb each piece of the information as it is shown. This is especially true with complicated charts and diagrams.

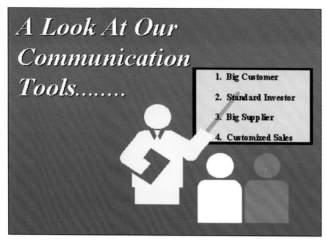

Figure 3.9 A Look at Our Communication Tools

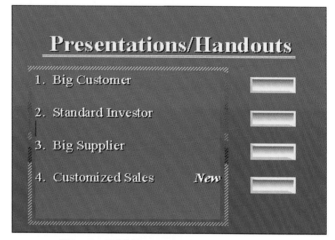

Figure 3.10 Presentations/Handouts

Figure 3.11 Big Customer Presentation

POINT, CLICK & *WoW!!*

Figure 3.12 Standard Investor Presentation

Figure 3.13 Big Supplier Presentation

Figure 3.14 Customized Sales Presentation - *New*

Figures 3.15 through 3.18 show the creative use of transitions. The first depicts the growth in the stock price of Silicon Valley Inc.

➤ The first visual (Figure 3.15) sets the frame and can be used to develop a sense of anticipation in the audience. (This simple chart is easy to understand. If you have a complicated chart, you can use the first visual to explain the axis.)

➤ The second visual (Figure 3.16), introduced with a "wipe right" transition, shows the chart in a way that gives the impression of it "growing" from left to right on the screen.

➤ The third visual (Figure 3.17) in the sequence delivers the main point and guides the eye to the appropriate place on the chart. This approach allows the story and visuals to build together. It is considerably more effective than introducing the third slide by itself and letting it remain on the screen while the story is told.

Figure 3.18 illustrates the sales growth by region for National Distributors Inc. The visual, shown here without its build stages, comprises nine stages that support the presenter's story. She introduces the subject (using a map without any yellow bars). Then she separately introduces each of the seven regions. Finally, she shows the total company performance. By using wipe up transitions between each visual, she creates the impression of each new bar growing on the screen. By using builds the presenter can talk about each region before she goes on to the next one.

More advanced programs, such as Astound, allow these builds to take place on one visual by defining specific entry and exit times and transitions for each element. Astound also offers a chart feature that controls the way charts "grow." The overall effect is similar.

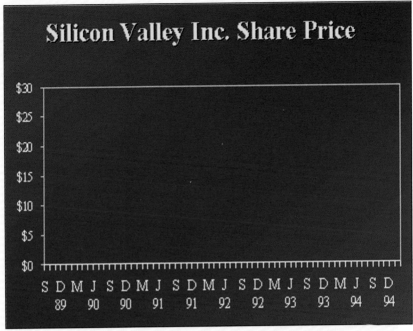

Figure 3.15 Silicon Valley Inc. Share Price

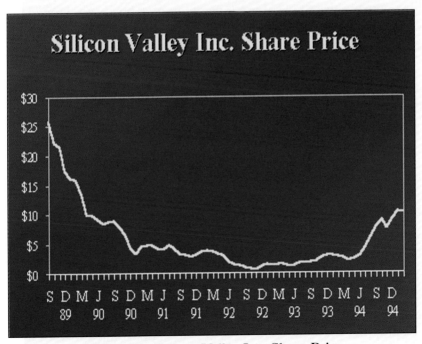

Figure 3.16 Silicon Valley Inc. Share Price

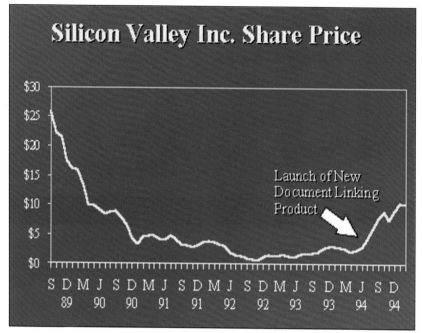

Figure 3.17 Silicon Valley Inc. Share Price

The opportunities to use these type of creative builds are limited only by time and imagination. But keep in mind, five build charts in a row is a lot. Intersperse them with other types of screens.

Pictures, Clip Art, Charts, and Video Clips

Pictures, clip art, charts, and video clips add variety to a presentation. They can make a presentation easier to understand. Keep in mind that most people are visually oriented. They grasp information better through pictorial images. Also be aware, however, that extraneous or inappropriate pictures can get in the way of your message.

The first issue to consider is whether your computer can support the type of presentation you are making. If you won't be using your computer for the actual presentation, are you sure the computer you will be using is able to support all your fancy graphics?

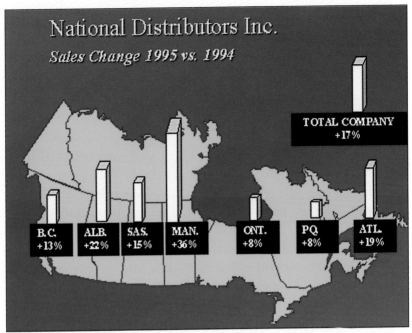

Figure 3.18 National Distributors Inc.

Following are some other questions to ask yourself when selecting pictures, photos, clip art, and video clips.

Why Am I Adding the Picture?

➤ Am I adding this picture, clip art, or video clip simply because I have access to it, or does it further my point?

➤ Is there anything in the picture that may offend or exclude part of my audience? Are there only men or only women in the pictures? Are the pictures only of a certain race? You must show variety in today's diverse workforce.

➤ Will the colors look the same at the presentation location as they do on my laptop in my office?

➤ Will adding these pictures increase the size of the file beyond what will fit on one backup disk? If not, do I have a way to compress it, or save it on multiple disks for a backup file?

The examples in Figures 3.19 to 3.22 illustrate how pictures, when carefully selected, are more interesting than text.

Am I Prepared to Explain and Comment on the Picture?

Have you ever suffered through a presentation in which the presenter just pointed out the visuals one after the other but never explained the point of each one? A picture may be worth a thousand words, but unless it is given context and meaning, it can be a different thousand words to everyone in the audience. Every picture needs to be accompanied by both a title or phrase the makes the point and an explanation by you.

Is Cartoony Clip Art Appropriate?

Photographs, arrows, symbols, and diagrams, if they support the message, are appropriate for all audiences, from conservative bankers to company employees. The same is not true of clip art. Many clip art pictures resemble cartoons and when included in a presentation conjure up a tone and style that does not fit all situations. You be the first judge, then get a second opinion.

Is This Chart or Graph the Best Way to Make a Point?

Just because your graphics program will make a graph of 12 lines across doesn't mean you should do one. Only use numbers if you truly believe your audience wants to see them. Sometimes a trend line is enough. After showing the trend line, you may want to bring onto the screen the key number that interests your audience.

As we said earlier, color-blind people will not be able to differentiate between red and green bars. Here are some other considerations for your charts and graphs:

Point, Click & *WoW!!*

Figure 3.19a Without Supporting Visual

Figure 3.19b With Supporting 10-Second Video Clip

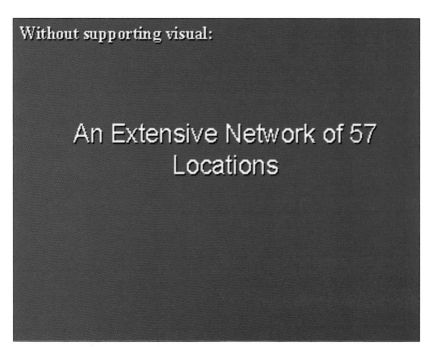

Figure 3.20a Without Supporting Visual

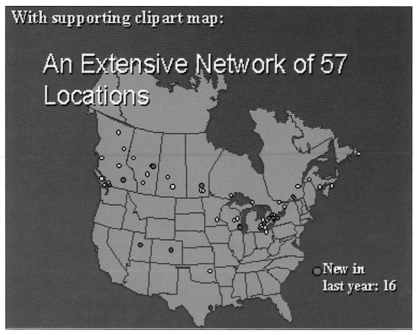

Figure 3.20b With Supporting Clipart Map

Figure 3.21a Without Supporting Visual

Figure 3.21b With Clipart Spotlight

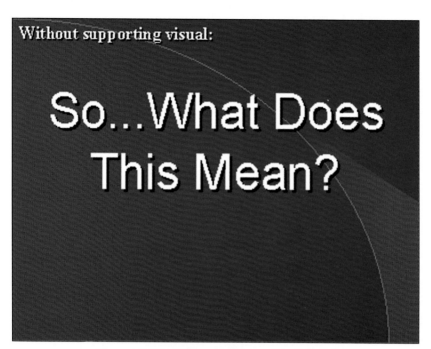

Figure 3.22a Without Supporting Visual

Figure 3.22b With Supporting Clipart Cartoon

- ➤ Make thick lines if you are showing trends. We see many narrow lines that are almost invisible on the screen.

- ➤ Make the lines in bright colors, but not yellow. No one can see yellow unless it's on a dark background.

- ➤ Don't put more than five lines or sets of bars on one chart. It confuses and they are too small.

- ➤ Guide the eye to the main point of the chart with an arrow, a different color, a box, or by the heading title.

- ➤ Shorten all the numbers as much as possible. For example, put '96 instead of 1996.

- ➤ Use rounded numbers that are as short as possible. Instead of $10,400.34, show 10 (or 10.4 if the .4 is significant) and change the axis to thousands.

See the following section on Visual Ideas for examples of charts that get the point across.

What Will the Audience Gain from Seeing the Video Clip?

Here are some ways video (and possible sound) clips can be of genuine value:

- ➤ Video clips of company employees introduce them to customers or to other employees.

- ➤ Displays of products and processes bring them to life.

- ➤ Video clips of plant locations take the audience to places they may not have an opportunity to visit.

- ➤ Customer or employee testimonials support your sales points.

As a low-cost, highly effective alternative to a video clip, use a "static talking head." This consists of a photograph of the person scanned into the PC and placed in the corner of the screen. To give the static talking head words, use either a recorded voice clip or text bullets attributed to the person in the photograph. These photos can add life to a presentation and can easily be inserted into most programs.

Visual Ideas

Looking at the way other people design visuals often helps stir the creative juices. We include here a few particularly effective visuals to give you some ideas for your own presentations.

U.S. & Canada Sales Growth (Figure 3.23)

Main point: The company's sales are growing strongly in 1996 in both Canada and the United States.

Features: The colors of the bars match those of the countries. This makes the chart easy to read and comprehend. There are not too many colors. There are no numbers on the bars to distract the audience. People like to see maps and charts—this combines both. The arrow guides the eye from the main point in the subheading to the part of the visual that makes the point.

Other applications: This approach can be applied to show trends by region or state in all types of sales, quality, production, and other presentations.

G7 GDP Forecast (Figure 3.24)

Main point: The United States and Canada are forecast to lead the G7 countries in economic growth in 1996.

Features: The chart clearly shows, in declining size from left

Figure 3.23 U.S. & Canada: Sales Growth %

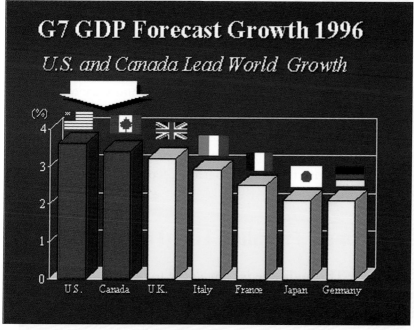

Figure 3.24 G7 GDP Forecast Growth 1996

to right, the forecast economic performance of the seven countries. Many charts of this type would have the countries in order of size or in alphabetical order. This approach is much easier on the eye. In this chart the eye is drawn to the important bars of the U.S. and Canada in two ways. First, they are in a different color. Second, the arrow from the sub-title directs the eye to them. Keeping all the other countries in one soft color, yellow, rather than a rainbow of colors, avoids distracting the eye from the two important bars. The flags of each country add an element of geographic interest.

Other applications: Use for any comparisons between countries, such as population growth, size, and various economic statistics.

Our Vision for Success Cascade (Figure 3.25)

Main point: This company has a comprehensive vision for success that includes a cascade of elements—from higher-level values to pragmatic agendas.

Features: The visual is an introduction to a presentation on the company's vision and plans. This is a main menu slide showing the items that will be discussed during the presenta-tion. It highlights the six key elements and links them with a visually attractive cascade. The more common way of show-ing this overview would be in a bullet slide or with interlink-ing circles. This is more interesting.

Other applications: The cascade can be used to show links between items in training programs, corporate plans, and quality processes.

Life 3 Single Premium Life (Figure 3.26)

Main point: The audience is now going to hear about another policy of Equitable of Iowa Companies called Life 3 Single Premium Life.

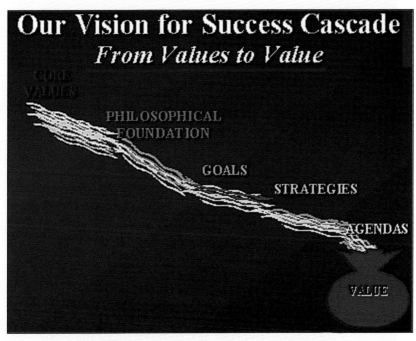

Figure 3.25 Our Vision for Success Cascade

Figure 3.26 Life 3 Single Premium Life

Features: Every time a new product is introduced, the background changes to yellow.

Other applications: You can change the background color when you introduce something that you have not as yet talked about, such as a new concept, product, feature, or teaching skill.

Product Features (Figure 3.27)

Main point: The audience is learning about Equitable of Iowa Companies' new product listed in the bottom righthand corner.

Features: The name of the product is always listed in the corner so the audience does not forget which product is now being discussed.

Other applications: In order not to have more than one heading

Figure 3.27 Product Features

Potnt, Click & WoW!!

at the top, you can put the product name, company name, or key concept being discussed in the bottom righthand corner. This keeps it in front of your audience but does not distract from the main point of the screen.

Information on the Data Base: Before and After Ideas (Figures 3.28a, 3.28b)

Main point: The audience sees how much information is entered in the data base.

Features: Listing the data is not a very interesting way to present information. This is especially true if you have to report on the progress and time frames of many projects. Time lines make information much easier to process and compare. You can show all the information at once or do a build. Use a build only if you have more than a few sentences to say about each one. Otherwise show all the data at once and then make a general overall comment.

Other applications: Use a time line for just one or two lines on your screen and then have a couple of other points in bulleted phrases. Always ask yourself whether there are ways to show the information that enable your audience to quickly compare data or dates.

Quality is the Vehicle (Figures 3.29a, 3.29b)

Main point: The visual ties "quality" and "vehicle" to a car.

Features: The clip art car is used to make a point. The second visual with VROOOOM! gives a feeling of movement. This works because the words mention a vehicle.

Other applications: Use clip art that links to the topic or point being made. You want it to be so obvious you don't have to say anything. Or, if you have to say something, you want what you say about the clip art to be relevant to your topic.

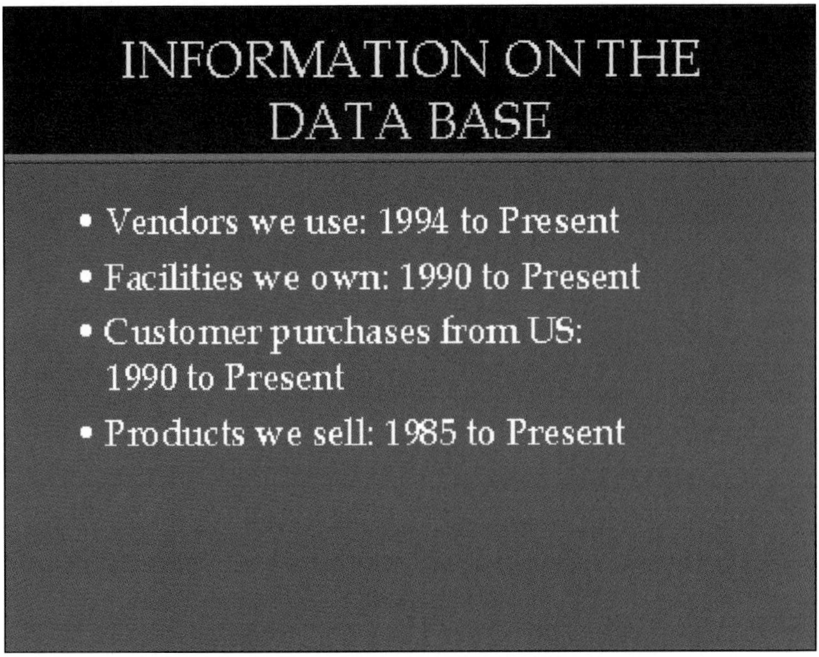

Figure 3.28a Information on the Data Base

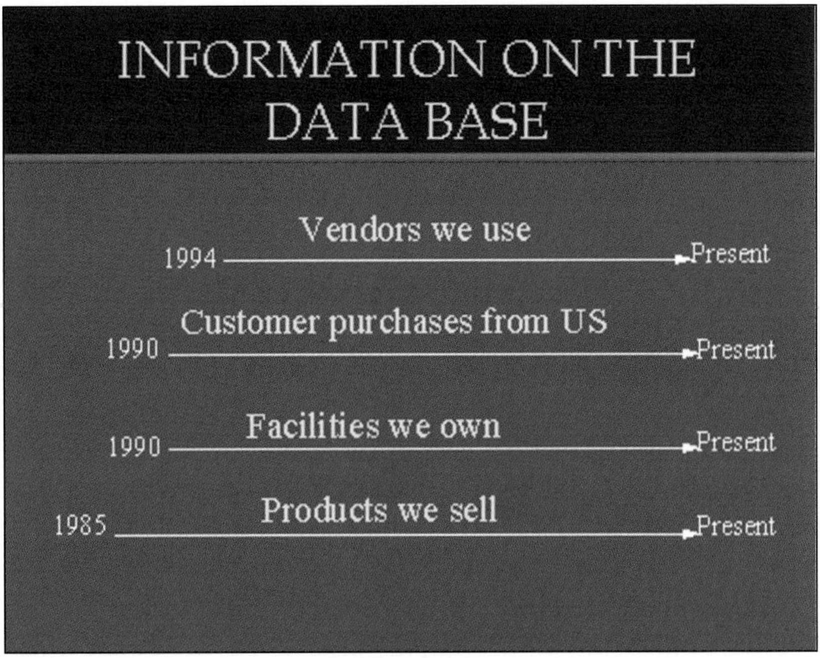

Figure 3.28b

Figure 3.29a Quality is the Vehicle

Figure 3.29b

Consumers Inc. Share Price (Figure 3.30)

Main point: The share price went up 433 percent from quarter 1 in 1994 to quarter 4 in 1995.

Features: Putting the arrows in and listing the percent increase focuses the audience on the main point. It's all there for them to see, instantly and automatically. Those who like trend lines can look at the line, while those who just want the bottom line number can see the number.

Other applications: When showing trends, ask yourself whether you need to put only one or two numbers on the screen so your audience does not have to struggle to figure out the key numbers.

Growth in U.S. Sales (Figure 3.31)

Main point: Sales are up 87 percent in 1994 in the United States.

Features: This visual shows the country of the sales, the figures since 1991 for those who want past data, and the key point that 1994 sales are up.

Other applications: Again, write out the main number your audience will want to know. Don't put too many numbers on your screen.

Multimedia Project (Figure 3.32)

Main point: Here is an update on the multimedia project.

Features: When you are listing what you have done and still have to do on a project, use checks and arrows. You can then say, "The checks are the items I have completed. The arrows are actions left to do." This makes it simple, as you don't have to read every item and say whether it is done or not. Your audience sees the situation in a quick visual glance.

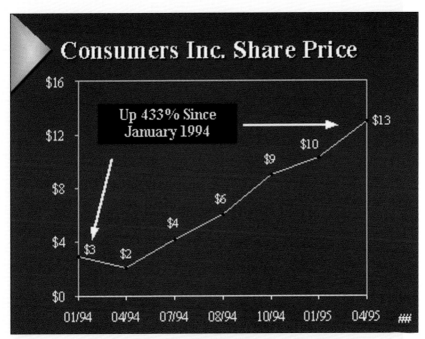

Figure 3.30 Consumers Inc. Share Price

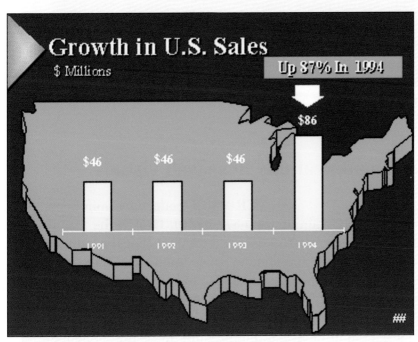

Figure 3.31 Growth in U.S. Sales

Other applications: Think about using symbols such as checks and arrows to convey the certain messages. Make up your own symbols for your particular presentation.

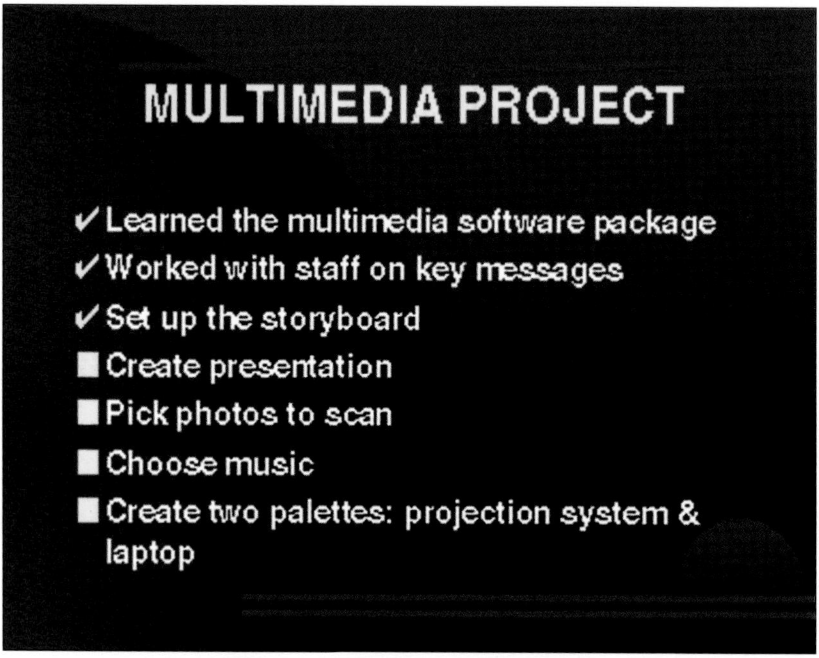

MULTIMEDIA PROJECT

✔ Learned the multimedia software package
✔ Worked with staff on key messages
✔ Set up the storyboard
■ Create presentation
■ Pick photos to scan
■ Choose music
■ Create two palettes: projection system & laptop

Figure 3.32 Multimedia Project

Telecommunications Research Visuals

TRA is a leader in communications technology training (800-872-4736). Due to the technical nature of their information and the fact that the subjects are sometimes not familiar to their audience, they have devised numerous methods, visuals, and other techniques to keep their audience interested and to train them in a short amount of time. On some of the visuals their instructors have created a system of icons. These icons keep the audience's

POINT, CLICK & *WoW!!*

interest and they very quickly tell the audience what to expect from the information on the visual. For example, they use the picture of a book with the words "Short Story" on it to say that this is a summary slide. They use a crystal ball icon to say that the visual is about the future. Here are three sample graphics.

Asynchronous Transfer Mode (Figure 3.33a)

Main point: Asynchronous Transfer Mode (ATM) specifies a formatting technique for information transport in which all information is carried in a similar fixed site container.

Features: The draft beer icon signals to the audience that there is not enough information on the visual to give them a full definition. The definition they see is just a "draft." This is a high level attempt to give the audience a first brush at the concept. This tells the audience that more information is coming, so just wait and some questions may get answered as the next visuals are presented.

They also use the familiar train analogy on this visual to make an unfamiliar concept easier for the audience to comprehend.

Virtual Circuits (Figure 3.33b)

Main point: A virtual circuit is a specific type of communication channel that is typically used for data transport.

Features: The Webster Dictionary icon tells the audience this is a full definition. There isn't additional information that needs to be presented. The audience has all the information on this slide. Consequently, if someone in the audience is confused, they need to ask now.

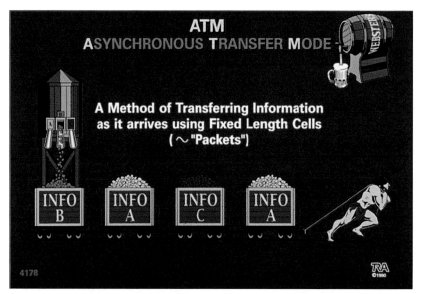

Figure 3.33a Asynchronous Transfer Mode

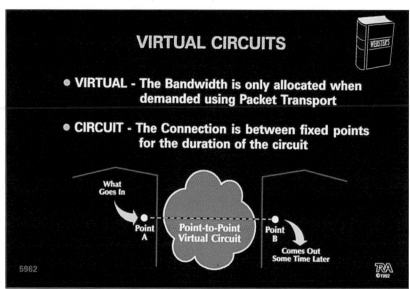

Figure 3.33b Virtual Circuits

LAN Interconnect Today (Figure 3.33c)

Main point: Users would have to wait up to six minutes for an image to be transferred if they were using a low-band-width communications channel.

Features: The icon of the man carrying a sign means that these are the user requirements. In this case, the user demands image transfer delays of less than six minutes.

Single Visual Checklist

Presenters tend to get involved in the details of designing their visuals. It is therefore important to sit back and take a second look at each one. Ask yourself these questions.

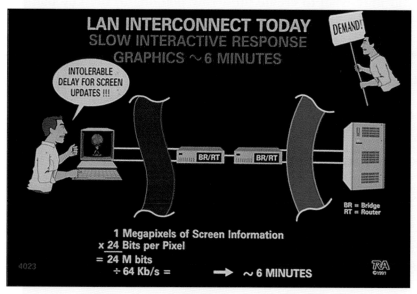

Figure 3.33c LAN Interconnect Today

Organization

❶ What is the major point of this visual?

❷ Does this visual have a heading that is different than the headings on the other visuals? You want to use different headings on each visual, making them easier to present from and easier for your audience to grasp the point.

❸ What information can I leave out of this visual? Could some of this information be given as a handout instead?

❹ Can any of this information be illustrated by a chart, symbol, or picture?

❺ Have I proofed this visual by starting at the bottom of the screen and reading it backward from right to left? This way you are more likely to see the mistakes.

❻ Do I use an arrow or some type of symbol that points to the important part of the chart or diagram?

❼ Can I highlight this information in such a way that I don't need to use a pointer to explain it? For example, with a chart you may wish to create an arrow pointing to the key data you are explaining.

Flow

❶ Will this photo work when I show it on my equipment? Will the colors show up?

❷ Am I going to show everything on this visual at one time or reveal the information separately as I talk?

❸ Where does my attention go when I look at this visual?

Look

❶ Do I use phrases, not sentences?

❷ Are the phrases parallel? Do they all start with verbs or start with nouns? It is easier to present when your starting words are set up this way.

❸ Have I left periods off the end of the phrases? Phrases do not need any punctuation.

❹ Have I included too many words that explain a picture? You can talk from the picture. If you include words that explain the picture as well, then why will your audience need to listen to you?

Total Visual Checklist

Once you have created all your screens, lay out a hard copy of your presentation on a table and look at it in its entirety. Yes, you can see it in sequence on the screen, but you don't get the same sense as when you lay it out and examine it all at once. You are seeing how everything looks together. Ask yourself these questions.

Organization

❶ Is there a logical organization to my presentation that an audience can follow? We are talking about your audience's ability to see the organization as you talk. For instance, you almost always need an opening screen with an agenda or overview.

❷ Did I use a format to organize the data?

Content and Flow

❶ Are there acronyms and abbreviations that are unfamiliar to my audience? Clarify anything that might be confusing.

❷ Are there human interest examples?

❸ Is there variety in the visuals? You don't want six pie charts in a row. Avoid repetition and monotony. Many people create electronic presentations that are just as dull as the overhead transparencies or slide shows they had previously created.

❹ What visuals can I cut out? You may discover that you don't need as many visuals to make your point.

❺ Do I have practical hints for the audience, if that is appropriate in the presentation?

❻ Is any of the clip art I used inappropriate for the audience?

❼ Where are the interesting changes in my visuals? Keep in mind the plot-point idea of showing visuals.

❽ Do I need all this information and detail? What could I leave out and hold as backup screens just in case I get a question?

❾ Did I include some questions to ask my audience in the middle of the talk to break it up? It is sometimes a good idea to pause midway, turn up the lights, and take questions. For a few minutes the dark room becomes light. People wake up and see you, and you have an opportunity to establish eye contact with your audience.

❿ Has my presentation been spell checked? Has it been carefully read by someone besides myself?

⓫ Have I numbered some of the phrases? You can show a list and say, "Here are some key points ... I will only talk about number four unless you want me to explain some of the other points."

⓬ What transition effects did I use?

Personalization

❶ Where have I personalized the visuals for my audience?

❷ Have I put my audience's name in the talk in different

places? For a small group it is fun to put people's names on some of the visuals. (See the personalized visuals example in Chapter 1, pages 11 and 12.)

❸ Is the wording and language appropriate for my audience? You might use technical words to your peers but nontechnical words to people unfamiliar with your area of expertise.

Look

❶ Are the font sizes large enough? Too large? Your answer to this question depends on the size of the screen. Obviously, with a gigantic screen you need larger sizes. A good rule is to avoid using fonts smaller than 24 points.

❷ Does every screen have a different heading on it? This makes it easy for the audience to quickly know the focus of the visual.

❸ Is the same typeface scheme followed throughout the entire presentation?

❹ Do I use all caps on the titles? That is acceptable. In bulleted phrases use caps only for the first letter of the word, not for the whole words.

❺ Did I use italics only occasionally for emphasis?

❻ Have I varied the layout styles used throughout the presentation? For example, you might include two-bullet columns, a one-bullet column, a chart, a picture and so on.

The Ten Don'ts for Visuals

Here is a summary of what not to do when creating visuals:

❶ Don't use a gradient template with a building scene, especially if you are showing charts and graphs. It is very difficult to read words and see charts superimposed over the buildings.

❷ Don't make your whole presentation a series of builds.

❸ Don't use so many colors that the presentation carries no consistency.

❹ Don't use so many different models and diagrams that your audience never has an opportunity to fix one or two models in their mind.

❺ Don't include so many words that you don't have anything to say besides what is written on the visuals.

❻ Don't use photos that take up too much memory for the size of your computer. Your computer will take a long time to bring them up on the screen. And don't show photos on equipment that doesn't have very good resolution. They will look blurred.

❼ Don't use a black background.

❽ Don't assume that you needn't look at the audience.

❾ Don't put so many numbers on a chart that your audience can't figure out the point of the chart.

❿ Don't include so many visuals that you know you will be short of time even before you start the presentation.

Finally, never assume that when you call a facility and ask about the equipment and the types of visuals you can show that the person you are talking to understands your questions or has the knowledge to answer them. People may tell you that your photos will show up fine on their equipment, yet when you arrive you find there isn't enough light for the photos to look anything but poor.

4

REHEARSE, REHEARSE, REHEARSE

*"If I'd rehearsed properly, I would have known
to turn off the screen saver."*

You must never kid yourself
that you don't need to practice your presentation out loud
using all your equipment and in the clothes you will be wearing. You may think you know how to use the technology. You
may think you know where you will stand so you can see
your laptop or the screen. But until you actually do the talk,
you don't know how you will give it. The only way you can
know is to practice in the same room with the same equipment you will be using. If you don't, you may be in for some
surprises.

In this chapter we will cover some of the technology issues
that you should check on during your rehearsal. We include
a real rehearsal flow chart for you to consider using, plus a
feedback sheet you can ask the people who come to your
practice to fill out. You'll also get some ideas on how to tame
the technology (or, if you can't tame it, at least how not to get
mauled by it). And finally, you'll get some general refresher
ideas on giving excellent presentations.

Check the Equipment and the Room

This section is a series of checklists. It reflects our philosophy (the same as that of the Boy and Girl Scouts): Be prepared. Based on our experience, everything goes wrong or fails to work at some stage in the life of a presenter. The best approach to dealing with all conceivable eventualities is to invest time up front in contingency planning and meticulous checking of details.

The Portable PC Checklist—For Traveling Presenters

See page 108 for the checklist form.

❶ *Saved disk and compression.* Have you saved your presentation onto a disk? If you are using a compression program that needs to be decompressed on retrieval, do you have a backup version of the software with you in case you need to use a PC that does not have the software to retrieve it? An alternative, if the file is too big to fit on one disk, is to simply split the presentation into segments and save each segment (without compressing it) on a separate disk.

❷ *Linked files.* Have you saved all related or linked files, such as video clips, that form part of your presentation?

❸ *Backup plan for a crash.* What is your backup plan in case your PC crashes? Have you made contingency arrangements to use an alternative PC from either your company or a local audiovisual firm? Do you know the PC specifications including the resolution settings you need?

❹ *Transferring files.* In the event you need to use a backup PC, do you have a way to transfer your presentation onto it? Does the backup PC have your presentation software on it? As a precautionary measure, do you have a copy of the viewer version of your presentation program that can be loaded onto the backup PC to run your presentation? (One of the authors, David, always travels with two backup copies of the presentation in different pieces of luggage, plus a copy of the viewer program in case it is needed to run the presentation disk.)

❺ *Overheads or a hard copy.* If it is not possible to organize a backup PC plan, are you at least traveling with overheads or paper copies that can be made into overheads? An overhead presentation will not be as effective as your electronic one, but at least you will still be able to present.

❻ *Electrical adapter.* If you are traveling internationally, do you have an electrical adapter kit, just in case the hotel or company does not have one? You also need a surge protector to use in all countries. Better safe than sorry!

❼ *Sufficient rehearsal time.* Have you scheduled sufficient time at the presentation location for a complete rehearsal and to allow for fixing all problems? Is there enough time to implement your backup plan if your PC crashes?

❽ *Items needed.* Are you traveling with the following items?

➤ 400-watt (4,000 to 6,000 lumen) light bulb for an overhead projector

➤ Extension cord and powerstrip

➤ A roll of tape (duct or electrical tape) to tape wires to floor to prevent people from tripping over them

➤ Name and phone number of audiovisual contacts in the city where you are presenting

➤ A spare mouse in case yours malfunctions

➤ A pointer—pointing with your hand usually blocks some people from seeing the screen, and standing in the light creates shadows (You can also use the pointer in the software program.)

➤ Extra batteries for your pointer

⑨ *Turned off screen saver.* Have you turned off the screen saver on your computer? Why? When you are presenting in front of an audience, do you want your screen saver to come up on the screen? It will be embarrassing.

⑩ *Screen and PC at same time.* Know which keys to press so you can show visuals simultaneously on the screen. Most PCs have 3 options: display on PC screen, display on screen, display on both screens.

⑪ *Turned off power-saving feature.* Most PCs when operating on a battery have a power-saver feature that puts them in "sleep mode," which means the screen goes blank. Make sure this is switched off.

The Location
(Meeting Room, Hotel, Convention Center) Checklist

See page 109 for the checklist form. It's 2:00 p.m. The lights dim and it's your turn. Are you ready? Here are the things that you should have done:

❶ *Equipment*
Ordered or brought all the required equipment, whether LCD panel and overhead, or projection system and computer, plus:

➤ Table for PC, and a chair

➤ Podium with working light

➤ Wireless lavaliere microphone

➤ Pointer

➤ Handouts

➤ Electric or duct tape for wiring

➤ Extension cord

➤ Powerstrip and cables

➤ Spare bulb for overhead or projection system

➤ Remote mouse

❷ *Screen.* Selected the right screen size, which is a critical factor. It depends on the size of the room, the size of the audience, and the size of type on your visuals. As a rule of thumb, the first row of seats should not be any closer to the screen than two times the screen height, and the farthest row should not be any farther than eight times the screen height. And is the screen high enough for everyone to see? If not, put the screen on a table. Why? Those in the back row will be able to see the bottom third of the screen.

❸ *Room access.* Ensured the room will be available when you want it. (Don't assume that just because you arrive in good time you will have access to the room. It may be occupied.)

❹ *Assistance.* Ensured that someone from the audiovisual department or AV company is on site to assist you—and that the person knows something!

❺ *Seats.* Sat in various seats to check that the screen and presenter will be clearly visible.

❻ *Podium.* Checked that the light from the podium does not cast rays on the screen; put the pointer at the podium and tried it out; arranged the podium or location where the speaker will stand to the left of the screen at a 45-degree angle to the audience, as shown in Figure 4.1.

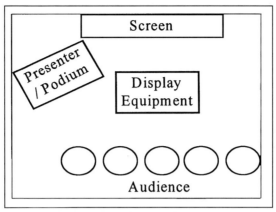

Figure 4.1 Podium Placement

❼ *Lighting.* Checked the lighting. Made sure no light is directly over the path of the projector or shining on the screen. Where possible, removed fluorescent lights and switched off or removed any spotlights above the screen. The best situation is nonfluorescent lighting that can be controlled with a dimmer switch.

❽ *Cords.* Taped over exposed floor cords and wires to avoid people tripping, and to conceal most wires

❾ *Microphones.* Tested the microphones.

❿ *Details.* Confirmed the schedule and time allotted. Checked the locations of the restrooms and fire exits. Some people walk the fire exits to be sure they are accessible.

⓫ *Screen saver.* Switched off your screen saver.

⓬ *Rehearsal.* Arrived in time to complete a run-through of the entire presentation and to correct any problems, which may include replacing the computer.

⓭ *Mouse.* Practiced using the mouse. If possible, use a remote mouse so you can walk around. Also, when it's dark, using a mouse eliminates the possibility of pressing the wrong key.

⓮ *Clothes.* Checked that everything is buttoned, zipped, etc.

⓯ *Water.* Put a glass of water where you will be speaking.

⓰ *Relax.* Breathed deeply and smiled, to yourself and others.

The Portable PC Checklist

The Portable PC Checklist for Traveling Presenters

Date of Presentation: _____   Contact: _____

Location: _____   Audience Size: _____

Item	Required
1. Have you saved your presentation on disk?	
2. If you compressed your files, do you have the software for retrieving the files?	
3. Have you saved all related or linked files (video clips, graphics)?	
4. Do you have a backup copy of your presentation software or a viewer version of your presentation software in case you have to use a backup PC?	
5. Do you have hard copy materials that can be made into overheads?	
6. Do you have an electrical adapter kit and surge protector for international travel?	
7. Have you allowed for sufficient rehearsal and setup time at the presentation site?	
8. Do you have the following items packed: • 4000 to 6000 lumen light bulb for overhead projector • Extension cord and powerstrip • Roll of electrical or duct tape • Names and phone numbers of audiovisual contacts in presentation city • Spare mouse • Pointer • Extra batteries (for pointer)	

The Location Checklist

CHECKLIST

The Location Checklist
(Meeting Room, Hotel, Convention Center)

Date of Presentation: _____   Contact: _____

Location: _____   Audience Size: _____

Item	YES	NO

1. Equipment
   Required equipment
   Projection system and computer
   Table for PC, and a chair
   Podium with working light
   Wireless lavaliere microphone
   Pointer
   Handouts
   Electric or duct tape for wiring
   Extension cord
   Powerstrip
   Spare bulb for overhead or projection system
   Remote mouse		

2. Screen		
3. Room access		
4. Assistance		
5. Seats		
6. Podium		
7. Lighting		
8. Cords		
9. Microphones		

10. Details
   Schedule
   Time alloted
   Washroom locations, fire exits		

11. Screen saver		
12. Rehearsal		
13. Mouse		
14. Clothes		
15. Water		
16. Relax		

The Real Rehearsal Flow Chart

You've created an effective electronic presentation. To give it with style, go through all the steps in Figure 4.2, The Real Rehearsal Flow Chart.

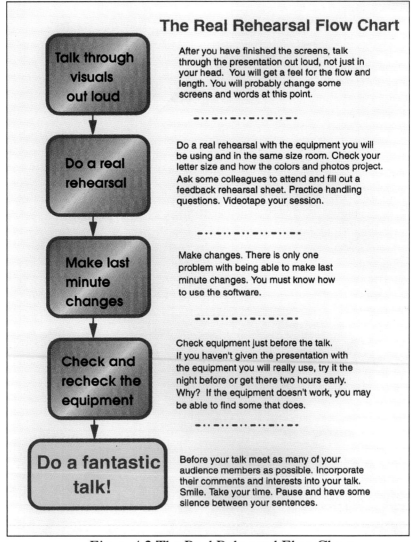

The Real Rehearsal Flow Chart

Talk through visuals out loud
After you have finished the screens, talk through the presentation out loud, not just in your head. You will get a feel for the flow and length. You will probably change some screens and words at this point.

Do a real rehearsal
Do a real rehearsal with the equipment you will be using and in the same size room. Check your letter size and how the colors and photos project. Ask some colleagues to attend and fill out a feedback rehearsal sheet. Practice handling questions. Videotape your session.

Make last minute changes
Make changes. There is only one problem with being able to make last minute changes. You must know how to use the software.

Check and recheck the equipment
Check equipment just before the talk. If you haven't given the presentation with the equipment you will really use, try it the night before or get there two hours early. Why? If the equipment doesn't work, you may be able to find some that does.

Do a fantastic talk!
Before your talk meet as many of your audience members as possible. Incorporate their comments and interests into your talk. Smile. Take your time. Pause and have some silence between your sentences.

Figure 4.2 The Real Rehearsal Flow Chart

Feedback Rehearsal Sheet

Figure 4.3 provides a sample feedback rehearsal sheet. Hand out these sheets to people who serve as your "guinea pig" audience for rehearsing the complete presentation.

FEEDBACK REHEARSAL SHEET

Thank you for watching me practice for my presentation. From your observations, please *check* or *circle* the ones you have noticed during my presentation. Your candid answers will help me enhance my communication style.

NON-VERBALS

____ Standing in front of the screen instead of beside it   ____ Shuffling notes
____ Fidgeting with a pen or pointer   ____ Juggling keys or coins in a pocket

Eye contact	just right	not enough	
Moving	just right	too much	too little
Expressions	just right	overly done	too deadpan
Posture	just right	too stiff	too loose

LANGUAGE

Technical words	just right	too many	too few
Examples	just right	too many	too few
Said too many "uhs" or "ums"	yes	sometimes	no

VOICE

Speed	just right	too fast	too slow
Sound	convincing tone	overly solicitous	unconvincing tone
Emotion	just right	too emotional	no emotion (monotone)

TECHNOLOGY

Spoke about words on the screen and didn't just read them

       yes   sometimes   no

Talked to the audience, not screen or laptop screen

       yes   sometimes   no

Clicked the right button at the same time

       yes   sometimes   no

Held the pointer still on the screen

       yes   sometimes   no

Please list two of my presentation habits or behaviors you see as effective.

1. _____

2. _____

Please list one suggestion for how I can use the technology more effectively:

1. _____

Figure 4.3 Feedback Rehearsal Sheet

Tame the Technology

Rehearsals with technology are a bit more complicated. It is sometimes hard to find all the equipment in order to practice, but be persistent and ask people to set up a room with the equipment. You will be happy you had the opportunity to get a feel for all that goes into using the equipment. If someone else will be helping you, you need to get your signals clear and to practice working together.

Here are some hints to help you always present with style and confidence. We have gathered these ideas from numerous experienced electronic presenters.

❶ *Keep your thumb quiet on the mouse.* Joan practiced using a remote mouse the night before her talk. She practiced sitting and looking at the screen. During the presentation the next day, she looked up at the screen several times only to be shocked to see that the next visual was already up there. It turns out Joan has a nervous habit of moving her thumb, and she was inadvertently clicking the forward mouse button as she talked. She never knew she moved her fingers so much when talking. Curing a moving thumb before getting up in front of an audience is a lot easier than trying to do it during the presentation.

❷ *Keep the arrow still on the screen.* Better yet, hide the arrow from the audience's view. Jim sometimes used the arrow to draw images on the screen. He was actually fairly good at the drawings, and his audience liked to see them. But after finishing the drawings, he inadvertently kept moving the arrow all over the screen. He needed to take the arrow off the screen when not using it.

❸ *Make sure the photos are clear on the screen and that the laptop you use has enough memory for your photos.* Michelle thought the photos looked great on the laptop. How could they look so different on the big screen? Everything was washed out.

POINT, CLICK & *WoW!!*

She had never considered that the size of the screen and the darkness of the room would make a big difference in how the photos would look.

❹ *Use a fast enough computer.* The fade ins and outs looked great on the laptop, but the actual equipment that Bob used for the presentation couldn't handle the speed. The transitions were unbearably slow. Bob felt awkward and didn't know what to say during the slow transitions.

❺ *Make sure the expert is an expert.* Susan's company was told by the catering office of the four-star conference center that the center had people who ran the electronic equipment and not to worry. Her company had spent thousands of dollars putting together a presentation to be given to a group of consultants. Susan hoped to obtain a great deal of business by impressing the consultants with her expertise.

Unfortunately, the so-called electronic "experts" at the conference center could not get the equipment to work. Susan never got to give her wonderful presentation. Don't be fooled. The expert you talk to ahead of time may be on vacation the week you are at the conference center. Qualify the person as an expert, then find out if he or she will be there the week you are using the facilities.

❻ *When speaking, have lights on you.* The conference center where Bill was speaking was not equipped to have a light focused on him while he gave a presentation using a laptop and LCD panel. Consequently, Bill was in the dark for the whole 45-minute presentation.

❼ *If there's no light on you, break up the talk.* Cut some of your visuals and spend more time answering questions. Divide the talk, and after every 15-minute segment, turn the lights up. Take 5 minutes of questions about the portion of the presentation just covered. The room energy will change, as the audience gets to see you and interact with you.

❽ *Get the right equipment.* Before you invest in an LCD panel and pay someone to create a fancy electronic presentation, find out whether your clients have the right kind of overhead projectors. Several presentation developers have discovered that over half their clients don't have the right kind of overhead projectors for an LCD panel. Some companies have said, "Until we can carry all the equipment with us, we will continue to use slides."

⑨ *Know the environment.* If the meeting is at a site you don't control, the odds of something going wrong increase dramatically. Low tech methods such as using overhead transparencies have fewer breakdowns. Dennis Belcher, financial consultant, says, "If the site is my site and under my control, then I use the high tech equipment. If the site is not my site, and not under my control, I go as low tech as I can get."

⑩ *Be sure the site has state-of-the-art equipment.* Never believe it when representatives for a conference site say they have the equipment needed for you to give a multimedia presentation. They may have equipment, but not state-of-the art. Find out the brands, types and capabilities of the equipment.

⑪ *Get a clear video projector.* Again, just because people say they have what you need, you can't be sure it works well or at all. Come prepared with a backup plan in case the equipment does not work.

⑫ *Check out the computer.* Check out the computer one last time just before the presentation. Then don't play with it, and don't let anyone else touch it. Don't leave the room with your computer on unless you put a sign on it that says, "Please don't touch the equipment. Thank you."

⑬ *Work with your hired graphics expert.* When you hire a consultant to create a presentation, you need to direct him or her. You need to explain the type of audience who will be seeing the presentation, give him or her a sense of your business, and describe the levels of expertise of the people who will be giving the presentation. Don't assume the expert is thinking of all these things. We have heard of companies spending thousands of dollars to have a presentation designed only to have to scrap it.

⑭ *Be sure you can run the software.* When you hire someone to make a sophisticated presentation, you need to know how to use the graphics package it was created with. Why? What if something happens during the middle of your talk and you haven't the faintest idea what to do? You should at least learn the program basics.

⑮ *Know the minimum requirements.* The presentation may run great on your 486 at work, yet on the laptop out at the customer's site the transitions are too slow. Save yourself the embarrassment and ask ahead of time whether on site equipment meets your requirements. Better yet, if you bring all your own equipment, you'll never have to worry about this issue.

⑯ *Use the partner system.* For high-level key presentations, always go in twos. If something happens with the technology, one of you can talk to the audience while the other troubleshoots the equipment. A good pairing consists of the speaker and the expert on the technology. It's not a good idea to pair two speakers who are novices concerning the equipment or software program, or two technical experts who are inexperienced speakers.

⑰ *Carry an extra bulb for the projection system.* Projection systems usually have two bulbs. Sometimes one of the bulbs burns out and no one replaces it. Consequently, you may have a false sense of security, thinking you have an extra bulb when you don't. Always check to be sure both bulbs work. Bob Weaver of Action Direct Marketing, a Polaroid dealer, says, "The only bulb that always works is the one in your pocket."

Present With Total Confidence

You've now created a clear, easy-to-follow electronic presentation. If you want to give it with style, follow these simple guidelines. If you really want to be sure you are ready, get someone to watch you and ask the person to fill out the feedback sheet in Figure 4.3.

The Pointer

When you use a laser pointer, you must hold it still on one point on the screen. And you must leave it in one place long enough for your audience to focus their eyes on the spot you are pointing to. Follow these same guidelines when using the pointer from the software program. Never leave the pointer on and wave it in your audience's eyes. People don't like that! Using a laser pointer takes practice—but not when you are in front of your audience. Practice using the pointer and have someone watch you and tell you if you are using it effectively.

Clothes

Practice in the actual clothing you will wear. You may have to climb up and down a platform, so don't wear anything too tight that won't let you take big steps. If you have gained or lost weight, be sure the clothes aren't so loose that they bag or so tight that seams will rip open or the zipper pop. (Not a pleasant experience when you are presenting in front of a hundred people!) Women, don't wear bracelets with loose jangling pieces, or every time you push the mouse button your jewelry will make a noise against the mouse.

Standing

You should plant your feet toward the audience. How you view your visual depends on how you have set up the room and the size of the screen. You can stand by the screen and use the screen as your visual. You will probably not be standing by the screen if it is gigantic; you may not even be able to read from the screen effectively. In that case, you will need to see the images on your laptop. Consequently, you need to position your laptop so you can see the images. You may find that the table is too low for the laptop, and you will have to get a box to put the laptop on. You only find out these kinds of things when you practice out loud with all your equipment.

Speaking

- ➤ Stand so everyone can see you.

- ➤ Ask, "Shall I say some more about this now?" If the audience says no, go on. Don't bore them.

- ➤ Ask, "Do I need to move back so you can see?" Don't ask, "Can everyone see?" They will be polite and say, "Yes."

- ➤ Put the pointer down when you are not using it.

- ➤ If your hand shakes, get someone else to move the arrow on the screen.

- ➤ Say something else besides reading off the screens.

- ➤ Talk to the audience, not the visual.

- ➤ Write up and then ask some interactive questions to involve the audience.

- ➤ Practice the whole talk out loud so you will know how long it is.

- ➤ Get a massage the day before your talk so you will feel relaxed.

- ➤ Don't ask, "Can you hear me?" People will be polite and say yes. Ask, "Shall I speak a little louder?" Better yet, have a person in the audience cue you to let you know if your voice volume is loud enough.

One last word. Let's say you have done everything we suggest. You are totally prepared, and still something goes wrong. What could go wrong you ask? The electricity in the hotel goes off. The company has a fire drill. Someone walks by and spills coffee all over your laptop. No matter what occurs, have a sense of humor. Get your audience to laugh with you. No one who laughs becomes or stays upset. Laughter gets everyone on your side. You can also remind yourself that whatever you're experiencing will make a great story in a few days. May you enjoy your fun, sophisticated presentations!

The LCD Panel / Projector Checklist

CHECKLIST

The LCD Panel / Projector Checklist

Date of Presentation: _____   Contact: _____

Location: _____   Audience Size: _____

Item	YES	NO
1. Is there a backup LCD unit or at least a spare bulb for the overhead projector?		
2. Do you have a plan if the LCD does not work?		
3. Have you checked that the bulb in the overhead projector generates at least 4,000 lumens and is not an incandescent bulb? (6,000 lumens is better) 3a. You want metal-halide or halogen bulbs. Do you have an extra overhead projector bulb? 3b. Does it work?		
4. Have you left sufficient time in the schedule to rehearse with all the equipment and replace the LCD (or a bulb) if it does not function effectively? Don't leave the rehearsal to the last minute.		
5. Do you have the name of a local audiovisual contact in case you run into a technical problem?		
6. Have you specified exactly the type of overhead projector you need—one for LCD panels?		
7. Do you know how to start up the LCD panel? Do you know which buttons adjust the colors and the postition on the screen?		
8. Have you rehearsed with the same type of equipment you will be using for the presentation?		
9. Do you have a remote mouse?		
10. Have you cleaned the projector equipment—the LCD lens or projector system lens?		
11. Do you have a wireless lavaliere microphone (the only kind to use!)? Are you wearing clothing you can clip the microphone pack to?		

RESOURCES

Ongoing Presentation Ideas and Technology

Presentations: Technology and Techniques for Better Communications.
This monthly magazine discusses the latest technology, gives
a company case study, and provides ideas on presenting.
Very informative and easy to read. Subscription information:
800-328-4329.

Time Devices

The Pacesetter. This small device helps you time your talk.
It vibrates or beeps to alert you of the time. Information:
800-950-1397.

Software Training

For information about software training, here are some
numbers to call.

Astound from Gold Disk. The software company is just
starting to put some type of training together. 800-835-5889.

Freelance Graphics from Lotus. The operator will give you
a list of training partners. 800-346-6409.

Director from Macromedia. The operator will give you the
names of authorized training centers. 800-279-8412.

PowerPoint from Microsoft. When you call select the
Windows 95, Office for Windows 95 option. 800-426-9400.

Presentations from Novell. The operator can give you
names of training centers. 800-233-3382.

Harvard Graphics from Software Publishing Corp. They
can tell you about their authorized training centers.
800-234-2500.

INDEX

Po!nt, Cl*ck & *WoW!!

Wilder Management Services

Discover the exquisite feeling of confidence when you deliver an outstanding presentation. Wilder Management Services is a unique consulting firm specializing in business presentations. Our firm's combination of expertise in both content organization/graphic design and delivery gives you everything you need to be a successful presenter.

3 wks   927.

Caesar

Caesar

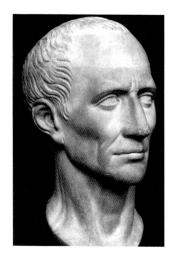

Nigel Cawthorne

HAUS PUBLISHING • LONDON

First published in Great Britain in 2005 by Haus Publishing Limited
26 Cadogan Court
Draycott Avenue
London SW3 3BX

Copyright © Nigel Cawthorne, 2005
The moral rights of the author have been asserted
A CIP catalogue record for this book is available from the British Library
ISBN 1-904950-11-6

Designed and typeset in Garamond by Falcon Oast Graphic Art
Printed and bound by Graphicom in Vicenza, Italy
Front cover: Courtesy akg-Images
Back cover: Courtesy akg-Images

Contents

The Road to Power – 100 to 59 BC

Gaius Julius Caesar was born on 12 or 13 July probably in the year 100 or, perhaps, 102 BC; sources differ. Or rather he was born on 12 or 13 Quintilis in 638 or 640 as Quintilis – the fifth month in the Roman calendar whose year began in March – was later renamed July in his honour and, until the Christian era, the Romans numbered their years from the legendary foundation of the Roman calendar by Romulus in 738 BC.

Gaius was Julius Caesar's given name. His family name was Caesar, though later emperors of Rome adopted the name and gradually the name Caesar became a title. It is the origin of the later titles Kaiser and Czar. Caesar's *gens*, or clan name, was Julius.

The Julii were patricians – that is, they were members of Rome's original aristocracy – and the Julii Caesars traced their lineage back to the goddess Venus. However, by the time Gaius was born, they were not rich or particularly influential.

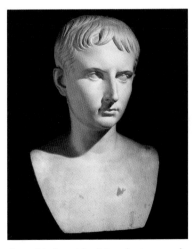

Caesar's father, Gaius Caesar died when Caesar was 16, having only reached the rank of praetor, or magistrate. His mother, Aurelia, of the prominent family of Cotta, was particularly influential in the development of

A marble bust idealising the image of the young Julius Caesar

According to legend, Rome was founded when Amulius deposed his older brother Numitor as king of Alba Longa. To secure his position against his brother's family, Amulius forced Numitor's only daughter, Rhea Silvia, to take the Vestal's vow of chastity. However, she was raped by Mars, the god of war, and gave birth to the twins, Romulus and Remus. Amulius ordered them to be drowned in the River Tiber, which separates the Etruscan land of Etruria from Latium to the south, but were washed ashore and suckled by a she-wolf until they were discovered by the shepherd Faustulus who raised them. As men, Romulus and Remus killed Amulius, put Numitor back on the throne, and founded the city of Rome on the site where they had been saved. Romulus built the city wall, but when Remus jumped over it, Romulus killed him. So the city was named Rome after the surviving brother, Romulus.

the young Caesar. According to the 1st-century historian Tacitus (AD 54–120), she was a typical Roman matron of her day.

'It was her particular honour to care for the home and serve her children . . . and no one dared do or say anything improper in front of her,' he said. 'She supervised not only the boys' studies but also their recreation and games with piety and modesty. Thus, tradition has it, Cornelia, mother of the Gracchi [social reformer Tiberius Gracchus (c167–133 BC)], Aurelia, mother of Julius Caesar, and Atia, mother of Augustus [Roman emperor (63 BC–AD 14), brought up their sons and produced princes.'[1]

Down on their luck, the family lived in an *insula*, or multi-storey apartment house, in the poor, multi-ethnic area of Subura. They did have servants, though. One was a slave from Gaul, a region still mostly outside Roman control. The young Caesar received a fine education under one of Rome's most important teachers, Marcus Antonius Gnipho, who was also the tutor of the famous orator Marcus Tullius Cicero (106–43 BC).

Rome was in political turmoil throughout Caesar's childhood.

According to the 2nd-century Greek historian Appian of Alexandria: 'Repeatedly parties openly took sides against each other, and often carried daggers; from time to time a tribune or praetor or consul, or a candidate for these offices would be murdered in a temple, or in the assembly, or in the Forum. Undisciplined arrogance soon became the rule, along with a shameful contempt for law and justice . . . Some refused to give up control of the armies entrusted to them by the people, and others even recruited foreigners on their own account, without public authority, to fight against their rivals. If one side took possession of Rome first, the other made war in theory against the rival faction, but in fact against their own country; they attacked it as though it were enemy soil, mercilessly slaughtered those who stood in their way, and proscribed, banished, and confiscated the property of the rest, some of whom they even tortured horribly. No sort of atrocity was left undone . . . '[2]

The founders of Rome were all men. To prevent the city from extinction after a single generation, they needed women. But the peoples of the surrounding tribes considered Romulus and his men little more than criminals and would not let their daughters intermarry. So Romulus invited the neighbouring Sabines to the games in Rome and abducted all their women in the famous rape of the Sabine women. Rome was then ruled by seven kings, but when Sextus Tarquinius, the son of the seventh king, Tarquin the Proud, raped the beautiful Lucretia in 509 bc, the royal family were expelled by Lucius Junius Brutus. A Republic was then established, which endured for the next 478 years.

The great hope for Caesar's family was Gaius Marius (157–86 bc), who had married Caesar's paternal aunt Julia in 113 bc. Marius was sometimes called the Third Founder of Rome – the first being Romulus, the second Lucius Junius Brutus. Marius was a 'new man' – that is, he did not have a distinguished family of his own. One of the most successful Roman generals in history, he had defeated the armies of Celts from Gaul and Germania in 102 and 101 BC and had been consul – one of two men elected to rule Rome each year – six times between 107 and 100 BC. His wealth and influence brought prestige back to Caesar's family and, vitally for Caesar's career in the long run, Marius had forced reforms on the Roman army. For the first time, men without property were encouraged to serve as soldiers. After Marius, poor men followed any general who offered them plunder and advancement.

In 90 BC the Social or Italic War broke out when Rome's Italian allies – the *socii*, who were denied Roman citizenship – rebelled. They felt that, though they had fought for Rome, they had never received a fair share in the spoils of the Roman empire, which extended in those days across Andalusia, southern Castile, Catalonia, Provence, Italy, the Dalmatian coast, Greece and Macedonia, Asia Minor, Cyprus, Crete and modern Tunisia. In the Social War of 90 to 89 BC, the Roman army crushed the revolt, while legislation instigated by Caesar's distant cousin, consul Lucius Julius Caesar (died 87 BC), granted Roman citizenship to those who had not rebelled. The effect was to unite the whole of the country south of the River Po, which runs from the Cottian Alps to the Adriatic across northern Italy. The conflict also put more generals in the field who were unwilling to relinquish command once the war was over.

Marius was locked in a deadly rivalry with his former protégé Lucius Cornelius Sulla (138–78 BC). He joined forces with Lucius Cornelius Cinna (died 84 BC) and captured Rome, while Sulla was away fighting King Mithridates VI (reigned 120–63 BC) of Pontus – north-eastern Anatolia – who had invaded Greece. Marius and Cinna took the consulships in 87 BC. There followed a massacre of Sulla's followers.

Caesar married Cornelia, the daughter of Cinna, and they had a daughter, Julia. When Sulla marched on Rome for a second time and became its dictator in 82 BC, after Marius and Cinna died, he ordered the 18-year-old Caesar to divorce Cornelia as a demonstration of loyalty to the new regime. Caesar refused. Sulla was impressed with his courage and spared him, saying, 'in this young man there is more than one Marius'.[3]

However, it was still politic to stay out of Sulla's way, so Caesar went out east to do military service. Between 81 and 79 BC, Caesar served in Asia Minor on the personal staff of Marcus Minucius Thermus, who was praetor in Asia Minor. Caesar was sent on a diplomatic mission to King Nicomedes IV (reigned c94–c74 BC) of Bithynia – north-west Anatolia – and seems to have had a homosexual affair with him.

Eventually Caesar won his laurels for taking Mytilene, the capital of Lesbos. Or at least he was awarded the *corona civica*, a wreath of oak leaves and acorns traditionally given to the first soldier, or centurion, to scale the walls of a besieged city. (It was said that Caesar enjoyed winning such wreaths because he was going bald. To hide this, he brushed his hair forward in a style later copied by Napoleon, who did not suffer from hair loss.) Soon after, Caesar was captured by Cilician pirates from south-eastern Asia Minor, who infested the Mediterranean at

Caesar's affair with King Nicomedes of Bithynia left a stain on his character. A notorious poem by Gaius Licinius Calvus (82–c47 BC) began: 'Whate'er Bithynia and her lord possess'd, Her lord who Caesar in his lust caress'd' According to Cicero, royal attendants conducted Caesar from his own bedroom to that of the king. There he had been laid 'upon a bed of gold with a covering of purple, where the flower of youth and innocence of him who was descended from Venus became defiled in Bithynia'. Later, when Caesar pleaded the cause of Nysa, the daughter of Nicomedes, before the Senate, he recounted the king's many kindnesses to him. In reply, Cicero said: 'Pray tell us no more of that. We all know what he gave you and what you gave him in return.'

the time. As they provided slaves for Senators' plantations, the Roman Senate largely tolerated the Cilicians. Caesar had to pay the standard ransom of 25 talents – some 500 kilograms – of silver. After this incident, he continued his studies.

When Sulla died in 78 BC, Caesar felt safe to return to Italy, where he started a career as a criminal lawyer. This was a shrewd political move. He won support among the clients he defended and gained a reputation for being on the people's side by prosecuting several prominent Romans for corruption. His first target was Dolabella, a leading follower of Sulla.

Considered a superb advocate and orator, second only to Cicero in skill and eloquence, Caesar spoke Greek fluently – essential for an educated Roman. He was well versed in Greek philosophy, literature and art, and he exhibited great magnetism and personal charm, and knew everyone in the centres of power in Rome. He also dressed ostentatiously and was extravagant with money.

In 75 BC, Caesar left Rome to study rhetoric in Rhodes, a necessary step in a political career. On the way there, he was once again captured by pirates, who demanded the usual tariff. Caesar insisted that the price be doubled – he was, after all, an aristocrat. He was held captive for 40 days while his men set about borrowing the ransom – 50 silver talents or 12,000 gold pieces. While they were away, Caesar joked with his captors, ordering them about and often promising, with a smile on his face, that he when he was free he 'would soon capture and crucify them – and this is exactly what he did'.[4] Once the ransom was paid and he was released, Caesar hired some ships, returned, captured the pirates and, good to his word, had them crucified.

In 74 BC, King Mithridates VI of Pontus attacked the Romans again. On his own initiative and expenses, Caesar raised a small army and defended some towns, giving the official Roman commander Lucius Licinius Lucullus (c118–56 BC) time to organise an army and attack Mithridates in Pontus.

Returning to Rome a war hero in 73 BC, Caesar began his political career in earnest. He was elected to the college of pontifices, which gave him high office in the Roman priesthood. Even so, he continued his spendthrift ways. He is thought to have built an expensive country house on Lake Nemi to the south of Rome, only to have it pulled down when he found it unsatisfactory. He was an avid collector of fine art and handsome young slaves. It was said that his debts approached eight million denarii – over $2.5 million – a fabulous sum for a young man without means.

He also began acquiring a reputation as the seducer of wives of men in his own social class, which added to his early reputation of being gay. Curio the Elder called him: 'Every woman's husband and every man's wife.'[5] It is difficult to find one of Caesar's later enemies – Cato, Pompey, Crassus, Bibulus – who was not thought to have been cuckolded by him. 'That he was unbridled and extravagant in his intrigues is the general opinion, and that he seduced many illustrious women,' Suetonius wrote, but beyond all others Caesar loved Servilia, the mother of Marcus Brutus, for whom in his first consulship he bought a pearl costing six million sesterces. During the civil war, too, besides other presents, he knocked down some fine estates to her in a public auction at a nominal price, and when some expressed their surprise at the low figure, Cicero wittily remarked: "It's a better bargain than you think, for there is a third off." And, in fact, it was thought that Servilia was prostituting her own daughter Tertia to Caesar. That he did not refrain from intrigues in the provinces is shown in particular by this couplet, which was also shouted by the soldiers in his Gallic triumph:

> "Men of Rome, keep close to your consorts,
> here's a bald adulterer.
> Gold in Gaul you spent in dalliance, which
> you borrowed here in Rome."

Caesar was elected military tribune in 72 BC, the first office he gained by popular vote. In 69 BC he served as quaestor – finance officer – under the governor of Further Spain – Andalusia and Portugal – an area of the Iberian Peninsula only recently brought under Roman control. Suetonius recorded that, in Gades – modern Cadiz – Caesar saw a statue of Alexander the Great in the Temple of Hercules and 'was overheard to sigh impatiently: vexed, it seems, that at an age when Alexander had already conquered the whole world, he himself had done nothing in the least epoch-making'.[6] Alexander had died at the age of 32; Caesar was already 31 or 33.

That year, Caesar's aunt Julia, Marius's widow, died. Caesar delivered the funeral oration, during which he took the opportunity to praise Marius and Cinna. He also detailed his aunt's lineage from gods and the ancient kings of Rome – and this lineage was, of course, also his own. He even carried prohibited images of his uncle Marius in the funeral procession in a blatant attempt to assume Marius's political mantel.

Soon afterwards Caesar's wife, Cornelia, died, leaving him with an infant daughter, Julia. He seized the opportunity to marry Pompeia, Sulla's granddaughter and a relative of the great general Gnaeus Pompeius Magnus – Pompey the Great – who had recently re-conquered Spain. This marriage made Pompey and the Optimates – the conservative elements in the Senate – Caesar's political ally, even though Caesar and Marius were seen as prominent members of the opposing party, the Populares, or populists, who sought popular support against the oligarchs.

As a quaestor, Caesar could attend meetings of the Senate after 67 BC. In a populist move, he championed the cause of citizenship rights of northern Italians just as his relative Lucius Julius Caesar had. Caesar also voted to give Pompey the powers to seek out and destroy the pirates of the eastern Mediterranean and the powers to wage war on Mithridates once more in the east.

Caesar himself became Curator of the Appian Way, the road

Cicero denounces the Catiline conspiracy from the floor of the Senate

that ran from Rome to southern Italy. Despite his huge debts, he maintained the thoroughfare at his own expense, which again made him very popular.

In 65 BC Caesar – with Marcus Calpurius Bibulus – was elected *curule aedile*, an urban magistracy in Rome that involved taking control of market trading, the upkeep of temples and public buildings, and holding public games on holidays. Caesar and Bibulus funded lavish building projects and threw a spectacular gladiatorial games, where 320 pairs of gladiators clad in silver armour fought in honour of Caesar's own father. This left Bibulus led sidelined. He complained that Caesar got all the credit for their aedileship, saying 'the joint liberality of Caesar and myself is credited to Caesar alone'.[7]

In 63 BC Caesar was elected *pontifex maximus* – highest of all priests – a position held for life. This irritated a number of Optimates – the majority party in the Senate – who had expected the job. But, as always, no one could match Caesar's bribes. Caesar had, in fact, run up such massive debts to get elected to the pontifcate that, when he left home on the morning of the election, he told his mother he would either return as *pontifex* or not at all. As it was, he polled more votes than all the other candidates put together.

Lucius Sergius Catilina (c109–63 BC) ran against Cicero for consulship twice and lost. He then began to enlist malcontents on both sides of the political divide. Cicero was kept fully informed of the growing conspiracy by a network of spies and informers. On 21 October 63 BC, Cicero denounced Catilina to the Senate in an impassioned speech, charged him with treason and, with the backing of the Senate, declared martial law. Catilina fled. It was only on 3 December that Cicero had proof that Catilina had secretly sought the support of the Allobroges, a Gallic tribe. Those co-conspirators still in Rome were arrested and executed on 5 December. Catilina's army tried to cross the Apennines into Gaul in January 62 BC but was destroyed by a Republican army at Pistoia and Catilina was killed.

When the Catilinarian conspiracy was uncovered in late 63 BC, Caesar strongly opposed Cicero, who wanted to execute several conspirators without trial. Caesar managed to persuade the Senators against abrogating of Roman law, which made him Cicero's lifelong enemy. And in any event, Caesar's inveterate enemy Cato the Younger (95–46 BC) succeeded in swinging the vote back to execution. Rumours circulated that Caesar had taken part in the Catilinarian conspiracy. From that time on, Caesar was at odds against the political leadership in the Senate. Cicero later wrote that it was then that he realised Caesar was capable of destroying the Republic.

In 62 BC a great scandal erupted when a group of women gathered at Caesar's house to celebrate Bona Dea, a religious festival celebrated exclusively by women. One of Caesar's friends, a dissolute youth named Publius Clodius Pulcher (c93–52 BC), dressed as a woman and managed to get into the house, only be to unmasked by Caesar's mother, rhe sharp-eyed Aurelia. However,

The triumph of Caesar ascribed to Peter Paul Rubens

gossip circulated that Pulcher had seized the opportunity to consummate an affair with Caesar's wife, Pompeia. In the ensuing brouhaha, Caesar – now urban praetor, just one step down from the consulship – calmly divorced Pompeia, claiming that it was not enough to know that she was innocent of adultery; Caesar's *wife must be above suspicion*.[8]

Caesar's extravagance had practically bankrupted him. He persuaded Marcus Licinius Crassus (c115–53 BC), the richest man in Rome, to bail him out with 830 talents – 17,500 kg – of silver. To rescue himself financially, Caesar got elected governor of Further Spain in 61 BC and, on the pretext of restoring order, he overran several towns and looted them. Then he made a lightning attack up the west coast of what is now Portugal and plundered the silver mines of Galicia.

In 60 BC Caesar returned to Rome a wealthy man. His successful campaign in Iberia meant he was entitled to a triumph.

A triumph promised to boost Caesar's popularity. However, many of his actions in Spain had been unjustified, and he was at risk of being prosecuted as a war criminal. The only way to avoid prosecution was to be elected consul, which would give him immunity. Cato the Younger

The triumph was a procession from Campus Martial, the Field of Mars, to the temple of Jupiter on the Capitol, where the triumphator gave thanks for his victory, which must have been substantial to merit this sort of celebration. At least 5,000 of the enemy must be dead. The campaign had to be conducted by a magistrate of Rome and the war concluded. The triumphator also needed permission to retain his military rank inside the boundaries of the city. He rode on a four-horse chariot, festooned with laurels. He wore a toga of purple and gold and held a laurel branch in his right hand and an ivory sceptre in his left. A slave held a golden crown over his head and whispered, '*memento mori*' – 'remember you must die' – in his ear. Even at the moment of glory, he must remember he was merely mortal.

had already announced the day of the consular elections, and Caesar would have to be a private citizen – not a provincial governor or a Senate-appointed general – to stand. So Caesar was forced to forego his triumph to become consul, the highest and most revered office in the Roman Republic.

The First Triumvirate – 60 to 58 BC

Not only did Caesar need the consulship to avoid prosecution, he also needed it for the money. The post of being one of the two leaders of Rome usually came with the post of a lucrative provincial governorship. But in order to discourage Caesar from seeking office, the conservatives in the Senate plotted that he would receive the unprofitable position of supervising cattle trails and forests in Italy if elected. They also resorted to a massive bribery campaign to secure the election of Caesar's bitter enemy, archconservative Marcus Calpurnius Bibulus. But Caesar had a plan of his own.

'So as soon as he entered the city he assumed a policy which deceived everyone except Cato, Plutarch wrote. This policy was to reconcile Pompey and Crassus, the most influential men in the city. These men Caesar brought together in friendship after their quarrel, and by concentrating their united strength upon himself, succeeded, before men were aware of it, and by an act which could be called one of kindness, in changing the form of government,'. 'For it was not, as most men supposed, the quarrel between Caesar and Pompey that brought on the civil wars, but rather their friendship, since they worked together for the overthrow of the aristocracy in the first place, and then, when this had been accomplished, they quarrelled with one another. And Cato, who often foretold what was to come of their alliance, got the reputation of a morose and troublesome fellow at the time, but afterwards that of a wise, though unfortunate, counsellor.'9

Caesar fought back against the conservatives in the Senate by forming the so-called First Triumvirate with Crassus and Pompey, an informal and more or less secret pact. The name 'Triumvirate' was only coined after Caesar was dead by the Roman historian Livy (c59 BC–AD 17) who was born the year Caesar came to the consulship. The idea was to thwart the Senate's will and, with Caesar in the consulship, the two older men would help steer Roman policy behind the scenes. Although Crassus and Pompey were traditional enemies, Caesar agreed that, if he gained power, he would promote their programmes, and the three decided that they would do nothing unless it benefited all three of them. With their help, Caesar was unstoppable.

An early bronze bust of Cato

Crassus had fled from Rome when Marius seized the city in 87 BC, and he subsequently became a colonel in Sulla's army. He fell out with Pompey, who was clearly Sulla's favourite, but his support for Sulla in the field gave him the opportunity to make his fortune once Sulla became dictator. He became a leading banker and the richest man in Rome. In 72 BC Crassus, as praetor, had put down Spartacus's slave revolt, crucifying six thousand slaves along the Appian Way. Later, he had supported Catilina in his planned coup but avoided the fate of the conspirators. Caesar was already indebted to Crassus, who had helped him had secured his profitable Spanish command. And Crassus was happy to back Caesar if he agreed to push laws through the Senate that favoured his business interests in the East.

The other triumvir, Pompey, was Rome's leading general. He, too, had started his career in Sulla's army and had gone on to suppress a rising of Marius's followers in Spain. Despite their rivalry, Pompey had helped Crassus finish off Spartacus's revolt. With the backing of Caesar in the Senate, Pompey had defeated the pirates in the eastern Mediterranean, then proceeded to defeat Mithridates, beating the king of Pontus decisively on the battlefield and forcing him to commit suicide. He then annexed Syria, invaded Palestine and captured Jerusalem. As a result of these victories, his soldiers called him 'Pompey the Great'. No one disputed his right to the title '*Magnus*', as he had vastly expanded the Roman empire and doubled Rome's annual income. In 62 BC Pompey returned to Rome and promptly fell out with the Senate, which was slow to ratify his conquests in the East and opposed his efforts to secure land for his veterans.

Pompey the Great

Together, these three conspirators would run the Republic. The deal was sealed by intermarriage: Pompey married Caesar's daughter Julia, and Caesar married Calpurnia, whose father, Lucius Calpunius Piso (died c33 BC), was a close friend of Crassus and took over as consul in 58 BC, becoming known as Caesonius.

In December 60 BC Caesar was elected to the highest office in the Roman Republic, alongside Bibulus. He saw to it that the Senate quickly amended the tax codes to favour Crassus's business in the East. They endorsed Pompey's actions in the East and passed an agrarian act distributing land among Pompey's soldiers, along with the urban poor who were essentially Caesar's constituency. When Bibulus tried to oppose this, Pompey's veterans rioted.

Although Caesar and Bibulus were not on speaking terms, they agreed to publish the proceedings of the Senate and passed a law against extortion. Eventually, though, Caesar lost his patience and had Bibulus driven from the Forum. The following day, when Bibulus complained in the Senate, Caesar's bodyguards were on hand to ensure that no-one dared to support his fellow consul. Similarly, when Cato opposed one of Caesar's proposals, Caesar had him dragged out the Senate building and jailed.

Then came the matter of the provinces assigned to each consul. These were the places that the consuls were supposed to fight wars in defence of Rome. Caesar's opponents in the Senate feared him. The last thing they wanted was for the army to fall into his hands. Even so, Caesar forced through a law that gave him command of Illyricum, the province along the Dalmatian coast; Cisalpine

In 73 BC, Spartacus was one of 78 gladiators who managed to escape from the fighting school of Gnaeus Lentulus Batiatus at Capua. According to Plutarch: 'Spartacus was a Thracian from the nomadic tribes and not only had a great spirit and great physical strength, but was, much more than one would expect from his condition, most intelligent and cultured, being more like a Greek than a Thracian.'[10] Runaway slaves flocked to join Spartacus. Together they fought off eight armies sent by Rome, crisscrossed the Italian peninsula from South to North and back, before arriving in the 'toe' in the winter of 72/71 BC. With the help of Cilician pirates, Spartacus wanted to conquer Sicily, but the Cilicans let him down. Meanwhile Crassus, with eight legions – 32,000 men – under his command built wall 38 miles long from the Tyrrhenian to the Ionian Sea, trapping the rebels, but the Senate sent Pompey, who defeated the slave army. Spartacus's body was never found, but six thousand of his men were captured alive and crucified along the Appian Way, from Capua to Rome.

Gaul, the plains along the River Po in northern Italy; and Transalpine Gaul, southern France, which the Romans had held since the end of the 2nd century BC. Here his writ would run for the years 58 to 54 BC. As these provinces protected Italy from attack from the north, four legions were stationed there. Now, with 20,000 men under his command, Caesar was safe against any enemy.

In early 58 BC, Caesar left Rome. His consulship was taken over by his father-in-law Piso, who would take care of the affairs of the triumvirate in the capital. Caesar was now free to seek his fortune in the north.

The Conquest of Gaul – 58 to 55 BC

To the Romans, Gaul consisted of what are now northern Italy, Switzerland, France, Belgium, southern Holland and Germany west of the Rhine. The population were a Celtic people the Romans called Gauls. There were, in fact, numerous tribes of different ethnic origin, but during the Iron Age, through a process of trade and exchange, they had begun to develop a common culture.

In the 4th century BC, Gallic warriors from had settled along the River Po in northern Italy and had invaded central Italy, capturing Rome in 387 BC. The Cisalpine Gauls had advanced into central Italy again the following century, but in 284 BC the Rome struck back, taking Milan and establishing colonies there to create a buffer zone. During the Second Punic War (218–202 BC), the Gauls in northern Italy sided with the Carthaginian general Hannibal. Once Carthage was defeated, the Romans decided that they must secure their northern border against any further attack, and by 181 BC, all of Cisalpine Gaul had been subjugated.

The Celtic tribes in southern

Julius Caesar is our primary source on the manners and customs of the Gauls, including the druids.

They are engaged in things sacred, conduct the public and the private sacrifices, and interpret all matters of religion . . . The Druids do not go to war, nor pay tribute together with the rest; they have an exemption from military service and a dispensation in all matters. Induced by such great advantages, many embrace this profession of their own accord, and many are sent to it by their parents and relations. They are said there to learn by heart a great number of verses: accordingly some remain in the course of training twenty years.[11]

France were also influenced by the burgeoning civilisation to the south. Familiar with elements of Greek and Roman culture for centuries, they lived in walled towns, had their own coinage and were adept at agriculture, mining, metallurgy and the decorative arts. The southern tribes had already adopted Roman ways of government, abandoning hereditary kingship for annually elected magistrates that were answerable to councils and public codes of law. Even so, the Romans feared a new Gaulish invasion. In 120 BC they entered into an alliance with Aedui against the Arverni and the Allobroges and took control of the Rhône valley. This became the Province, modern-day Provence. Then, in 118 BC, the Romans established the colony of Narbo – the modern city of Narbonne – and named the new province Gallia Narbonnesis or Narbonne Gaul.

To the north, though, Roman influence was not so strong. The northern Celts still retained their kings. Even so, the Rhône-Saône-Rhine corridor was fast becoming the most important trade route in pre-industrial Europe. Britannic tin was traditionally transported along the rivers Garonne and Seine, and the Gallic tribes in the area were beginning to get a taste for the goods coming from the south. However, the hardy Germanic tribes beyond the Rhine positively rejected the luxuries offered by Roman traders, fearing that these indulgences would make them soft and unmanly.

In the 2nd century BC a mass migration began with Germanic peoples moving westwards into Gaul. In 102 BC two Germanic tribes, the Cimbrii and the Teutones, had crossed the Rhine only to be defeated on a battlefield by Caesar's uncle Gaius Marius. By the time Caesar came to power, the Helvetii from Switzerland and the Suevi from the Germanic tribes were on the move, and the Romans were once again terrified of a invasion by Germanic tribes. This allowed Caesar to pretend that his annexation of the rest of Gaul was a defensive move.

Caesar's military base was in the valley of the Rhône, which had been Roman territory from 123 BC. To the north were the Aedui, Rome's allies who occupied the valley of the Saône. When Caesar became governor of Transalpine Gaul, the Helvetii invaded. Caesar seized the opportunity to show that he was the true heir to Marius. He raised two extra legions and defeated the Helvetii as they were crossing the Saône. Although the Romans were vastly out-numbered, the Helvetii, who were thought to number some 270,000, had women and children with them, which hampered their movements. Caesar engaged them again at Bibracte – modern Mont Beuvray in Saône-et-Loire, then the capital of the Aedui – leaving only an estimated 130,000 of them alive. The survivors fled back to what is now Switzerland.

After these victories, the Aedui and other Gallic tribes asked Caesar to help them push back Germanic tribes under their leader Ariovistus, who had crossed the Rhine and settled in Alsace. However, Ariovistus was officially honoured as a 'Friend and Ally of the Roman People', so Caesar tried to solve the problem with diplomacy. But Ariovistus would not listen to reason and Caesar moved against him, only to find his own men were afraid of fighting the Germanic tribes. He told his men that, under Marius, the Romans had beaten the Germanic peoples and, under Caesar, they would do it again. He led a charge that routed the Germanic right wing in a great battle near modern-day Besançon. Many Germanic warriors were slaughtered. The rest were driven back across the Rhine. The victorious Caesar wrote with understandable pride: *Two campaigns were thus completed in a single summer*.[12]

Caesar's men were quartered for the winter near the battlefield, while Caesar himself returned to Cisalpine Gaul. This was because he was fighting a war on two fronts – one in Gaul, the other in the Senate. So he needed to be nearer to Rome to get orders through to Piso.

Although Caesar's campaigns against the Germanic tribes had been successful, his victories were not spectacular enough to give him an unassailable reputation in the capital. During the winter of 58/57 BC, he conceived a larger plan. He knew that he could not pull his troops back into the old provinces of Transalpine Gaul without losing all the ground he had gained. Before he withdrew, he would have to pacify the whole of Gaul. Fearing his intentions, the Belgic tribes, who lived to the north between the River Moselle and the North Sea, armed themselves and prepared for war. This gave Caesar the excuse he needed to attack.

Julius Caesar and Ariovistus exchange greetings before battle

He raised two more legions and, together with his other troops, moved up to the River Marne. His movement was so swift that he surprised the Belgic tribe of the Remi, who lived in the area of modern Reims. His sudden appearance prevented the Remi from joining the other Belgae, and they formed an alliance with the Romans.

By this time, 15 Belgic tribes were united under Galba, the king of the Suessiones, who could now field 300,000 men. He decided to attack the Remian town of Bibrax on the river Aisne.

Caesar sent a force of auxiliaries – Balearic slingsmen and archers from Crete and Numidia (modern Algeria) – to break the siege.

The Belgae responded by marching on the Roman camp. Roman cavalry stopped them about two miles out. Caesar ordered ditches dug to protect his flanks, which Roman artillery machines defended. Two legions were left to protect the camp, while another six went out to face the Belgae.

A marsh lay between the two armies, and neither side was eager to cross it. Seeing the strength of the Romans, the Belgae decided to break off. Each tribe would go home and defend its own territory. This decision was ill-conceived, as the fragmentation allowed Caesar to pick the tribes off one by one. He laid siege to the Suessione town of Noviodunum. It surrendered. Caesar then attacked the Bellovaci, then the Ambriani. Both gave in.[13]

Even though the Belgic union had disintegrated, the blood-thirsty Nervii tribe, who lived along the Somme, were determined to continue the fight. The Nervii were lead by a man named Boduognatus and joined by the Atrebates and Viromandui. The Aduatuci were on their way to help them. In the Battle of Sambre, they were annihilated. Barely 500 of their army of 60,000 survived.[14]

As Caesar moved into the territory of the Nervii, he learnt from prisoners that their army were camped along the River Sabis. Now known as the Sambis, it is about three feet deep in that area. On the side where the Nervii massed, the ground was open for about 200 yards, then flanked by wooded slopes. On the other side of the river, the Romans began building a camp on a hill. As the legions marched into it, they were harassed by Belgic cavalry who emerged from the woods, galloped across the river, attacked, then retreated back into the safety of the woods again, where the Romans dare not follow them. So Caesar then sent cavalry along with light infantry, archers and slingers across the river to attack the Belgic camp. Then the Roman baggage train arrived and the Nervii forces came rushing out of the forest at full tilt in the hope of plundering it. *The Nervii ran down to the river with such incredible speed that they seemed to be in the woods, the river, and close upon us almost at the same time. And with the same speed they hastened up the hill to our camp,*[15] said Caesar.

The Romans in camp were taken completely by surprise. Few had enough time to even put on their helmets or grab their shields. However, the IX and X legions on the Roman left flank met the Atrebates on higher ground and managed to push them back across the river. The legions crossed the Sabis and defeated the enemy there. Legion XI and VIII fought the Viromandui in the centre and also managed to force them back towards the river. But Boduognatus led his Nervii infantry in a narrow column through the middle of the Roman line, completely overrunning the Roman camp. The XIII and XIV legions at the rear of the baggage train rushed up in to join the fighting. Even so, it was touch and go and Caesar, resplendent in his blood-red cloak, had to intervene personally to rally his troops. Titus Labienus, who was commanding the left flank, eventually took the Belgic camp and sent the X legion back across river to help. This move renewed the Romans' spirits. Caught front and rear, the Belgae were all but wiped out.

Caesar ascribed his victories in Gaul, the Roman Civil War and in Asia Minor to two things – luck and leadership. But it is clear that his own personal courage inspired his men. In his *Commentaries on the Gallic War*, written in the third person, he said: *The situation was critical and as no reserves were available, Caesar seized a shield from a soldier in the rear and made his way to the front line. He addressed each centurion by name and shouted encouragement to the rest of the troops, ordering them to push forward and open their ranks so they could use their swords more easily. His coming gave them fresh heart and hope. Each man wanted to do his best under the eyes of this commander despite the peril.*[16] This description may sound self-serving, but there are other instances when Caesar turned up in the front line at the crucial moment.

The Aduatuci showed up too late to help the Nervii and, seeing their allies slaughtered, they returned home. Caesar pursued them long the Sambre and the Meuse. Eventually they surrendered, but then tried to escape. To punish them, Caesar sold the 53,000 surviving men, women and children into slavery.[17]

After subduing the Atrebates, Caesar named Commius, a man whose courage and conduct he admired, their king. Commius the Atrebate was then sent as an ambassador to the other Celtic tribes of Gaul and later to Britannia to invite these peoples *to embrace the protection of the Roman people, and apprise them that he* [Caesar] *would shortly come thither.*[18]

Meanwhile, a smaller Roman army under Crassus's son Publicius Licinius Crassus (died 53 BC) had marched through the west of modern France, and had subdued Armorican tribes in Normandy and Brittany. After successfully completing its Belgian campaign, Caesar's army swept around to the west to join up with them and establish winter quarters along the Loire. Back in Rome, the Senate ordered a public thanksgiving in Caesar's honour lasting 15 days. No one had been granted such an honour before.

Caesar spent the winter in Illyricum, but when he crossed the Alps back into Cisalpine Gaul, the Gauls in Brittany rose up. Before returning to crush them, he met Crassus and Pompey in Lucca. The triumvirs decided that Caesar's generalship in Gaul would have to be prolonged until the end of 50 BC. In return, Caesar was to support Crassus's and Pompey's bid to become consuls in 55 BC.

Caesar had already decided that he would have to invade Britannia, which had become a safe haven for rebellious Gauls who fled there when he threatened from the south. He had first to secure the Channel by putting down the Veneti, a seagoing people who live in Brittany. So he started a shipbuilding programme, then went back over the Alps to put down the rebels.

The campaigns of 56 BC began with Caesar dividing his forces, which he rarely did. Legions were stationed throughout Gaul to prevent other tribes from helping the Veneti. Meanwhile, the Roman fleet under the command of Decimus Junius Brutus (died 43 BC) attacked the Veneti by seas. The Bretons and their allies in Britannia had a fleet of light, manoeuvrable sailing ships that initially ran rings around the lumbering oar-powered Roman galleys. But the Romans soon developed new a tactic. They would employ suppressing fire from archers, row close alongside a Veneti vessel, hook the mast with a grappling iron, then row away, breaking off the enemy ships' mast. Without a mast, the Veneti ship was helpless, and the Romans could board it and overwhelm the enemy crew. Aided by a calm weather that summer, the Roman galleys destroyed the Veneti. The tribe was sold into slavery while Caesar's colonels undertook mopping up expeditions in Aquitaine and Normandy. The legions over-wintered again in Gaul, while an invasion fleet was built and Caesar returned to Cisalpine Gaul.

The Invasion of Britannia – 55 to 54 BC

The following year, 55 BC, was one of the most successful in Caesar's career. While he was in Italy, he heard that two Germanic tribes, the Usipetes and Tencteri – some 430,000 men – had crossed the Rhine to aid the Belgae. Caesar raced to the scene. When he confronted the tribes' leaders, they claimed that they had been forced to cross the Rhine against their will. During the negotiations, however, the Germanic horsemen attacked Caesar's cavalry. The following day, when the leadership of the Germanic tribes came to apologise for breaking the truce, Caesar arrested them, then attacked their position 12 miles away. Leaderless and taken by surprise, the Germanic tribes stood no chance. Tens of thousands of them were forced back towards the confluence of the Rhine and the Meuse. Thousands were slaughtered. Others drowned trying to swim across the river.

But though Caesar chalked up another victory, his methods drew criticism from his enemies in Rome, who condemned him as duplicitous and underhanded. Caesar silenced his critics with an act of daring. In just ten days, he built a trestle bridge across the Rhine near modern-day Coblenz and marched his legions across it. For 18 days, he terrorised the German countryside, burning villages, cutting down corn and intimidating the population. He then marched his army back across the bridge, dismantled it and returned to Gaul. Even his critics in the Senate were impressed.

Caesar marched his men to his new port Itius, near modern-day Boulogne, where a large fleet was waiting. The VII and X legions and 500 cavalry were loaded on into 98 transports and set

'His expedition against the British was celebrated for its daring. For he was the first to launch a fleet upon the western ocean and to sail through the Atlantic sea carrying an army to wage war. The island was of incredible magnitude, and furnished much matter of dispute to multitudes of writers, some of whom averred that its name and story had been fabricated, since it never had existed and did not then exist; and in his attempt to occupy it he carried the Roman supremacy beyond the confines of the inhabited world. After twice crossing to the island from the opposite coast of Gaul and in many battles damaging the enemy rather than enriching his own men – for there was nothing worth taking from men who lived in poverty and wretchedness – he brought the war to an end which was not to his liking, it is true; still, he took hostages from the king, imposed tributes, and then sailed away from the island.'

PLUTARCH OF CHAERONEA[19]

off across the Channel to Britannia on 26 August 55 BC. It was the first invasion of the benighted isle in Roman history.

By nine o'clock on the morning of the 27th, Caesar's invasion force was off Dover and saw massed Britanni warriors lining the tops of the White Cliffs, waiting for the Roman fleets to land. *The nature of the place was this: the sea was confined by mountains so close to it that a spear could be thrown from their summit upon the shore*, wrote Caesar. *With wind and tide favourable at the same time, the signal being given and the anchor weighed, he advanced about seven miles from that place, and stationed his fleet over against an open and level shore.*[20]

The fleet moved off northwards, and Caesar ran the ships ashore on an *open and level shore*[21] – probably Walmer Beach at Deal. The Britanni cavalry and charioteers had followed them along the coast and were soon in a position to oppose the landing. The shelving beach required the soldiers in heavy armour to leap out of the transports into waist-high waves. Some hesitated, but the standard-bearer of the X Legion cried out: 'Leap, fellow soldiers, unless you wish to betray your eagle to the enemy. I, for my part, will perform my duty to the commonwealth and my general.' Then *he leaped into the water and proceeded to bear the eagle towards the enemy.*[22] On shore, the Roman soldiers lined up behind the? standard-bearer, and their determined charge drove off the Celts. However, without the cavalry, which had failed to complete the crossing, Caesar could not pursue them.

A frenzied depiction of the first Roman invasion of Britain

The battle was maintained vigorously on both sides, wrote Caesar. *Our men, however, as they could neither keep their ranks, nor get firm footing, nor follow their standards, and as one from one ship and another from another assembled around whatever standards they met, were thrown into great confusion. But the enemy, who were acquainted with all the shallows, when from the shore they saw any coming from a ship one by one, spurred on their horses, and attacked them while embarrassed; many surrounded a few, others threw their weapons upon our collected forces on their exposed flank. When Caesar observed this, he ordered the boats of the ships of war and the spy sloops to be filled with soldiers, and sent them up to the succour of those whom he had observed in distress. Our men, as soon as they made good their footing on dry ground, and all their comrades had joined them, made an attack upon the enemy, and put them to flight, but could not pursue them very far, because the horse had not been able to maintain their course at sea and reach the island. This alone was wanting in Caesar's accustomed success.*[23]

According to Caesar, the Britons immediately sued for peace and returned Commius the Atrebate, who they had seized and shackled the moment he set foot on the soil of Britannia. His arrest, they said, had been a mistake. Caesar complained that had they could have sent ambassadors to the Continent to sue for peace and *they had made war without a reason.* They handed over hostages to ensure their good behaviour. *In the mean time they ordered their people to return to the country parts, and the chiefs assembled from all quarters, and proceeded to surrender themselves and their states to Caesar.*[24]

Four days later, the Roman cavalry transports were finally spotted on their way from Gaul. But a great storm blew up. They failed to make landfall and limped back to port Itius. The storm had hit during a spring tide – a phenomenon that Mediterranean sailors were unfamiliar with – and Caesar's fleet was severely damaged. Some ships were saved by putting out to sea and heading back to Gaul. Others filled with water or crashed against the shore.

At a stroke, Caesar lost his only means of retreat. He was short of supplies and the local chieftains who had come to his camp to sue for peace had observed how few men he had with him. After renewing their promises of loyalty, the native leaders *slipped away one by one from the camp and secretly called up once more the men who had returned to the fields.*[25]

The Britanni refused to hand over the hostages they had promised and, while foraging some distance from the camp, a Roman legion was attacked. Caesar was alerted by the cloud of dust heading towards his men and set out with two cohorts – a cohort is one tenth of the legion or 400 men – to relieve them. *When he had advanced some little way from the camp, he saw that his men were overpowered by the enemy and scarcely able to stand their ground, and that, the legion being crowded together, weapons were being cast on them from all sides.*[26]

Caesar wrote extensively on the Britannis' methods of combat: *Their mode of fighting with their chariots is this: firstly, they drive about in all directions and throw their weapons and generally break the ranks of the enemy with the very dread of their horses and the noise of their wheels; and when they have worked themselves in between the troops of horse, leap from their chariots and engage on foot. The charioteers in the mean time withdraw some little distance from the battle, and so place themselves with the chariots that, if their masters are overpowered by the number of the enemy, they may have a ready retreat to their own troops. Thus they display in battle the speed of horse, the firmness of infantry; and by daily practice and exercise attain to such expertness that they are accustomed, even on a declining and steep place, to check their horses at full speed, and manage and turn them in an instant and run along the*

A seventeenth-century English engraving of British charioteers attacking the invading Roman legions

pole, and stand on the yoke, and thence betake themselves with the greatest celerity to their chariots again.[27]

The Romans had never before encountered chariots in battle and had no defence against them. Even so, when Caesar turned up, the Britanni charioteers paused. Caesar stayed his hand, not daring to provoke the enemy. He soon managed to withdraw the legion and get it back to camp. The storm prevented the Britanni from pressing home any advantage they had gained from this encounter. When it passed, Caesar drew up his legions in battle order in front of his camp, and when another attack came, it was easily dispersed.

When the action commenced, the enemy were unable to sustain the attack of our men long, and turned their backs; our men pursued them as far as their speed and strength permitted, and slew a great number of them; then, having destroyed and burned every thing far and wide, they retreated to their camp,[28] said Caesar.

According to Caesar, the Britanni sued for peace again, and he demanded double the number of hostages he had previously asked for. By this time, the fleet had been patched up well enough to transport the army back to Gaul. The autumnal equinox was fast approaching, and Caesar knew it would bring with it more storms. For the moment, though, the weather was fair, so one night, a little after midnight, the fleet slipped out to sea and headed back to port Itius.

On the way, two of his ships got detached from the flotilla and landed a little further down the coast. The three hundred men on board were surrounded by six thousand of the local Morini tribe *excited by the hope of spoil,*[29] who ordered them to lay down their arms. For four hours, the Romans fought them off. Then Caesar sent in the cavalry. When the Morini saw them, they threw away their arms and fled. A great many of them were killed.

Even though Caesar's expedition to Britannia was hardly an unblemished success, the Senate could not fail to be impressed by the general who had finally reached the edge of the known world. Crassus and Pompey, now consuls, ordered an unprecedented 20 days of thanksgiving in Caesar's honour in Rome.

'His expedition into Britain was the most famous testimony of his courage,' said Plutarch. 'For he was the first who brought a fleet into the western ocean, or who sailed into the Atlantic with an army to make war; and by invading an island incredible magnitude, and furnished much matter of dispute to multitudes of writers, some of whom averred that its name and story had been fabricated, since it never had existed and did not then exist; and in his attempt to occupy it he carried the Roman empire beyond the limits of the known world.'[31]

'From Britain he had won nothing for himself or for the state except the glory of having conducted an expedition against its inhabitants; but on this he prided himself greatly and the Romans at home likewise magnified it to a remarkable degree. For seeing that the formerly unknown had become certain and the previously unheard-of accessible, they regarded the hope for the future inspired by these facts as already realised and exulted over their expected acquisitions as if they were already within their grasp; hence they voted to celebrate a thanksgiving for twenty days.'
CASSIUS DIO[30]

But not everyone was impressed.

'I hear there is not an ounce of either gold or silver in Britain,' Cicero wrote to his protégé, Gaius Trebatius (died 43 BC), who was serving under Caesar. 'If that is true, my advice is to lay hold of a chariot and hurry back to us at full speed!'[32]

Back in Gaul, the legions established the winter quarters, this time in the territory of the Belgae. Before Caesar left for Italy, he ordered another, larger fleet to be built, ready for a second invasion of Britainnia the following year. He also altered the ships' design, making the transports broader and lower to make them better fitted for the tidal waters of the Channel. More equipment was to be bought from Spain.[33]

When Caesar returned to Gaul in the spring, 28 new galleys and 600 new transports had been built, and he began to assemble a new invasion force at port Itius. But first he had to secure his rear. The Treveri, in what is now Luxembourg, had formed an alliance with the Germanic tribes across the Rhine and were preparing to attack the Roman forces in Gaul while Caesar was in Britannia. He marched with four legions and 800 cavalry into the Ardennes and demanded 200 Treveri hostages, including the chief's son and other close relatives.[34]

Caesar then sailed to Britannia with 2,000 cavalry and five legions on over 800 ships. This was the biggest sea-borne invasion force until D-Day in 1944, nearly 2,000 years later. Seeing the invasion fleet coming, the Britanni fled from the coast and hid inland. This time, the Romans landed unopposed. Once they had set up camp, Caesar left ten cohorts of 300 to guard the ships, which lay at anchor on a *even and open shore*,[35] while the rest of the force struck inland in a lighting night march. Having advanced some 12 miles, they found themselves under attack with chariots and cavalry swooping down on them from higher ground.

Repulsed by the Roman cavalry, the Britanni force concealed themselves in a forest, where they had a wooden fort built for an earlier civil war. Soldiers of VII Legion formed themselves up into the classic *testudo* – a 'tortoise shell' formed out of overlapping shields – and threw up a rampart to overwhelm the fortifications. The Britanni were driven out of their fort and fled into the wood. But Caesar stopped his men pursuing them, for they did not know the terrain, and he was keen to build fortifications of his own.[36]

The next day, men were sent out to pursue the Britanni, but the Romans were recalled when Caesar heard that his ships had once again been badly damaged by another freak storm. Heading back to the beach, he found that 40 ships had been lost and many more damaged. The ships were brought up on shore and his men set about repairing them behind heavy fortifications.

He also sent word to his commander in Gaul, Titus Labienus, to build more ships.

To the Britanni, it seemed that the Romans had turned back out of fear. They held a great assembly and elected as their war leader Cassivellaunus, chief of the Catuvelluini. The Catuvelluini occupied the region north of the River Thames and, before the arrival of the Romans, Cassivellaunus had taken on the combined forces of all the other Britanni states. Caesar now had a clearly defined enemy and, after 10 days of repair work, he set out after Cassivellaunus, leaving his ships heavily guarded.

Britannia was still largely unknown to the Romans, and Caesar took great interest in its

The interior portion of Britain is inhabited by those . . . born in the island itself: the maritime portion by those who had passed over from the country of the Belgae for the purpose of plunder and making war and having waged war, continued there and began to cultivate the lands. The number of the people is countless, and their buildings exceedingly numerous . . . They use either brass or iron rings, determined at a certain weight, as their money. Tin is produced in the midland regions; in the maritime, iron; but the quantity of it is small: they employ brass, which is imported... They do not regard it lawful to eat the hare, and the cock, and the goose; they, however, breed them for amusement and pleasure. The climate is more temperate than in Gaul, the colds being less severe.

GAIUS JULIUS CAESAR[37]

geography. *The island is triangular in its form,* he said, *and one of its sides is opposite to Gaul. One angle of this side, which is in Kent, where almost all ships from Gaul landed, faces east, while other side faces south. This side extends about five hundred miles. Another side lies toward Spain and to the west, there is Ireland, which, it is reckoned, is about half the size of Britain. The distance from Britain to Ireland is equal to the distance Britain is from Gaul. In the middle of this passage is an island, called Mona: many smaller islands besides are supposed to lie there. The length of this side, as their account states, is seven hundred miles.*[38]

Caesar believed that, at the time of the winter solstice, the night in Britannia lasted for 30 consecutive days, as if it were in the Arctic Circle. The Romans could not verify this theory but, with the use of a water clock, they discovered that the nights in Britannia were shorter than those on the Continent in the summer.

The third side faces the north and no land opposite it, wrote Caesar, but an angle of that side looks principally toward Germany. This side is estimated to be 800 miles in length. Thus the whole island is some 2,000 miles in circumference.[39]

Caesar was also interested in the inhabitants.

The most civilised of all these nations are those that inhabit Kent, which is entirely a maritime district, and their customs do not differ much from those in Gaul. Few of the inhabitants inland sow corn. Instead they live on milk and flesh, and are clad with skins. All the Britons dye themselves with woad, which gives them a bluish colour to make then look more terrifying when they are fighting. They wear their hair long, and have every part of their body shaved except their head and upper lip. Ten and even 12 have wives common to them, and particularly brothers among brothers, and parents among their children; but when one of these wives has a child, it is taken to be the child of the man who she was first married to when a virgin.[40]

The Romans spread out across Kent, driving the Britanni from the woods and hills, killing many of them. But they did not have it all their own way. The Britanni were good at feinting a retreat, luring the Romans on, then turning and attacking when they were over-stretched. And foragers again found themselves under attack by charioteers.

When Caesar reached the Thames, he found it could be forded in just one place and there only with difficulty. This would have made the crossing point near the present site of London, thought to be Brentford. On the far bank, Cassivellaunus had mustered his forces. The bank was bristling with sharpened stakes and Caesar learnt from prisoners and deserters that there were more sharpened stakes under the water line. Even so, *the soldiers advanced with such speed and such ardour, though they stood above the water by their*

*heads only, that the enemy could not sustain the attack of the legions and
of the horse, and quitted the banks, and committed themselves to flight.*[41]

Cassivellaunus dismissed most of his men and committed a
small force of around 4,000 charioteers to guerrilla warfare. They
observed the legions as they advanced and pulled the people and
their cattle back into the woods. Then, as the Romans foraged,
the chariots would attack. Caesar ordered that his men should
only scavenge close to the main column, and they took their
revenge on the enemy by ravaging the land.

A number of tribes who were traditional enemies of
Cassivellaunus made peace with Caesar, handing over hostages and
corn. They told Caesar that Cassivellaunus had a fortified wooded
stronghold, probably at Wheathampstead, near the current site of
St. Albans. The legions attacked him there. Cassivellaunus's men
fled and the Romans took a large number of cattle.

With Romans over 80 miles from their base, Cassivellaunus
sent orders for the Britanni in Kent to launch a surprise attack on
Caesar's beachhead camp. The attack failed. A great many
Britanni were killed and the leader of the assault was captured.
Cassivellaunus then sued for peace. Commius the Atrebate nego-
tiated the terms, fixing the number of hostages Cassivellaunus
should hand over and determining the tribute the Britanni should
pay Rome. Cassivellaunus was also forbidden to make war on
other Britannic tribes. Meanwhile, there was trouble in Gaul.
After two months of campaigning in southern Britannia, Caesar
withdrew, never to return. Britannia would only become a
province of the Roman empire when the Emperor Claudius
invaded 97 years later.

The Pacification of Gaul – 53 to 52 BC

On the Continent, there had been a drought that summer, resulting in a shortage of corn. This meant that Caesar had to pass the winter with his men in small groups spread thinly across Gaul. He himself remained in Samarobriva – modern Amiens – in case of trouble. One legion under Quintus Titurius Sabinus and Lucius Aurunculeius Cotta, newly raised in northern Italy, was stationed near modern Liege in the territory of the Belgius Eburones, who occupied most of the land between the Meuse and the Rhine. The Eburones, under their leader Ambiorix, rose up. Terrified of attack by both the Gauls and Germans, Sabinus tried to reach the forces under Quintus Tullius Cicero – the orator's brother – some 30 miles away near Namur. But as soon as the legion left its fort, it was attacked and wiped out by the Gauls.

Ambiorix then persuaded the Nervii and their allies to attack Cicero. Some 60,000 men ambushed? him using siege tactics they had learned from the Romans. Cicero managed to hold out, even though the Gauls fired balls of red-hot clay and heated javelins, setting the fort on fire. Cicero tried to get a message to Caesar, who was almost 120 miles away near Amiens, but his messengers were captured and tortured to death. After a week, the slave of a Gallic defector managed to get through the lines with a letter.[42]

Caesar sped to Cicero's rescue with just two legions – 7,000 men. As the relief column approached, the Gauls turned to attack Caesar's legions. Caesar, inferring that the siege had been lifted, quickly fortified his camp and sent out cavalry to lure the enemy to him. As soon as they had engaged the Gallic horsemen, the

Roman cavalry turned and raced back to the fort, as if frightened. Fooled by this feint, the Gauls drew up a line in front of the fort in a disadvantageous position, while heralds invited Caesar's men to defect. Caesar's cavalry then came racing out of the fort and cut the Gauls down. Later that day, Caesar's forces reached Cicero and Caesar commended him and his men on their courage.[43]

Caesar's position in Gaul had been considerably weakened, however. Having lost one complete legion and suffering heavy losses to a second, he went to work raising two new legions from Cisalpine Gaul and borrowed a third from Pompey, which arrived before the end of winter. They brought with them news that Caesar's daughter Julia had died in childbirth, which meant that his alliance with Pompey could not longer be relied on. Caesar offered Pompey a new marital alliance through one of his numerous grandnieces. Pompey rejected this suggestion, as he had his own fish to fry. Violence on the streets of Rome had made it impossible to hold the consular elections and there was talk of making Pompey dictator – in a crisis, the Romans appointed a dictator and granted him extraordinary powers, though his tenure of office lasted just six months.

But Caesar could not be distracted by the goings-on in Rome. His political future depended on his success in Gaul. He ordered the convocation of Gallic chiefs in Lutetia – modern-day Paris. It would be emphasized that those who did not attend planned to continue their resistance. Afterwards, Caesar sent out forces under Trebonius and Labienus to slaughter the Manipii and Aduatuci. Back in Rome, when Cato heard of this policy of deliberate genocide, he said that Caesar ought to be handed over to the Germanic tribes.

Meanwhile, Caesar marched back into Eburone territory in search of Ambiorix. Once again, he bridged the Rhine to harass the Germanic people in case Ambiorix had sought refuge with them. He subsequently returned to Gaul to search the vast Ardennes Forest, where Ambiorix was said to be hiding, but

Caesar found himself harried by guerrillas. He therefore offered bounty to all Celtic tribes who joined him in pillaging the territory of Eburones. A large force quickly gathered, as there were always Gauls ready to attack and plunder one another with the Romans' assistance. Unfortunately, members of Germanic tribes heard about this scheme and decided to join in. The Sigambri, who lived nearest to the Rhine, crossed the river and attacked the hapless Cicero, whose troops were guarding the baggage at Aduatuca, modern Tongeren, or Tongres, in Belgium. Against orders, Cicero sent out foraging parties and two cohorts were destroyed before Caesar returned and saw the Germanic raiders off.[44]

In frustration, Caesar devastated the lands of the Eburones, but Ambiorix still eluded capture. Finally, Caesar ordered another great Gallic convocation at the Remi's capital Durocortorum – modern-day Reims. There he seized Acco, one of the tribal leaders. Accusing him of being one of the leaders of the insurrection, Caesar had Acco flogged to death, the customary Roman punishment for such an offence. Caesar then left his legions in their winter quarters and returned to Cisalpine Gaul, believing that the Gauls had finally been pacified. In reality, however, Caesar's severity had merely made the Gauls more determined to fight. They were now willing to put aside their tribal difference and unite behind a leader who would be capable of taking on Caesar. That man was Vercingetorix, chief of the Arverni, who occupied the region now known as the Auvergne in central France.

While Caesar was fulfilling his regular judicial duties in Cisalpine Gaul in the winter of 53-52 BC, Rome was in turmoil following the murder of Publius Clodius Pulcher, whose job it was to keep Pompey on Caesar's side and stop him from joining Cicero and the Optimates. With Caesar's political future looking very shaky indeed, events in Gaul overtook him again. The Carnutes – the Celtic tribe who gave their name to Chartres, which had been their Druidic headquarters – rose up and massacred all

Roman citizen traders along with Caesar's supply officer in their *oppidum* (fortified town) of Cenabum, modern-day Orleans. This was the signal to the Senone people to the north-east to form guerrilla forces and begin disrupting the Roman army's food supply. Elsewhere, other Gallic forces moved against the Roman legions in their winter quarters. In late February, Caesar sped across the Alps and defied heavy snows in the Cevennes mountains to arrive unexpectedly at Agedincum, modern-day Sens in Burgundy – where he assembled his legions. Titus Labienus was sent with four legions to suppress the Senones and the Parisii to the north, while Caesar himself led six legions towards Gergovia, the hilltop stronghold of the Arverni near modern-day Clermont-Ferrand.

Vercingetorix was not just a formidable fighter. He was also a skilled politician who had secured the support of Caesar's former allies the Aedui tribe. The Aedui had served for years in the legions as auxiliaries and were highly valued by Caesar as cavalry. While Caesar was besieging Gergovia, the Aedui rebelled and massacred Roman troops and all Roman citizens in Cabillonum – modern-day Chalon-sur-Saône – to his rear. His siege of Gergovia now imperilled, Caesar attempted to storm the hill-fort, but he was repulsed with heavy losses. This was the first outright defeat Caesar had suffered in Gaul and he was forced to withdraw.

Tribal leaders once loyal to Caesar now switched their allegiance to Vercingetorix, who was elected commander-in-chief; some sources say he was named King of Gaul. Even Commius the Atrebate joined the rebels and it is thought that as many as 45 tribes joined the struggle against Rome. They set fire to the army depot at Noviodunum – modern Nevers – and massacred the Roman merchants there.

Caesar now found himself in a critical situation. His tribal allies had deserted him. The Arverni, elated by their victory at Gergovia, were at his rear. The Bituriges, from modern Bordeaux, were on his left flank and the Aedui barred his front. According to the military theoretician J.F.C. Fuller, one of the founders of modern tank warfare: 'One thing alone saved him – his own invincibility.'[45]

With his supply lines under attack, Caesar fell back towards the Loire, where he managed to reunite with the legions of Labienus and replenish his cavalry with Germanic auxiliaries. The Aedui in particular viewed their replacements with horror, considering them brutal barbarians. Vercingetorix now had superior numbers, but Caesar managed to hold him off with his Germanic horsemen.

Without a clear victory that summer, Vercingetorix had difficulty maintaining his leadership. The tribes under his control were accustomed to warring with each other for territory and loot. At the best of times, they had problems co-operating with one another. Vercingetorix urged them to adopt a scorched-earth policy and pleaded with the tribal leaders to destroy their grain stores to deprive the Romans of food during their campaign. The Bituriges burnt more than 20 of their own towns in one day, but begged that Avaricum – modern Bourges – be spared as it was *the fairest city in the whole of Gaul* and could easily be defended.[46] It was taken by storm within a month.

Vercingetorix was now on the defensive and withdrew his huge army to the hill-fort of Alesia, the capital of the Mandubrii. This *oppidum* was on the top of Mont

'Most of the people who escaped from the battle took refuge with their King in the city of Alesia. The place was regarded as impregnable because of the size and strength of the walls and the great numbers of its defenders. Caesar besieged it, however, and while doing so, was threatened from outside by a quite indescribable danger. Three hundred thousand men, the best fighting troops from every nation in Gaul, assembled together and marched to the relief of Alesia. Caesar now found himself caught between two enormous forces; he was himself besieged and was compelled to build two systems of fortification, one facing the city and one facing the relieving army, since he knew well that, if the two forces should combine, everything would be over with him.'

PLUTARCH OF CHAERONEAX[47]

Auxois above the present-day village of Alise-Sainte-Reine, 30 miles north-west of Dijon.

Quickly grasping the changed situation, Caesar surrounded Alesia in an attempt to isolate Vercingetorix from his allies. Key to Caesar's strategy was his army's engineering ability. The entire plateau of Alesia was quickly encircled by a series of walls ten miles long. His men dug an 18-foot-wide ditch. Alongside this was a trench, filled with water. 'Mantraps' were dug. These were carefully concealed holes in the ground, several feet deep, with a sharpened spike in the middle that could impale anyone who fell into it. Then a second nine-foot wall, capped with breastworks, was built far behind the first line of defence. At regular intervals were square towers where the Roman's awesome siege equipment was mounted. These elaborate constructions were all designed to keep Vercingetorix and his army trapped inside.

Caesar's bicircumvallation of the Gaullish armies at Alesia was an awesome military achievement

But Caesar also expected other Gauls to rally to Vercingetorix's cause. So he began constructing an entire second line of fortifications between 13 and 15 miles long, parallel to the first, facing outwards. The Gauls could scarcely believe their eyes when they saw the scale of this feat of military engineering and Caesar's army was now safe between the two rings of fortifications.

While the construction was underway, Vercingetorix sent out cavalry detachments to harass the building work and foraging parties. As the siege tightened, there were cavalry battles in the three-mile gap corridor between the outer wall of the hill-fort and the inner wall of Caesar's circumvallation. The night before the Roman fortifications completely encircled Alesia, Vercingetorix sent out all his cavalry, telling them to go back to their own tribes and conscript all the men of military age. The lives of 80,000 men inside the fort were in their hands. The horsemen escaped through the last remaining gap in the Roman lines and rode off to raise reinforcements.[48]

Vercingetorix had worked out that there was barely enough corn to hold out for a month and introduced strict rationing. As stocks ran low, he decided to eject all the townspeople who could not bear arms from the hill fortress and march them out into no-man's-land. The women, children and aged cried out pitiably begging the Romans to take them as slaves, but then the Romans would have the problem of feeding them. Caesar posted guards to ensure that his troops would refuse them admission and he let them starve between the lines.

Meanwhile, Commius and the other tribal chieftains arrived with what Caesar said was a quarter of a million men.[49] Modern scholars

As long as the Gauls were at a distance from the entrenchments, the rain of javelins which they discharged gained them some advantage. But when they came nearer they suddenly found themselves pierced by the goads or tumbled into the pits and impaled themselves, while others were killed by heavy siege spears discharged from the rampart and towers. Their losses were everywhere heavy and when dawn came they had failed to penetrate the defences at any point . . . The besieged lost much time in bringing out the implements that Vercingetorix had prepared for the sortie and in filling up the first stretches of trench, and before they reached the main fortifications heard of the retreat of the relief force, so they returned into the town without effecting anything.

GAIUS JULIUS CAESAR[50]

believe the warriors numbered somewhere between 80,000 and 100,000. Seeing them, a great cheer went up inside the hill-fort. As these fresh troops encamped on a hill a mile outside the Roman outer wall, Caesar and his lieutenants, including Gaius Trebonius and Mark Antony, braced themselves for a battle on two fronts.

Fighting began on the first day with a cavalry battle, which ended with a Roman victory, thanks to the daring the Germanic horsemen. After a day's rest, the Roman fortifications were attacked simultaneously from inside and out, but they held firm. Around midday on the fourth day, the Gauls attacked again from both sides. After a terrible battle, the Romans won a great victory. As Caesar charged the relief force from the front, the Germanic cavalry hit them in the rear and scattered them. Completely routed, they were pursued from the field by the Germanic auxiliaries.

The following day, Vercingetorix surrendered. He gathered the tribal leaders and told them he had not made war for personal reasons, but for the freedom of Gaul. They must now decide whether to kill him to appease the Romans, or hand him over alive. A deputation was sent to Caesar, who ordered the defeated

Vercingetorix surrenders to Caesar after his defeat at Alesia

Gauls to lay down their arms and bring their tribal chiefs to him. Then he sat on the fortification in front of his camp and waited.

'Vercingetorix, after putting on his most beautiful armour and decorating his horse, rode out through the gates,' said Plutarch. 'Caesar was sitting down and Vercingetorix, after riding round him in a circle, leaped down from his horse, stripped off his armour, and sat at Caesar's feet silent and motionless, until he was taken away under arrest to be kept in custody for the triumph.'[51]

Vercingetorix was taken to Rome in chains. He remained in an honoured prisoner in Roman captivity for the next six years while Caesar fought Pompey in the Civil War. Once Caesar was in sole control of the Roman world, he had Vercingetorix exhibited in Caesar's Gallic triumph in 52 BC. Then, according to custom, the Gaul was strangled in the depths of the Mamartine Prison in Rome. Nineteen centuries later, Emperor Napoleon III of France, mindful of the contribution of Germanic cavalry to the defeat of Vercingetorix, had a massive statue of the Gallic leader erected on the site of the ruins of the Alesia fortifications, which had recently been rediscovered. Vercingetorix had come to symbolise the courage of France in fighting her enemies. Napoleon III fell from power after being defeated by the Germans at Sedan in 1870.

Some 20,000 Aedui and Arverni were separated from the prisoners and returned to their tribes in an attempt to regain their loyalty. The Arverni also had to hand over some hostages to ensure future good behaviour. The other survivors were divided among Caesar's soldiers and enslaved.

In Rome, the Senate honoured Caesar with another 20-day thanksgiving. The defeat of Vercingetorix at Alesia essentially ended any hope of an independent Gaul. But Caesar had two more years of mopping up before he had completed the pacification of Gaul.

To do this, he changed policy. Problems with the Bituriges in late 52 were handled with unprecedented leniency. Then he Caesar aided both the Bituriges and the Suessiones against the

Carnutes and Bellovaci, destroying the Gallic confederacy and encouraging inter-tribal rivalry. However, when Caesar heard that Ambiorix was on the warpath again, he destroyed whatever remained of the Eburones to remind them of the misfortune Ambiorix had brought on them.

A crowd of Gallic fugitives under Drapes and Luterius marched south to plunder the Roman Province. Caesar besieged them in the natural fortress of Uxellodunum, modern-day Puy d'Issolu on the Dordogne. This stands on a plateau on top of a rocky hill that rises 600 feet above the flood plain of the Dordogne River. Caesar distracted the defenders by pretending to erect great siegeworks against what was essentially an impregnable position. Meanwhile, his engineers found and diverted all sources to the spring that supplied water to the hill-fort. Without water, Uxellodunum surrendered.

An idealization of Gaul under Roman occupation, painted by Octave Penguilly L'Haridon, 1870

The lives of the survivors – perhaps 2,000 men in all – were spared. But they had both hands amputated. These cripples were then dispersed throughout Gaul to remind the inhabitants how severe Roman punishment could be.

'The campaigns by which he subjugated Gaul proved him to be as good a soldier and commander as any of those who have been more admired for their leadership and shown themselves to be the greatest generals . . . we shall find that Caesar's achievements surpass them all. He may be considered superior to one because of the difficulty of the country in which he fought; to another because of the extent of his conquests; to another because of the number and strength of the enemy forces which he defeated; to another because of the savage treacherous character of the tribes whose goodwill he won; to another because of the reasonable and considerate way in which he treated prisoners . . . he surpassed them all in the fact that he fought more battles than any of them and killed greater numbers of the enemy.'

PLUTARCH OF CHAERONEA[55]

The Gallic Wars ended with the fall of Uxellodunum. During the campaign in Gaul, Caesar had taken more than 800 cities by storm, subdued 300 nations and fought pitched battles at different times with three million men. According to Plutarch, 'he killed one million of them in hand to hand fighting and took as many more prisoners, with more than a million being sold into slavery.'[54] So three million were lost out of a population of an estimated 12 million.

Caesar organised the new territories, which now had to pay tribute of 40 million sesterces a year. By the end of his term as governor, he had added a vast, new and profitable province permanently to the empire. It adopted Roman culture within a few generations, and there was no further rebellion in Gaul until the Roman empire went into decline four centuries later. In fact, the Romanisation of Gaul survived the fall of Rome itself and remains one of Julius Caesar's most enduring legacies.

Crossing the Rubicon – 51 to 49 BC

While Caesar was away fighting in Gaul, things had changed in Rome. With the death of Julia in 54 BC and the murder of Publius Clodius Pulcher in 52 BC, Caesar could no longer rely on Pompey as a political ally. Meanwhile, Crassus became governor of Syria and, seeking to emulate the military successes of his two fellow triumvirs, he attacked the Parthians, who lived to the east in modern Iraq. Defeated at the Battle of Carrhae in 53 BC, Crassus was killed when his Parthian gave him what he desired most – gold. The liquefied metal was poured into his mouth. After this cataclysm, Pompey married Crassus's widow Cornelia, the daughter of the leading Optimate Metellus Pius Scipio (died 46 BC). He was fast becoming the conservatives' champion.

Clodius had been killed by the followers of Titus Annius Milo, whose consulship candidacy Clodius and Pompey had resolutely opposed. Violence erupted on the streets of Rome with renewed vigour and the Senate house was burned down by a mob. The Senate implored Pompey to restore order and made him sole consul in 52 BC, which gave him near-dictatorial authority. He summoned troops from the rest of Italy and quickly passed laws to contain the violence. Milo was prosecuted under these new emergency measures. Cicero, Milo's defender, was prevented from making a concluding speech by Pompey's soldiers. Milo was banished to Massilia – modern Marseilles.

After Crassus's death, the Senate feared a war between Caesar and Pompey, with the winner declaring himself king. That said, Pompey was considered less of a threat. The Senate passed laws against bribery in elections, making them retrospective to 70 BC. These were directed at Caesar, though Pompey denied it. Several attempts to recall Caesar to Rome in the years 51 and 50 BC failed ashe was liable for prosecution under the bribery acts, if not for war crimes in Spain and Gaul.

In the run up to the consular elections of December 50 BC, the Senate passed a motion by a majority of 370 to 22, asking both Pompey and Caesar to lay down their commands before standing. After some deliberation, Pompey obeyed the Senate. But Caesar was in no position to do so. He was ineligible to run for the consulship while still in command of the army in Gaul – to stand, he had to be in Rome itself. The compromise Pompey proposed was unacceptable to Caesar, who used the wealth he had amassed in Gaul to bribe Senators.

When the consul Gaius Claudius Marcellus tried to have Caesar declared an enemy of the state, the Senate opposed him. Even so, on 2 December 50 BC, Marcellus visited Pompey and handed him

Caesar and his cohorts cross the Rubicon

a sword. Pompey accepted this gesture as an invitation to raise an army to defend Rome against Caesar and his Gallic veterans.

On 7 January 49 BC, the Senate demanded that Caesar hand over his ten battle-hardened legions to the new governor they had just appointed. Caesar was in Ravenna when he heard the news. He now had to decide whether to rebel or to face prosecution. The conqueror of Gaul saw no real choice in the matter. Quoting his favourite poet Menander, he said: *Alea iacta est! (The dice is cast).*[55]

On 10 January, Caesar advanced with ten cohorts towards Ariminum – modern-day Rimini – where he could control the passes across the Apennines. In doing so, he had to cross a small stream called the Rubicon – now Rubicone – which marked the border between Cisalpine Gaul and Italy. Crossing the Rubicon was an act of war in itself. Caesar reached the river at dawn and hesitated for a long time on the bank. Caesar never underestimated the momentousness of crossing the river into Italy. He told his men: *We may still draw back but once across that little bridge, we shall have to fight it out.*[56]

For Caesar's men, after crossing the Rubicon, they had to emerge victorious – otherwise they would be condemned as traitors.

They [the hostile senators] *have alienated Pompey from me*, said Caesar, *and led him astray, through jealous belittling of my merits. I ask you to defend my reputation and standing against the assaults of my enemies.*[57]

They crossed.

As it turned out, the Senate had misjudged the situation. The Senators believed that the issue was between a rebellious enemy of the state and Rome's legitimate rulers. The Senators had expected the towns of Italy to send troops to defend the liberties of the Roman people and the authority of the Senate. But Caesar was a hero who had given Rome great victories in Gaul, while most people were sceptical about the self-serving patricians in the Senate.

Unable to raise armies, the Senate was helpless. City after city fell to Caesar. Within weeks, he took all of northern Italy without a serious battle. Pompey announced that he and the supporters of the Republic in the Senate were leaving the city. Pompey allegedly decreed that anyone who remained behind would be considered an ally of Caesar and, henceforth, his enemy. He intended to regroup in Asia, where he thought that he could depend on the many client-kings he had installed there in his campaign between 67 and 62 BC.

Caesar pursued Pompey and his army to Brundisium – modern-day Brindisi – but he arrived too late to stop Pompey, his senatorial followers and the army, who sailed across the Adriatic to the Balkans on 17 March. But although he had fled Italy, Pompey was far from beaten. He had, after all, a fleet, and Caesar did not. Unfortunately, though, in the scramble to flee Rome, Pompey and the Senators forgot to take the Roman treasury with them. They would have no money to raise armies in Asia or bribe client-kings with.

The treasury was stored under the Temple of Saturn. Caesar found it untouched when he arrived in Rome and promptly seized 15,000 gold bars, 30,000 bars of silver and 30 million sesterces. When a young Tribune named Marcellus said that the money belonged to the legitimate government of Rome, Caesar merely pointed out that it would be easier for him to kill Marcellus than to threaten to kill him. No more was said. Caesar's war chest was now much larger than Pompey's.

One of the few who did not flee Italy was one of Caesar's sternest critics Cicero. But then again, he had no particular fondness for Pompey.

'When all of us feared Caesar, Pompey was his friend,' he wrote. 'Now that he has started to fear him he expects us all to be Caesar's enemies.'[58] Cicero told his friend Titus Pomponius Atticus (110-32 BC), who lived in Athens: 'Do you think that there is no understanding between them, that no agreement has ever been possible? Today there is a possibility. But neither of them has our happiness as their aim. They both want to be kings.'[59]

Remaining in Italy was a brave move. When Sulla marched on Rome a generation earlier, he had been ruthless with his enemies, killing them, banishing them and seizing their property. Many were convicted that Caesar would act the same way. Instead, he instituted a policy of *clementia* – mercy.

On 5 March, while on the march to Brundisium, Caesar wrote the wealthy writer and statesman Lucius Cornelius Balbus, a friend of Caesar, Pompey and Cicero, saying: *I had of my own accord decided to show all possible clemency and to do my best to reconcile Pompey. Let us try whether by this means we can win back the goodwill of all and enjoy a lasting victory, seeing that others have not managed by cruelty to escape hatred or to make their victories endure, except only L. Sulla, whom I do not propose to imitate. Let this be the new style of conquest, to make mercy and generosity our shield.*[60] This letter was almost certainly meant for circulation.

Caesar pardoned armies and whole cities that had stood against him. He told his enemies to go join Pompey if they wished. This liberality won many Romans over – in the short term. Later, most of his murderers were men who had fought against him in the Civil War and been pardoned.

To Cicero himself, Caesar wrote on 26 March: *You rightly surmise of me (you know me well) that of all things I abhor cruelty . . . I am not disturbed by the fact that those whom I have released are said to have left the country in order to make war against me once more. Nothing pleases me better than that I should be true to my nature and they to theirs.*[62]

'Do you see what sort of man this is into whose hands the state has fallen? How clever, alert, well prepared? I truly believe that if he takes no lives and touches no man's property those who dreaded him most will become his warmest admirers.'

MARCUS TULLIUS CICERO[61]

On 28 March, Caesar visited Cicero in Formiae – now Formia in the Gulf of Gaeta, 72 miles south-east of Rome. He plainly wanted Cicero to return to Rome with him to lend some weight to the members of Senate that had remained there. Cicero said that if he returned to Rome, he intended to propose to the Senate that Caesar should not pursue the war against Pompey. Cicero also insisted that Caesar restore the pre-war status quo of the Republic.

After the interview, Cicero wrote Atticus: 'We were wrong in thinking him accommodating. I have never found anybody less so. He said I was passing judgement against him . . . After a long discussion, Caesar said, *Come along then and work for peace.* "At my own discretion?" I asked. *Naturally*, he said. *Who am I to lay down rules for you?* "Well," I said, "I shall take the line that the Senate does not approve of an expedition to Spain or of the transport of armies into Greece and," I added, "I shall have much to say in commiseration of Pompey." At that he protested that this was not the sort of thing he wanted said.'[63]

In Rome, Caesar pardoned his enemies instead of massacring them, and he created a new Senate to authorise whatever he chose. Before it had assembled, Caesar was already en route to Spain, leaving his lieutenants Mark Antony and Marcus Aemilius Lepidus (89-13 BC) in charge with instructions to a law-giving Roman citizenship to the inhabitants of Cisalpine Gaul.

To Caesar, as a military commander, the situation was clear. Pompey had left seven legions in Spain without a commander, while their commander was in Greece without army. Before leaving, Caesar told his household: *I am off to meet an army without a leader; when I return I shall meet a leader without an army.*[64]

With no transports, Caesar's army had to march to Spain. But first he had to break the resistance of the port of Massilia – Marseilles – which supported Pompey. The city was besieged by Trebonius by land and by Decimus Brutus by sea, with a small fleet of hastily constructed warships. They had orders not to take the port by storm. Instead Trebonius began building huge fortifications that cut the city off to the landward. The sheer scale of these military works eventually intimidated the Massilians into surrender.

Meanwhile, Caesear mustered his legions and crossed the Rhône and the Pyrenees. In northern Spain there were five legions – roughly 30,000 men – and 5,000 cavalry under Lucius Afranius (died 46 BC) and Marcus Petreius (115-46 BC). Despite their superior numbers, they made no attempt to block the Pyrenees as Caesar's advance guard approached. Instead they took up positions at Ilerda, near the site of modern Barcelona. There they were besieged by Caesar's entire army, supported by 7,000 cavalry. The ensuing Battle of Ilerda was a series of indecisive skirmishes that caused a huge toll of casualties on both sides.

In late July, the Pompeians attempted a surprise evacuation to positions south of the Ebro River. By a forced march, Caesar's troops overtook the retreating army and dug entrenchments in front of and behind the Pompeians. Cut off from water

'The place was craggy in the front and steep on either side, and was so narrow that . . . no relief could be sent on the flanks . . . From the town, indeed, the precipice inclined with a gentle slope for near 400 paces. Our men had to retreat this way, as they had, through their eagerness, advanced too inconsiderately. The greatest contest was in this place, which was much to the disadvantage of our troops . . . yet they exerted their valour and patience, and bore every wound. The enemy's forces were increasing, and cohorts were frequently sent to their aid from the camp through the town, that fresh men might relieve the weary. Caesar was obliged to do the same . . . [O]ur men had suffered much from superior numbers, having spent all their javelins, they drew their swords and charged the enemy up the hill, and, having killed a few, obliged the rest to fly.'

GAIUS JULIUS CAESAR[65]

Marcus Terrentius Varro, one of Rome's greatest scholars and satirists, studied with the philosopher Antiochus of Ascalon at Athens, then served under Pompey in Spain in 76 BC and in the war against the pirates. In 59 BC Varro wrote a political pamphlet entitled *Trikaranos* – 'The Three-Headed' – on the still-to-be named triumvirate. After surrendering to Caesar in Spain, Varro joined Pompey in Greece, where he saved many lives Corcyra after the battle. Although Mark Antony wanted Varro proscribed, Caesar pardoned him in 47 BC and appointed him to design a new library in Rome. After Caesar's death, Mark Antony outlawed Varro, and his books were burned, but Emperor Augustus later restored his property. Varro wrote books on the law, astronomy, geography, literature, education and other subjects, as well as satires, poems, orations and letters. His only complete surviving work is the Res rustica – 'Farm Topics' – a practical guide to husbandry.

sources and besieged in open terrain, they capitulated on 2 August. Again, Caesar showed clemency. He disbanded the defeated legions and spared the commanders on the condition that they did not serve in war again. However, Afranius and Petreius broke their oaths and joined Pompey in Greece. Caesar then marched on southern Spain, where the two legions under Marcus Terrentius Varro (116-27 BC) at Corduba surrendered without a fight. Varro, too, was pardoned and made his way to Greece.

Returning to Rome, Caesar was named dictator. He filled vacant religious and administrative posts and arranged for the celebration of deferred religious festivals. Citizenship was extended to Latin communities in Spain as well as Cisalpine Gaul and, later, Gaul itself, and he issued a grain ration to the people of Rome. Then, in late December, he laid down the dictatorship and went to join his armies in Brundisium. He was now ready to go after Pompey.

The Destruction of Pompey – 48 BC

Pompey had not been wasting time in Greece. Drawing on the resources of the eastern provinces and client-kings, he had raised an army of eight legions, along with some 500 warships and light galleys. The fleet was commanded by Caesar's old enemy Marcus Calpurnius Bibulus. Pompey was now in a position to re-invade Italy. But Caesar beat him to it.

Reaching Brundisium, Caesar found he was suffering from a critical shortage of ships. Despite of six months of procurement throughout Italy, his men had only managed to muster transport for 6,700 cavalry and 15,000 legionaries. This meant his force would have to be taken across the Adriatic in two shifts. Despite the dangers of travelling by sea in winter, Caesar set off across the Adriatic with the first part of his army on 4 January 48 BC, under the noses of Bibulus's patrols. He landed at the small harbour of Palaesate – modern-day Palasë – the following day, and then sent the transports back to pick up the second tranche.

Realising that he had been outsmarted, Bibulus increased patrols along the whole coast of Epirus-Illyricum – north-west Greece, Albania and Yugoslavia – thereby blocking the passage of Mark Antony and the rest of Caesar's army.

Although his leading elements were outnumbered by Pompey's by as much as seven to one, Caesar did not wait around. Instead he marched directly north through Epirus towards Pompey's arsenal and depot at Dyrrhachium – modern Durrës, in Albania – taking several small towns, including Apollonia – near modern-day Vlorës – on the way. Pompey was soon aware of

Caesar's movements, as Caesar made a political gamble and sent a peace offer to Pompey with Vibellius Rufus, one of Pompey's engineers captured by Caesar. Vibellius caught up with Pompey on the Egnatian Way as he was making his way towards winter quarters near Dyrrhachium.

Caesar's gamble failed. Because he had the upper hand, Pompey was not interested in making peace. Forewarned of Caesar's intentions, he moved into position north of the River Apsus – modern-day Aóös River – and blocked Caesar's route to his supply depot. Caesar drew up his army south of the Apsus, where he awaited Antony's arrival with reinforcements. He was now in an extremely vulnerable position. He had lost his chance to seize the supplies in Dyrrhachium, and Bibulus's fleet was menacing his supply lines across the Adriatic.

Caesar did what he could to prevent Bibulus from re-supplying his fleet by picketing the coastline. He sent a message to Antony to be careful attempting his landing. Even so, Caesar was desperate for the balance of his legions, and there is a story that he tried to sneak back to Brundisium across a storm-tossed sea to fetch them himself, convincing the sceptical captain that he could succeed because he carried *Caesar and Caesar's luck*.

The two armies were close enough for fellow Romans to fraternise easily. Caesar made an effort to persuade Pompey's men to join him, but his old second-in-command from Gaul, Titus Labienus, who had sided with Pompey, declared that the war would only end when he was brought Caesar's head.

Caesar's fabled luck held and Pompey did not attack. The winter was over when Antony was finally able to land his army three months after Caesar had set off. With three legions of veterans, one of recruits and 800 cavalry, he sailed for Apollonia. In what Caesar himself calls *an incredible piece of luck*,[67] the south winds blew Antony north of his goal, nearer to Caesar's camp. He landed safely near Lissus landing on 10 April. The same winds drove

16 of Bibulus's galleys onto the rocky coasts with the loss of the ships and most of their crew. Again Caesar was merciful and sent the survivors home. Pompey's men were less lenient. When one of Antony's transports fell into their hands, the 220 soldiers on board were promised that their lives would be spared if they surrendered. When they complied, the Pompeians killed them all.

Thanks to the capture of the transport, the news that Antony had crossed the Adriatic reached Pompey first and he moved to attack at Lissus. Even though he had a vastly larger army, Pompey abandoned the chase as soon as he realised that he had made the elementary mistake of having Antony in front of him, while Caesar was to his rear. As Pompey withdrew northwards to his stronghold at Dyrrhachium, Caesar's two armies linked up. Although still outnumbered by Pompey's forces, Caesar was now in command of

Between Pompey's and Caesar's camp was only the river Apsus, and the soldiers frequently conversed with each other, with no weapons thrown during their conferences. Caesar sent Publius Vatinius, one of his lieutenants, to the riverbank to make such proposals conducive to peace. After speaking in humble language, Vatinius received the enemy's answer: Aulus Varro proposed to hold to a conference that deputies from both sides might attend without danger. When a great multitude of deputies from both sides assembled the next day, expectations were high, with most people disposed towards peace. Titus Labienus and Vatinius were arguing when darts from all sides interrupted their conversation. Several men were wounded, including Cornelius Balbus, Marcus Plotius, Lucius Tiburtius, centurions, and some privates; hereupon Labienus exclaimed: 'Forbear, then, to speak any more about an accommodation, for we can have no peace unless we carry Caesar's head back with us.'

GAIUS JULIUS CAESAR[66]

34,000 infantry and 1,400 cavalry. He sent the XI and XII legions, along with some cavalry under Gnaeus Domitius Calvinus, to intercept Metellus Scipio, son of a famous military family, who was on his way from Syria to reinforce Pompey. Calvinus held Scipio at Thessaly, in eastern Greece. A detachment of the Roman fleet under Pompey's elder son Gnaeus sailed in and destroyed Caesar's transports at Oricum – modern Orikum in Vlorës Bay – then did the same to Antony's vessels in Lissus. Every ship Caesar had was now out of action, and he could not even send a message back to Italy for help.

Ever audacious, Caesar raced for Dyrrhachium, beating Pompey's advance guard by just an hour. Caesar pitched camp on the north side of a waterway called the Shimmihl Torrent, while Pompey's army occupied the south bank. Even though Caesar had reached Dyrrhachium first, his supply problem was not yet over. The surrounding countryside had already been cleaned of food-stuffs, and there was little for his cavalry to forage.

Pompey could re-supply by sea, but he had a larger cavalry force. By denying his horses forage, Caesar could make Pompey look weak in the eyes of eastern client-kings who supported him. Caesar worked on building a wall around Pompey's forces, enclosing him in an enclave of just 22 square miles. As soon as he realised what was happening, Pompey began fortifications of his own. These eventually ran to 15 miles in length. Caesar's were larger, however, and he had Pompey pinned with his back to the sea. And Pompey did not even move his cavalry outside of the stockade, where they could have prevented Caesar's men foraging. Instead he had to feed them himself inside.

Meanwhile, Caesar's men ran out of grain to make bread, and they began using a root they called *kelkass* instead. Lumps of this unappetising substance were smuggled through the lines by deserters. After tasting it, Pompey said: 'What kind of wild beasts are we fighting with?'[68]

But it was not just a war of attrition. There were numerous skirmishes. Caesar recorded that six engagements happened in one day, three at Dyrrhachium and three at the fortifications.

He estimated that some 2,000 had been killed on Pompey's side, several of them volunteer veterans and centurions and six military standards were taken.

Of our men, not more than 20 were missing in all the action, said Caesar reported. *But in the fort, not a single soldier escaped without a wound; and in one cohort, four centurions lost their eyes. And being desirous to produce testimony of the fatigue they under went, and the danger they sustained, they counted to Caesar about 30,000 arrows which had been thrown into the fort; and in the shield of the centurion Scaeva, which was brought to him, were found 230 holes. In reward for this man's services, both to himself and the public, Caesar presented to him 200,000 pieces of copper money, and declared him promoted from the eighth to the first centurion. For it appeared that the fort had been in a great measure saved by his exertions; and he afterward very amply rewarded the cohorts with double pay, corn, clothing, and other military honours.*[70]

A root called chara, discovered by Valerius's troops, greatly relieved soldiers' hunger when mixed with milk and made into a sort of bread. 'They had great plenty of it; loaves made of this ... And there were frequently heard declarations of the soldiers on guard ... that they would rather live on the bark of the trees than let Pompey escape from their hands. [Pompey's men] could scarcely maintain their horses, and that their other cattle was dead: that they themselves were not in good health from their confinement within so narrow a compass, from the noisome smell, the number of carcasses, and the constant fatigue to them ... But Caesar's army enjoyed perfect health and abundance of water, all sorts of provisions except corn, and they had a prospect of better times approaching; and saw greater hopes laid before them by the ripening of the grain.

GAIUS JULIUS CAESAR[69]

However, being outside the line of fortification, Caesar could deprive the enclave of water. His engineers began damming and diverting the streams flowing down from the mountains. Inside the enclave Pompey's men began digging wells, but as summer drew on, these dried up in the heat. Lack of provisions soon became so urgent that Pompey evacuated his cavalry by sea.

A deserter from Dyrrhachium contacted Caesar and offered to reveal the layout of the town to him. Late one night, Caesar took a small force between the marshes and sea to the gates of the Temple of Artemis to meet the turncoat, expecting the town to be betrayed by its defenders. However, in the narrows, he was attacked both front and rear by a large force that had landed along the shore in boats. Caesar lost many men and barely escaped with his own life. Not surprisingly, he makes no reference to the plot in his own account of the Civil War. At the same time, Pompey made a night assault on the wall. He captured a portion of it and killed a large number of men, but Caesar's troops eventually repulsed the attackers.[71]

Soon afterwards, two Allobrogian Celts named Raucilus and Egus, who had served with Caesar in Gaul, were caught embezzling the legions' pay and escaped through the lines. They told Pompey that the weakest point in Caesar's defences were at the southern end, just south of the Lesnikia River. At that point, there was no cross-stockade between the double walls to bar entry.

Pompey attacked the inner wall with 60 cohorts. At the same time, a force of soldiers and archers were sent by sea to attack the rear of Caesar's defences and move up the gap between the two sets of fortifications, outflanking the defenders. Caesar's smaller force was quickly routed. Antony was sent with 12 cohorts to reinforce them. However, by the time they arrived, Pompey had breached the circumvallation and built a fortified camp to the south, outside Caesar's carefully constructed stockade.

Caesar counterattacked and drove Pompey's forces back to within a mile of the coast. He regained the part of fortifications he had lost and plugged the gap in his lines with two cohorts. Then he attacked Pompey's new camp to the south with 33 cohorts, who quickly overwhelmed its defences. But Pompey's force still overwhelmingly outnumbered Caesar's. He sent five legions – 50 cohorts – and his cavalry. Caesar's right column was already fighting within the camp when it was threatened to the rear. His men panicked and tried to flee. The panic infected the second column which had pushed Pompey's troops back almost to the western – seaward – gate.

Caesar grabbed the standards of his fleeing troops and tried to rally them, but he was unable to stem the retreat.

However, Pompey's men did not pursue them. In a moment of hubris, they hailed Pompey as *Imperator* – 'Emperor' – and he sent out messengers throughout the East proclaiming his victory. Meanwhile, Labienus killed every prisoner the Pompeians had captured.

Dyrrhachium was one of Caesar's rare defeats. He readily admitted: *Today my enemies would have finished the war if they had a commander who knew how to win a victory.*[73]

He had lost 32 tribunes and centurions, 960 soldiers and 32 army standards. Many of these had been trampled to death by fleeing comrades. It was a defeat, but not a catastrophe. Caesar still had over 20,000 men and pulled

'His soldiers showed such good will and zeal in his service that those who in their previous campaigns had been in no way superior to others were invincible and irresistible in confronting every danger to enhance Caesar's fame . . . Such a man . . . was Cassius Scaeva, who . . . had his eye struck out with an arrow, his shoulder transfixed with one javelin and his thigh with another . . . In this plight, he called the enemy to him as though he would surrender. Two of them, accordingly, coming up, he lopped off the shoulder of one with his sword, smote the other in the face . . . and came off safely . . . [I]n Africa, Scipio captured a ship of Caesar's that Granius Petro . . . was sailing . . . [Scipio] told [Granius] that he offered him his life. Granius, however, remarking that it was the custom with Caesar's soldiers not to receive but to offer mercy, killed himself with a blow of his sword.

PLUTARCH OF CHAERONEA[72]

away to the southeast towards Thessaly, where he could find food and forage and join up with Domitius Calvinus.

Pompey's followers were so elated by his victory that they wanted to set off after Caesar. However, while Pompey wrote to distant kings, generals and cities in the tone of a victor, he feared a new encounter. His men were exhausted and he was old. With Caesar in flight, some of his lieutenants wanted to pursue him and finish him off. Others wanted to cross over into Italy. Some of them were already sending their attendants and friends to Rome to take houses near the Forum, as they hoped to become candidates for office.

A Senate was assembled and Afranius gave his opinion that first they should secure Italy, which was the greatest prize. Once they held Italy, they would also become masters of Sicily, Sardinia, Corsica, Spain and Gaul. Pompey said that it might damage his reputation to run away from Caesar a second time. Nor would it be right to abandon Scipio in Thessaly. He would stand no chance against Caesar, who would be strengthened by Scipio's money and men. Pompey had no choice. He had to set off in pursuit of Caesar, though he wanted to avoid a battle. He hoped simply to harass Caesar, keeping him short of supplies and in a permanent state of siege.[74]

Along the way, Pompey joined up with Metellus Scipio and his reinforcements from Syria. Together they followed Caesar southwards into Greece, catching up with him at the small trading town of Pharsalus, near modern-day Farsala, on 9 August 48 BC by the old Roman calendar. Caesar was camped on the plain outside the town, on the north bank of the River Enipeus. His estimated 23,000 men were recuperating after a harsh seven-day march over the Pindus mountains of central Greece when Pompey's army of over 50,000 appeared on the heights overlooking the plain. They were in high spirits. After Dyrrhachium, Caesar's legendary legions no longer seemed so invincible.

Once again, Pompey was slow to take the initiative. He wanted to fight a war of attrition. More men and supplies were on their way from the East, while Caesar was expecting no reinforcements. So Pompey saw no advantage in risking open battle until he was good and ready.

'On the most prudent calculation, he decided to protract the war and drive the enemy from famine to plague,' said Appian. 'But he was surrounded by a great number of senators, of equal rank with himself, by very distinguished knights, and

An engraving of Gnaeus Pomeius Magnus, Pompey the Great

by many kings and princes. Some of these, by reason of their inexperience in war, others because they were too much elated by the victory at Dyrrhachium, others because they outnumbered the enemy, and others because they were quite tired of the war and preferred a quick decision rather than a sound one – all urged him to fight, pointing out to him that Caesar was always drawn up for battle and challenging him.'[75]

Indeed, for several days, Caesar made a great display on the four-mile plain separating the two armies, in the hope of luring Pompey into battle. And finally, against his better judgement, Pompey decided to fight. He was confident of victory, and a great feast was prepared. He had already beaten Caesar at Dyrrhachium and now his men outnumbered Caesar's almost two to one. Pompey's army comprised 110 cohorts of legionaries and auxiliaries, some 45,000 men in all. These were supported by 1,200 slingsmen, 3,000 archers and about 7,000 cavalry from at least ten nations, including Gauls, various Germanic tribes, Syrians and Cappadocians from Asia Minor. However, many of the men supplied by Eastern potentates were slaves. Others were ill-trained with little knowledge of the Roman way of warfare.

Caesar had about 80 under-strength cohorts, amounting to about 22,000 soldiers, plus 1,000 cavalry and a small number of light troops. But they were highly disciplined soldiers, seasoned veterans from ten years campaigning in Gaul. And Caesar was delighted that Pompey was finally going to join him in battle. His supplies were running low, and every day of delay put him at more of a disadvantage.

Like Pompey, Caesar was confident. His password was 'Venus the Victorious'[76] – as he claimed descent from Venus. Pompey's was 'Hercules the Invincible'. However, Pompey appears to have experienced some last-minute misgivings. As he made preparations for battle, he said: 'Whichever should conquer, that day would be the beginning of great evils to the Romans for all future time.'[77]

At Pharsalus, two of the greatest generals of the Roman world faced each other. Pompey's right flank was protect by the steep banks of the Enipeus, and he placed mixed Spanish and Cilician troops – from Anatolia – there with Syrian legions holding the centre. His cavalry, under the command of Titus Labienus, was his great advantage. Pompey put them on his open right flank, along with massed archers and slingsmen. Caesar immediately understood what Pompey was trying to do. With only 1,000 cavalry at his disposal, Caesar's right risked being overwhelmed by Pompey's 7,000 horses. Once the right wing was lost, Pompey's men would encircle Caesar's army, push it back into the Enipeus and the battle would be lost.

To counter this, Caesar withdrew six cohorts from his rear line and positioned them in a diagonal behind the cavalry on the right wing. This placement made it difficult to see infantry when they are hidden behind mounted cavalry. Caesar gave a rousing speech, pointing out that the whole battle might depend on these men. He told them to use their lances and strike at the faces of Pompey's horsemen, who would, in turn, protect their eyes, leaving them vulnerable.

Mark Antony would hold the left with the VIII and IX Legions. Domitius Calvinus was in the centre with XI and XII, while Publius Sulla would be on the right with X, with Caesar himself directly behind him. He also pointed out that, facing odds of over two to one, victory depended on timing. No man was to move without his specific signal.

Pompey knew that Caesar was eager to fight and ordered his troops to stand firm, in the hope that Caesar's men would exhaust themselves in the initial charge across the plain. Caesar thought that this was a mistake. Pompey's multinational army had lost the psychological advantage it would have got from making the first charge. As it was, Caesar's veterans spotted the trap. They stopped short of Pompeian lines to rest and reform their lines.

Once the armies engaged, Pompey's archers and slingsmen attacked Caesar's right. As his massed cavalry struck, they almost broke the line and spilled around Caesar's exposed flank. At that moment, Caesar raised a flag, signalling the six cohorts hidden on the right to counterattack. This masterful stroke routed Labienus's cavalry, trampling the archers behind them. Those left standing were defenceless. Caesar then wheeled his troops around Pompey's exposed left. At the same time, Caesar poured reinforcements through into his first and second ranks. Pompey's exhausted men were struck on the front and flank by fresh troops. They broke and streamed back into the shelter of Pompey's fortified camp.

His cunning not yet exhausted, Caesar saw a way to end not just the battle, but the entire war. He sent heralds out onto the battlefield to tell his men not to harm their fellow Romans. Instead they were to sweep through the enemy ranks, killing only the foreign auxiliaries. 'As Pompey's left wing began to give way his men retired step by step and in perfect order, said Appian, 'but the allies who had not been in the fight, fled with headlong speed, shouting, "We are vanquished," dashed upon their own tents and fortifications as though they had been the enemy's.... Then the rest of Pompey's Italian legions, perceiving the disaster to the left wing, retired slowly at first...but when the enemy, flushed with victory, pressed upon them they turned in flight. Thereupon Caesar, in order that they might not rally,... with greater prudence than he had ever shown before, sent heralds everywhere among the ranks to order the victors to spare their own countrymen and to smite only the auxiliaries. The heralds drew near to the retreating enemy and told them to stand still and fear not...'[79] As they had nothing to fear, the Italians in Pompey's army gave up the fight, while Caesar's men slaughtered their allies who crumbled, broke and ran.

Seeing the rout, Pompey went back to his tent, which had already been decorated with laurels in anticipation of his victory. For some time, he seems to have gone quite mad with depression. Although it was nearing noon on a very hot day, Caesar rallied his men for the final push and led them up to the fortifications of Pompey's camp. News of the attack roused Pompey, who said: 'So they're at our camp as well?' He disguised himself and, with four companions, fled on horseback to the port of Larissa. That night, Caesar dined in Pompey's tent, and 'the whole army feasted at the enemy's expense'.[80]

Caesar described the scene: In Pompey's camp could be seen artificial arbours, a great weight of silver plate laid out, tents spread with fresh turf and . . . covered with ivy, and many other indications of extravagant indulgence and confidence in victory; so that it could readily be judged that they had no fears for the outcome of the day.[81]

Pompey's remaining forces surrendered the next day. Caesar was thought to have lost just 30 centurions and 200 legionaries, though Appian quoted some authorities who put Caesar's losses as high as 1,200. Caesar himself estimated that 6,000 Roman citizens were killed, though Appian quoted that figure as Roman losses on Pompey's side alone. That included ten hostile Senators, among them Lucius Domitius Ahenobarbus (died 48 BC), the former consul appointed by the Senate to take over from Caesar as governor of Gaul. No one counted the foreign dead. Caesar estimated their number at 15,000. Other authorities put it as high as 25,000.[82] Caesar said simply: *They brought it on themselves. They would have condemned me regardless of my victories – me, Gaius Caesar – had I not appealed to my army for help.*[83]

The first-century Roman poet Lucan mourned the death of the Republic on Pharsalus plain with the lines: 'The loser bears the burden of defeat/ The victor wins, but conquest is a crime.'[84] The soldier and historian Velleius Paterculus called the Battle of Pharsalus 'that day of carnage so fatal to the Roman name, when so much blood was shed on either side, the clash of arms between the two heads of the state, the extinction of one of the two luminaries of the Roman world'.[85]

From Larissa, Pompey took a small boat to the sea, then a ship to Mitylene, capital of the Greek island of Lesbos. There he joined his wife, Cornelia, and they embarked on four triremes, which had come from Rhodes and Tyre.[86] He planned to rally his supporters and continue the fight against Caesar in North Africa, Spain and the East. But first he headed for Egypt.

With Caesar in hot pursuit, Pompey lost contact with his own fleet. He decided to land at Pelusium, a port at the eastern edge of the Nile delta, long since silted up. There he would seek the assistance of the ten-year-old king Ptolemy XIII (63-47 BC), his former client, who was involved in a civil war with his sister, Cleopatra (69-30 BC). Having offered his assistance to Ptolemy, Pompey had every reason to expect a friendly reception.

But Ptolemy was surrounded by powerful advisers – notably Potheinus the Eunuch, Achillas the Egyptian and Theodotus of

Chios, a Greek hired to teach the young king rhetoric. Some counsellors thought they should welcome Pompey; others wanted to drive him away. And while Pompey anchored some distance from the shore, Theodotus pointed out that neither course was safe for the young king. If he received Pompey, he would make Caesar his enemy and Pompey his master. But if he rejected him, Pompey would blame him for casting him aside, and Caesar would blame him for making him continue his pursuit. The best course, therefore, was to kill him. That way, Caesar would be grateful, and Ptolemy would have nothing to fear from Pompey. Theodotus added with a smile: 'A dead man does not bite.'[87]

King Ptolemy marched down to the coast, ostensibly to welcome Pompey. A small fishing boat was sent out to meet him. On board was Septimus, who had once been one of Pompey's tribunes. He greeted Pompey in Latin and hailed him as *Imperator*. Achillas saluted Pompey in Greek and invited him on board. Also with them was Salvius, a centurion. Pompey's aides were worried, for their leader was not being greeted with sufficient pomp, but Achillas explained that the water was too shallow for a larger boat to reach the shore.

Pompey embraced Cornelia and got on board the fishing boat with two centurions and his freedman Philip. Despite her misgivings about the number of armed men on shore, Cornelia took heart when she saw many of Ptolemy's men assembling at the landing point, as if to give her husband an honourable welcome. Pompey recognised Septimus and tried to make small talk with him. But Septimus merely nodded and the journey continued in silence.

When they reached the beach, Pompey took Philip's hand to steady him as he stepped ashore. At that moment, Septimus drew his sword and stabbed Pompey from behind. Then Achillas and Salvius drew their daggers and struck him, too.[88]

'And Pompey, drawing his toga down over his face with both

hands, without an act or a word that was unworthy of himself, but with a groan merely, submitted to their blows, being 60 years of age less one, and ending his life only one day after his birthday,' said Plutarch.[89] The date was 28 September 48 BC.

When the people on board the ship saw what had happened, they let out a wail that reached the shore. Then they weighed anchor and fled. The Egyptians cut off Pompey's head and threw his naked body from the boat. Philip recovered it, collected some wood and built a funeral pyre. An old Roman walking down the beach, who in his youth had served in campaigns with Pompey, asked Philip who thought he was to give burial rites to Pompey the Great. When Philip said that he was Pompey's freedman, the man said: 'But you shall not have this honour all to yourself; let me share in this privilege, that I may not altogether regret my stay in a foreign land and, in return for my many hardships I find this happiness at least – to touch with my hands and array for burial the greatest of Roman *Imperators*.'[90]

The Egyptian Adventure – 48 to 47 BC

Caesar pursued Pompey across the Mediterranean and reached Alexandria on 2 October. He refused to look at Pompey's severed head, though he accepted his signet ring and was said to have shed a tear as he did so. Although he claimed that the Egyptians had robbed him of the opportunity to pardon Pompey, Caesar must had been relieved, as he still faced hostile Republican forces in North Africa, Spain and the East. But, ever the politician, Caesar still persuaded Ptolemy to release the friends and companions of Pompey he had arrested and offered them his help and friendship. Naturally, he did not let this gesture go unnoticed and wrote to his friends in Rome saying that, of all the results of his victory, what gave him the most pleasure was *that he was so often able to save the lives of fellow citizens who had fought against him*.[91]

Despite the hostile forces still ranged against him in the rest of the Roman world, Caesar remained in Egypt for the next nine months. This extended delay undoubtedly had something to do with his romance with Cleopatra. But Caesar was a hard-headed pragmatist as well. He badly needed money to pay his troops, and Egypt was the richest country in the ancient world.

Caesar had arrived in Alexandria with just 4,000 men. He set up residence in the royal palace and prepared to mediate the dispute between Ptolemy and his sister. Whichever of them sat on the throne, he maintained, owed him money promised by their father.

The Cleopatra of Michelangelo's artistic imagination

Cleopatra was the last of the Ptolemaic dynasty in Hellenised Egypt that began when Alexander the Great's general Ptolemy I took over the kingdom after Alexander's death in 323 BC. The Ptolemys adopted Egyptian royal ways, including incestuous marriage, which horrified Europeans but preserved the Macedonian bloodline. Cleopatra VII was born in 69 BC, the third daughter of Ptolemy XII and his sister, Cleopatra V. Ptolemy had ordered his daughters Berenice IV and probably Cleopatra VI murdered when they had tried to seize the throne. When he died in 51 BC, 12-year-old Cleopatra V ascended to the throne to rule jointly with her seven-year-old brother Ptolemy XIII, whom she was expected to marry. Instead she took sole control. In the Civil War, she supported Pompey, sending ships and grain. In 48 BC, ministers who supported her younger brother ousted Cleopatra, who retreated to Arabia and began raising an army.

Alexandria was in the hands of Ptolemy's ministers, so he had Caesar's ear so Caesar had to listen to him. Cleopatra wanted to plead her case, but she could not get past the guards into her own former palace.

'So Cleopatra, taking only Apollodorus the Sicilian from among her friends, embarked in a little skiff and landed at the palace when it was already getting dark,' said Plutarch, 'and as it was impossible to escape notice otherwise, she stretched herself at full length inside a bed-sack, while Apollodorus tied the bed-sack up with a cord and carried it indoors to Caesar. It was by this device of Cleopatra's, it is said, that Caesar was first captivated, for she showed herself to be a bold coquette, and succumbing to the charm of further intercourse with her.'[93]

Caesar was 52; Cleopatra, 21.

Although Cleopatra has long had the reputation of being a great beauty, a recent forensic reconstruction showed that she looked like the inbred Macedonian she was. Even existing busts show she had a prominent, hooked nose and full lips. She was Greek in facial features and dress. According to Plutarch, her charms lay elsewhere.

'Her beauty, so we are told, was not of that incomparable kind which struck all those who saw her,' he said. 'But conversation with her had an irresistible charm, and her presence, combined with the persuasiveness of her discourse and character ... had something stimulating about it.'[94]

Her verbal dexterity was particularly impressive.

'There was sweetness also in the tones of her voice,' said Plutarch, 'and her tongue, like an instrument of many strings, she could readily turn to whatever language she pleased.'[95]

She could speak with 'Ethiopians, Troglodytes, Hebrews, Arabians, Syrians, Medes or Parthians' without a translator. And she spoke Egyptian and Greek, though most of the Ptolemic pharaohs before her had not even given up their Macedonian dialect.[96] Caesar, like all educated Romans, spoke Greek, so they had a common language.

'As for the war in Egypt, some say that it was not necessary, but due to Caesar's passion for Cleopatra, and that it was inglorious and full of peril for him. But others blame the king's party for it, and especially the eunuch Potheinus, who had most influence at court, and had recently killed Pompey; he had also driven Cleopatra from the country, and was now secretly plotting against Caesar. On this account they say that from this time on Caesar passed whole nights at drinking parties in order to protect himself. But in his open acts also Potheinus was unbearable, since he said and did many things that were invidious and insulting to Caesar.'

PLUTARCH OF CHAERONEA[92]

Caesar decided that Ptolemy and Cleopatra should share the throne, and he held a great banquet to celebrate the reconciliation. But Caesar's barber overheard Achillas and Potheinus the Eunuch plotting against Caesar. He had the banqueting hall surrounded. Potheinus was killed, but Achillas escaped.

The Alexandrians, who feared Roman influence in Egyptian affairs, rebelled and proclaimed Cleopatra's younger sister, Arsinoe, queen. A full-scale war broke out. Caesar and Cleopatra

In the 3rd century BC, Ptolemy I founded the famous Mouseion (Museum) of Alexandria, which included a magnificient library that became the most important in the ancient world, housing numerous rare poetic works. The first librarian Zenodotus of Ephesus (c325–260 BC) made the first critical edition of Homer. The fourth librarian, Aristophanes of Byzantium (c257–180), applied a systemic metrical theory to lyrical poetry and edited dramatists Aristophanes, Menander, Sophocles and Euripides. The sixth librarian, Aristarchus of Samothrace (c217–145), who wrote important monographs and commentaries, fled Alexandria during a persecution by Ptolemy VIII. The city's standing as a centre of learning never fully recovered. Although the great library survived the fire Caesar set in 47BC, the patriarch Theophilus of Alexandria later destroyed it in AD 391.

were besieged with the small Roman force in the royal enclave of the city, while Arsinoe and Achillas rallied their army outside.

The enemy dammed up the canals and Caesar's men were in danger of being cut off from their water supply. Then the Egyptians tried to intercept his communications by sea. Caesar responded by setting fire to the ships in the docks. But the fire spread from the dockyards and set fire to the great library at Alexandria. There was fierce fighting in the harbour of the island of Pharos, where the great lighthouse was topped by a huge statue either of Alexander the Great or Ptolemy I, one of the seven wonders of the world.

As a result, Caesar almost lost his life. He had sprung down from the mole into a small boat and was trying to help his men who were engaged in battle, but the Egyptians sailed up against him from all directions. His small boat was immediately sunk. He was forced to jump into the sea and swim, and he only just managed to escape. According to Plutarch, Caesar was holding a number of papers in his hand at the time and would not let them go, though he was being shot at from all sides and was often under water. Holding the papers above the surface with one hand, he swam with the other.[97]

Eventually, Ptolemy managed to escape and join the rebels. But in March 47 BC, reinforcements arrived, and Caesar promptly defeated the Egyptian insurgents. Ptolemy drowned in the Nile while trying to escape, but Arsinoe was captured and held prisoner to walk in Caesar's triumph in Rome the following year.

After the war, Caesar and Cleopatra set off on a two-month honeymoon cruise up the Nile. Caesar took his army and a fleet of 400 ships with him. The aim was both to impress and intimidate the Egyptians.

In June 47 BC, Caesar left Egypt at the start of the new campaigning season. He left Cleopatra was securely upon the throne, ruling alongside her 11-year-old brother, Ptolemy XIV, her only remaining sibling who, by tradition, she married. Three of Caesar's four legions were left behind as an occupying army.

Cleopatra bore her first child, a son, on 23 June 47 BC. Although later historians claimed that the child was not Caesar's, Mark Antony said that Caesar acknowledged him as his own. The Alexandrians called him Caesarion.[98] From the age of three – after Ptolemy XIV died, poisoned, it is said, by Cleopatra – the boy would reign with his mother as Ptolemy XV.

'I Came, I Saw, I Conquered' – 47 to 45 BC

After leaving Cleopatra in Egypt firmly under Roman control, Caesar headed north to pacify Asia. After the death of Mithridates, his kingdom of Pontus in northeast Anatolia had been incorporated into the Roman empire and Pompey had awarded Mithridates' son Pharnaces the kingdom of the Cimmerian Bosporus in the Crimea. But Pharnaces took advantage of the civil war to attempt to win back his father's empire. He swept around the eastern end of the Black Sea, across Asian Minor and defeated a Roman army under Caesar's lieutenant Domitius Calvinus at Nicopolis in Macedonia in late 48 BC. Caesar sent Calvinus to Africa and took charge of the situation himself.

Caesar marched on Syria – modern-day Israel, Jordan, Lebanon and Syria, east of the desert, west of the Euphrates and north of the Tarsus Mountains. He met with local leaders to ensure their support. In Palestine, he met King Herod, the man accused of the 'massacre of the innocents' in the Gospel of St Matthew, although there is no historical evidence. Caesar also met the governor Gaius Cassius Longinus, whom he pardoned for supporting Pompey – though his governorship was given to Caesar's own relation Sextus Caesar. During the trip, Caesar also took money from the rich aristocrats who lived in the area and had supported Pompey. And he collected a few royal crowns.

Boarding one of the ships that had followed him from Egypt, Caesar sailed to Tarsus, where he met all the leaders of the territories in the area. They quickly reached a settlement. Then he marched north to the city of Comana – modern Sahr in southern Turkey.

He also met King Deiotarus, who supported Pompey and then, after the Battle of Pharsalus, changed sides to back Calvinus in his campaign against Pharnaces. Deiotarus, too, was pardoned for supporting Pompey, and he was given a command in Caesar's army.

By this time, Pharnaces was feeling isolated and tried to make peace with Rome. He sent ambassadors with a gold crown 'to entreat that Caesar would not come as an enemy, for he would submit to all his commands'.[99] They pointed out that 'Pharnaces had granted no aid to Pompey, as Deiotarus had done, whom he had nevertheless pardoned'. In his sweep into Asia Minor, Pharnaces had been responsible for the deaths of many Roman civilians. But Caesar once again offered clemency.

Pharnaces should meet with the utmost justice, if he performed his promises, Caesar said, *but at the same time he admonished the ambassadors, in gentle terms, to forbear mentioning Deiotarus . . . He told them that he never did any thing with greater pleasure than pardon a suppliant, but that he would never look upon private services to himself as an atonement for public injuries done to the province . . .; that he was however willing to forgive the injuries done to the Roman citizens in Pontus, because it was now too late to think of redressing them; as he could neither restore life to the dead, nor manhood to those he had deprived of it, by a punishment more intolerable to the Romans than death itself. But that he must quit Pontus immediately, send back the farmers of the revenues, and restore to the Romans and their allies what he unjustly detained from them. If he should do this, he might then send the presents which successful generals were wont to receive from their friends.*[100]

But Pharnaces did not withdraw. In May 47 BC, his army was camped on a hill three miles from the Pontic town of Zela – modern Zile in eastern central Turkey – where his father Mithridates had defeated the Romans 20 years earlier. Caesar arrived and camped on a hill five miles away. He had just four legions with him – once of which was the VI, which had seen action in Egypt and had only 1,000 men left. Caesar assumed that

Caesar, astonished at his incredible rashness and confidence, and finding himself suddenly and unexpectedly attacked, called off his soldiers from the works, ordered them to arms, opposed the legions to the enemy, and ranged his troops in order of battle. The suddenness of the thing occasioned some terror at first . . . Our advantageous situation, but especially the assistance of the gods, who preside over all the events of war, and more particularly those where human conduct can be of no service, favoured us greatly on this occasion . . . Great numbers {of the enemy} being slain . . . such as had the good fortune to escape were nevertheless obliged to throw away their arms . . . Our men flushed with victory, did not hesitate to advance up the disadvantageous ground, and attack their fortifications . . . Almost the whole army was cut to pieces or made prisoners.

GAIUS JULIUS CAESAR[101]

Pharnaces was among the few to escape alive.

Pharnaces was not eager to join battle and set to work building fortifications. The following day, however, Pharnaces began moving his lines forward. Caesar thought the enemy was just testing him and deployed only a single defensive line, while the rest of his men continued building fortifications. Suddenly, he found the enemy rushing up the hill at him and hastily assembled the rest of the legions.

Pharnaces led the attack with scythed chariots, but Romans fought them off with javelins and mortars. The armies then engaged in hand-to-hand fighting. Soon Pharnaces had exhausted the surprise advantage, and his forces were fatigued from the uphill fight. Despite being depleted, the VI Legion on Caesar's right began pushing the enemy back. Then the centre and the left began to give way. The collapse turned into a rout. As the Romans chased Pharnaces's men down into the valley, the fleeing troops dropped their weapons and in their flight trampled many of those left behind to death.

When Pharnaces's men reached the other side of the valley wall, they could not stop the pursuing Roman legions. Pharnaces had left a few hundred men to guard his camp and the Roman easily them cut them down. Almost all the enemy army was killed or captured. Only Pharnaces and some of his cavalry escaped. He returned to Bosphorus, only to be killed in an insurrection by the new Roman client-king Asander.

Caesar gave the enemy camp to his troops as plunder and set up a monument to commemorate his victory. Suetonius remarked on the speed of his success, saying: 'Five days after his arrival' – that is, around 1 August 47 BC – 'and four hours after catching sight of Pharnaces, Caesar won a crushing victory at Zela; and commented dryly on Pompey's good fortune in having built up his reputation for generalship by victories over such poor stuff as this.'[102]

Caesar was so proud of his achievement that he reputedly sent the famous message to the Senate in Rome: *Veni, vidi, vici* – 'I came, I saw, I conquered.'[103]

Suetonius only records that, the following year, when Caesar was celebrating his triumphs in Rome, the wagon representing Pontic victory was not decorated

The Roman coin minted to honour Caesar's victory at Pharnaces

with scenes from the battle like the rest. It merely carried that simple three-word inscription.[104]

With Asia firmly back under Roman control, Caesar sailed for Rome, landing at Tarentum – modern Taranto – on 24 September 47 BC. There had been civil unrest in the capital for several months. When news of Caesar's victory at Pharsalus had reached Rome, the Senate had appointed him dictator once again. He appointed Mark Antony as his *magister equitum* – master of the horse. But Antony had let conflicts flare between his followers and those of his political rival Dolabella. There were riots and street fighting, in which around 800 Romans were killed. When he arrived in Rome, Caesar sacked Mark Antony who, though a favourite, did not serve in a significant position for another two years, and quickly quelled a veterans' mutiny on the Campus Martius.

Once order was restored, Caesar arranged for the elections of magistrates and consuls. He also substantially increased the number of Senators, whose ranks had been depleted by the defeat of Pompey. Previously, the Senators had been members of the august patrician families. Caesar's new Senators were men who had fought by his side on his campaigns and the Senate was now crammed with his supporters. They were centurions, men without name or reputation in Rome. In the controversy that followed his appoint-ments, it was said that even barbarians – supposedly in hairy breeches – were allowed to sit in the hallowed halls of the Senate. It is more likely that these men were in fact provincial Italians. But for the patrician families, it amounted to the same thing.

With the empire so enlarged, Caesar realised that its govern-ment had to be enlarged as well. He increased the number of

Julius Caesar's spectacular forum and Senate. A reconstruction of the front elevation by Olindo Grossi

Senators, who also served as judges, was increased from 600 to 900. The praetors – judicial officers – doubled in number, from eight to 16. Aediles – magistrates – rose from four to six, and quaestors – treasurers and tax gatherers – from 20 to 40.

Caesar also knew how to make himself popular with the Roman masses. He soon undertook a massive building programme. On the old Forum, the political heart of the empire, he rebuilt the speaker's platform, the courthouse and the Senate building. While the new Senate house was being built, the Senate met in the Theatre of Pompey. As this was located outside the city, Caesar's army could easily control its meetings. Caesar then arranged for a new state library under the auspices of Varro, the commander of Pompey's legions in Corduba. Caesar also conferred the privileges of citizenship on all doctors and teachers of the liberal arts, many of whom were Greek, to ensure that Rome remained a centre of learning.

The great Basilica Julia, alongside the Forum Julium – a huge complex of markets, temples and halls just outside the traditional Forum – was among the many projects under construction. Naturally, a little self-glorification was in order, so Caesar began building a temple to his ancestor Venus, the temple of Venus Genetrix (Mother Venus), in thanks for her assistance at Pharsalus. Caesar instituted all these civic improvements at his own expense.

In the meantime, he was also raising money for a new campaign in Africa, where a number of Republican Senators, including Caesar's arch-enemy Cato, still held out, with the help of Juba (85–46 BC), king of Numidia. The people in this region were mainly Berber, along with Carthaginians who had escaped after the Romans destroyed their city in 146 BC. Juba hated Caesar after being slighted by him when he had travelled to Rome in his youth as an ambassador for his father King Hiempsal (died 118 BC). During the Civil War, Caesar's tribune Gaius Scribonius Curio the Younger had proposed annexing Numidia and brought it into the Empire as a province. Curio occupied Sicily for Caesar, then crossed to Africa in 49 BC. He first confronted the Republican general Publius Attius Varus, beating him at a battle near Utica in modern Tunisia. But Curio was soon defeated and killed by Juba in a battle in the Bagradas Valley.

Around 23 December 47 BC, Caesar resigned the dictatorship once again and set sail with six legions, five of recruits, and 2,000 cavalry. After landing in Sicily, Caesar pitched his tent on the beach to make it clear that they were not staying there long. When a favourable wind blew up, Caesar put to sea with 3,000 men and a small contingent of horsemen. Once he had landed these unobserved, he set sail again to meet the main force while they were still out at sea, ensuring that they landed safely as well.[105]

As usual, Caesar had to fight a propaganda war alongside the military campaign. After the Battle of Pharsalus, Scipio had escaped to Africa along with Cato. The Republican forces drew much comfort from an oracle who said that the Scipio family could never be defeated in Africa – famously, Scipio Africanus the Elder (236-183 BC) had beaten Hannibal at the Battle of Zama in 202 BC, ending the Second Punic War, while Scipio Africanus the Younger (185-129 BC) destroyed Carthage in 146 BC, ending the Third Punic War. So Caesar put a minor member of the Africani family, Scipio Sallustio, at the head of his troops, as though Sallustio were the commander. Plutarch said that he did not know whether Caesar was trying to mock the omen or appropriate it for himself.[106]

The main force of the Republican army, under the command of Scipio and Labienus, was stationed near Utica. Caesar's force was considerably smaller, but he had encouraged his ally Bocchus (reigned 49–33 BC), the king of Mauretania – northern Morocco and western Algeria – and an Italian adventurer named Publius Sittius (died 44 BC) to attack Numidia from west, forcing Juba to divide his substantial army of infantry, cavalry and elephants.

Caesar had other problems, too. His men and horses were short of food and rations. His horsemen were forced to feed their mounts seaweed, which they washed free of salt and sweetened by mixing with grass.[107] Caesar's troops were also harassed by the Numidians, who controlled the country and attacked in great numbers. On one occasion, Caesar's horsemen were caught unawares. Having left their horses with slaves, they were off duty, sitting on the ground watching a Libyan show them 'how he could dance and play the flute at the same time in an astonishing manner', when the enemy suddenly surrounded them. Some men were killed and the Numidians 'followed hard upon the heels of the rest as they were driven headlong into camp'.[108] According to Plutarch, if Caesar himself and Gaius Asinius Pollio (76 BC–AD 5), who had been with Caesar since crossing the Rubicon, had not come from the ramparts to their aid and checked their flight, the war would have been lost then and there.[109]

On another occasion, when the enemy got the advantage in the encounter, Plutarch said that Caesar had to grab a fleeing standard bearer by the neck, turn him around and say: *Look, that's where the enemy are.*[110]

Even so, with Scipio Sallustio at the head of the column, Caesar continued to attack the enemy frequently and to force the pace of the fighting. He began besieging the seaport of Thapsus, some five miles east of present-day Teboulba in Tunisia.

However, Quintus Metellus Scipio was not greatly impressed by his namesake and decided to force a decisive battle. He left Afranius, who had served with Pompey since 76 BC. Juba encamped separately a short distance apart, while Scipio began fortifying a camp beyond a lake just inland from Thapsus. He intended to move the whole army into this camp. From it, they could sally out to the battle – and it would serve as a place of refuge if things went wrong. But while Scipio was busy with this project, Caesar and his men made their way rapidly through wooded area to catch 14 legions and 15,000 cavalry on a corridor of land that formed the northern approaches to the city. They outflanked some of the enemy, and made a frontal assault on the rest. Scipio's men were quickly defeated. Caesar could no longer restrain his men. They drove on to overwhelm the camps of Juba, who was killed, and Afranius, who escaped but was caught by Sittius and executed. Plutarch reported that, in a small part of one day, Caesar made himself master of three camps and slew 50,000 of the enemy, without losing 50 of his own men.[111]

'In all the civil wars he suffered not a single disaster except through his lieutenants, of whom Gaius Curio perished in Africa, Gaius Antonius fell into the hands of the enemy in Illyricum, Publius Dolabella lost a fleet also off Illyricum, and Gnaeus Domitius Calvinus an army in Pontus. Personally he always fought with the utmost success, and the issue was never even in doubt save twice: once at Dyrrhachium, where he was put to flight, and said of Pompey, who failed to follow up his success, that he did not know how to use a victory; again in Spain, in the final struggle, when, believing the battle lost, he actually thought of suicide.'

SUETONIUS[112]

Plutarch was not sure if Caesar was personally responsible for this slaughter. In some accounts of the battle, he said, Caesar was not in the action. 'While he was marshalling and arraying his army, his usual sickness' – epilepsy – 'took hold of him. Aware that it was beginning, before his already wavering senses were altogether confounded and overpowered by the malady, he was carried to a neighbouring tower, where he stayed quietly during the battle.'[113]

Whatever his condition during the fray, after it Caesar showed little mercy.

'Of the men of consular and praetorial rank who escaped from the battle, some slew themselves at the moment of their capture, and others were put to death by Caesar after capture,'[114] said Plutarch.

With his victory at the Battle of Thapsus in 6 April 46 BC,

Caesar had defeated the Pompeians so effectively that Republican opposition in Africa ceased. Eager to take Cato alive, Caesar raced towards Utica. But Cato had committed suicide upon hearing of the defeat. His dream of preserving the Republic was dead, and he wanted to avoid the humiliation of appearing in Caesar's triumph. Caesar was clearly annoyed by this cowardice. He said: *Cato, I begrudge you your death, as you begrudged me the opportunity of giving you your life.*[115]

The other Republican leaders, who fled, were tracked down and killed. However, Pompey's two sons, Sextus and Gnaeus, managed to escape to Spain.

The war in Africa, at least, was over, and Caesar returned to Rome on 25 Quintilis (July) 46 BC where he was appointed dictator again, this time for a 10-year term. The city was in a wretched condition. After three years of conflict, the Optimate oligarchy had been destroyed in the field. Italy had been ravaged by war. Large numbers of men were dead. The survivors had had their property looted and destroyed. They had been heavily taxed to finance the fighting. Uprisings in Rome in 48 and 47 BC had been forcibly suppressed and the victorious soldiers were clamouring for the spoils of war.

Later, Caesar wrote a treatise bitterly condemning Cato. This treatise, Plutarch wrote, did 'not seem to indicate that he was in a gentle or reconcilable mood. After such a pitiless outpouring of anger against the man when he was dead, one can scarcely imagine that he would have spared him when he was alive. And yet from his considerate treatment of Cicero and Brutus and thousands more who had fought against him, it is inferred that even this treatise was not composed out of hatred, but from political ambition, for reasons which follow. Cicero had written an essay praising Cato, which he called 'Cato'. This was widely read as it was composed by the ablest of orators on the noblest of themes. But it annoyed Caesar, who thought that Cicero's praise of the dead Cato was a denunciation of Caesar himself.

PLUTARCH OF CHAERONEA[116]

The work was called 'Anti-Cato.'

Despite these problems, Caesar was determined to redraw the Roman political structure. Now that the war was over, most everyone was calling to restore the institutions of the Republic. Cicero was particularly vociferous. But Caesar insisted that the empire could no longer be controlled by city-state. He had spent more than half his adult life in the provinces and saw the political enfranchisement of the people as a vital to the growth of empire. He reformed the tax system. For decades, Roman taxmen had looted the provinces for their own gain. In Sicily and Asia Minor, Caesar reinstated the earlier system that allowed the provinces themselves to collect their own taxes and pay tribute to Rome without middlemen taking their cut.

Although Caesar consulted the Senate and employed the consularship and the other offices of the old Republic, he used his dictatorial powers to push through reforms. There was little opposition left in the Senate, and many feared that Caesar was becoming an autocrat. In 48 BC, he had consented to petitioners from Asia Minor to be worshipped as a god. Even Cicero, who had been a bitter opponent for 20 years, turned his tongue to sycophancy.

'In this glory, O Gaius Caesar, which you have just earned, you have no partner,' he said in 46 BC in the Senate after Caesar had returned from Africa. 'The whole of this, however great it may be – and surely it is as great as possible – the whole of it, I say, is your own. The centurion can claim for himself no share of that praise, neither can the prefect, nor the battalion, nor the squadron. Not even that very mistress of all human affairs, Fortune herself, can thrust herself into any participation in that glory. She yields to you. She confesses that it is all your own, your peculiar private desert.'[117]

Caesar made his own contribution to this cult. He set about organising an unprecedented four triumphs – one each for Gaul, Egypt, Pontus and Africa – which were celebrated from 20 September to 1 October 46 BC. He had achieved victories on three continents – Europe, Asia and Africa – as well as vanquishing his enemies at home. The Roman people saw Vercingetorix, Cleopatra's sister Arsinoe and Juba's four-year-old son paraded through the streets. It was estimated that the jewels, crowns, gold, silver and other booty on display were worth over 300 million sesterces – nearly $10 million. An astonishing amount of booty was divided between his soldiers; each private soldier received 5,000 denarii – $6,250. Centurions got twice that, and tribunes four times as much. Ever the populist, Caesar was happy to share his booty with the people. Every Roman citizen received 300 sesterces – $100 – ten pounds of oil and ten pecks – 20 gallons – of grain.

Caesar put on the most bloodthirsty games Rome had ever seen. A thousand prisoners of war and criminals fought to the death in pitched battles. Hundreds of lions were killed in the arena and a great naval battle was fought on an artificial lake on the Campus Martius. Festivals took place across the city. Caesar himself hosted a lavish banquet for tens of thousands of Romans. Afterwards, he was escorted home by 20 torch-bearing elephants while the crowd cheered. And he declared a general amnesty for everyone who had sided with Pompey in the Civil War.

But controversy still dogged Caesar. In the summer of 46 BC, after having ruled Egypt successfully for more than a year, Cleopatra and her brother-husband – and her son Caesarion – left Alexandria in the hands of their ministers and travelled

'Before the dinner proper came sea hedgehogs; fresh oysters, as many as the guests wished; large mussels; sphondyli; field fares with asparagus; fattened fowls; oyster and mussel pasties; black and white sea acorns; sphondyli again; glycimarides; sea nettles; becaficoes; roe ribs; boar's ribs; fowls dressed with flour; purple shellfish of two sorts. The dinner itself consisted of sows' udder; boards head; fish-pasties; boar-pasties; ducks; boiled teals; hares; roasted fowls; starch pastry; Pontic pastry.'

Macrobius, on a dinning with Caesar[118]

Nineteenth century view of Cleopatra the seductress, presented to Julius Caesar

to Rome. Cleopatra moved into in Caesar's villa in Trastavere, across the Tiber from Rome, where she remained until Caesar's death. She was the target of Roman xenophobia and misogyny. Romans regarded the Egyptians – particularly the incestuous Ptolemaic dynasty – as degenerate. They had no time for monarchs, particularly oriental potentates. Reigning queens were an anathema, particularly one who claimed divinity. Here was a woman who did not defer to her husband and was reputed to be sexually voracious.

While Caesar continued to live with his wife, Calpurnia, he visited Cleopatra regularly and it was known that Caesarion was his bastard son. Although used the bulk of her time in Rome to develop her diplomatic contacts, Cleopatra's reputation for ruthless ambition had long preceded her. The more conservative factions in Rome viewed her with distaste and suspicion. Cicero, typically, found her appalling, although some suggest he was not entirely impervious to her charms. However, Roman sensibilities were offended even more deeply when Caesar unveiled his magnificent new temple of Venus Genetrix. In it, he had placed a life-size gold statue of Cleopatra. No foreign king or queen had ever been honoured this way in Rome before, let alone such a notorious one.

Back in Rome, Appian wrote, Caesar held four triumphs: 'one for his Gallic wars . . . ; one for the Pontic war against Pharnaces; one for the war in Africa . . . Between the Gallic and the Pontic triumphs he introduced a kind of Egyptian triumph, in which he led some captives taken in the naval engagement on the Nile . . . 60,500 silver talents was borne in the procession and 2,822 crowns of gold weighing 20,414 pounds, from which wealth Caesar paid the army all that he had promised and more. Each soldier received 5,000 Attic drachmas, each centurion double . . . He gave also various spectacles with horses and music . . . There was a combat of elephants, 20 against 20, and a naval engagement of 4,000 oarsmen, where a thousand fighting men contended on each side. He erected the temple to

Venus, his ancestress . . . He placed a beautiful image of Cleopatra by the side of the goddess.'[119]

Caesar then put a programme of social reform into action. Rome had long had a problem with the landless poor. First Caesar thoroughly assessed the problem by taking a census. He then founded dozens of colonies overseas, both military and civilian. Cities that the Romans had destroyed, such as Carthage and Corinth, were to be rebuilt. Landless veterans and some 80,000 of the city's poor were to be settled there. Civil war veterans were given small farms and his own soldiers a silver talent – that is, 21 kilos of the metal, equivalent to 26 years' pay. One third of farm workers on landed estates were to be free men rather than slaves, to stop landless workers from being forced into the overcrowded towns. Eventually the number of people receiving the dole – in the form of free grain – was reduced from 300,000 to 150,000.

Caesar prepared standard regulations for the municipal constitutions and even planned to codify all existing civil laws – a project not completed until AD 438. Jews, who had helped him during the Alexandrine War in Egypt, were to be protected. He also reorganised of the calendar. The old Roman Republican year had been 355 days. Whenever the calendar slipped out of kilter with the seasons, an extra month was added. On the advice of Cleopatra's astrologer, Caesar added four extra months to the year 692 (46 BC). Then from 1 January 691 (45), a calendar of 365 days was to be used, with a leap year every four years. Due to misunderstandings, this new system was not in smooth operation until AD 8.

The Civil War had left the economy in tatters. Interest rates were sky high. Many called for the cancellation of debt – a popular move, but one which would have triggered economic collapse. Instead, Caesar issued an edict obliging creditors to accept in settlement land at pre-war values assessed by independent arbitrators. Whatever interest already had been paid was then deducted. This arrangement wiped out about a quarter of the debt and stimulated the economy without driving either debtors or creditors into bankruptcy.

Some of Caesar's reforms displayed an element of self-interest. He limited the tenure of office for proconsuls and provincial governors – perhaps to stop anyone else from amassing the wealth and power he had achieved in Gaul. He also passed sumptuary laws to try and prevent the sort of lavish display that characterized his triumphs, though these rules were largely ignored. Private guilds were abolished, as they had been recruiting grounds for the mobs that had followed Milo and Clodius. Determined not to be ruled by the mob or by the oligarchs, Caesar allowed only those of the rank of knight and senator to sit on juries.

Although Caesar was firmly in control of Rome, there was one last campaign of the Civil

The Julian calendar was in use until 1582, when Pope Gregory XIII reformed it. The calendar was advanced by ten days, to compensate for the slippage of the equinoxes. After that, centuries, though divisible by four, would no longer be leap years, unless they were divisible by 400. A further refinement making every year divisible by 4,000 a non-leap year will keep the Gregorian calendar accurate to within day for 20,000 years. The Gregorian calendar was adopted by the Italian states, Spain, Portugal and the Catholic states of Germany the following year. Protestant German states adopted it in 1699, England and its colonies in 1752, Sweden in 1753, Japan in 1873, China in 1912, the Soviet Union in 1918 and Greece in 1923. Muslim countries retain the Islamic calendar, which is a lunar calendar, rather than a solar calendar. It has 354 days for 11 years and 355 days for the other 19 years of a 30-year cycle.

War to fight. Gnaeus and Sextus Pompey and Caesar's former legate Titus Labienus had established themselves in Spain, where they had recruited 13 legions, along with some 6,000 cavalry and other auxiliaries.

In November 46 BC Caesar left Rome, arriving in Spain in

later that month or in early December with eight legions, some of whom had been with him since the Gallic Wars, and 8,000 cavalry. His arrival was completely unexpected and the element of surprise gave him an early advantage.

Over the next three months, the two sides did what they could to secure various cities and the loyalty of the Spanish tribes. There were a series of skirmishes that were both bloody and brutal. This campaign was the last hope for the Republicans. Neither side gave any quarter, and captives were executed by both sides.

The two armies finally met on the plains of Munda, near the city of Urso – modern-day Osuna – in southern Spain. The Republican army was camped in a hill, an unfavourable position for Caesar to attack. They remained in sight for a few days until 17 March 45 BC, when Caesar, never one to shrink from battle, gave command to march up the hill and engage the enemy.

Once the battle was joined, it became clear that this would be among the most ferociously fought of Caesar's career. Both commanders were forced to leave their command posts and join in the fray. When Caesar saw his veteran X Legion falter on his right wing, he went to rally them. Here was the man, who only a few months before had the world at his feet, now at risk of dying on some remote Spanish battlefield. His men remembered seeing 'the look of death on his face' as he plunged into battle. *On other occasions I fought for victory*, he said, *but today I fought for my life.*[120]

The Roman historian Velleius Paterculus wrote that the battle was 'the bloodiest and most perilous Caesar had ever fought. It was also to be his last.'[121] But his sudden appearance stemmed the rout. The X Legion began to push the enemy back. Gnaeus Pompey countered by moving a legion from his own right wing to reinforce his left. It was a mistake. Caesar sent his cavalry hard against Pompey's now depleted right.

At the same time, Caesar's ally, King Bogud of Mauretania (died 31 BC) – brother of Bocchus and co-ruler – now attacked

Pompey's camp in the rear. Titus Labienus, commander of the Pompeian cavalry, spotted the threat. He broke off from the main battle and rushed to secure the camp. The Pompeians were now under pressure on the left from Caesar's X Legion and on the right by his cavalry. They thought Labienus and the cavalry were fleeing. They panicked, turned and fled. Up to this point, both sides had about a thousand men in heavy fighting, but as the Pompeian army fled, pursued by Caesar's men around 30,000 were slaughtered in the carnage. Labienus was cut down, but Gnaeus and Sextus Pompey managed to escape.

Caesar caught up with them and the remnants of the army at Corduba. The city surrendered, but was not spared. An estimated 20,000 people were slaughtered. Once again, the brothers managed to escape, this time out to sea. Caesar's naval commander Gaius Didius then hunted down the Pompeian ships. Gnaeus Pompey sought refuge on land, was captured and executed. Sextus survived to become a pirate and harassed the governors Caesar installed in Spain. After the death of Caesar, he was rehabilitated and the Senate appointed him admiral of the fleet. However, in the Second Civil War, he fought with all three triumvirs: Lepidus, Mark Antony and Gaius Octavius, better known as Octavian and, later, Caesar Augustus. Sextus was eventually killed in Asia.

The Ides of March – 45 to 44 BC

Over the next few months, Caesar mopped up in Spain, brutally punishing anyone still loyal to the Republican cause. During this campaign, Caesar was joined by his great-nephew Gaius Octavius (63 BC–AD 14), better known as Octavian, who later became the first Roman emperor under the name Caesar Augustus.

Julius Caesar remained in Spain until June, reorganising the province's administration and planning a number of colonies, such as Seville, there. On his way back to Rome, Caesar travelled through Gaul and northern Italy, arranging for the foundation of more new colonies, including Arles. Arriving back in Rome in October 45 BC, he staged another triumph – to the great dismay of the Roman people, for it represented the first time a Roman celebrated victory over other Romans. By that time, Caesar had already changed his will. Instead of the patrician Mark Antony, he named Octavian as his heir. His great-nephew would inherit the bulk of Casear's estates. On the last page of the will, Caesar adopted as Octavian as his son. With this move, Caesar founded a dynasty and effectively ended the Roman Republic forever.

Caesar continued exercising *clementia* to woo the remaining Optimates. This policy was superficially successful. While complaining of his tyrannical intentions behind his back, the Optimates were sycophantic to his face. Even before his victory at the Battle of Munda, the Senate showered lavish honours on Caesar. The title '*Imperator*' would be adopted as his family name, and the dates of his victories would be national holidays. Already dictator for the next 10 years, Caesar was also granted a 10-year term as consul – alongside Mark Antony – guaranteeing that he would become the tyrant they accused him of being. Coins were minted with Caesar's head on the obverse. He was the first citizen to appear on Roman coins while still alive. They bore the inscription *Venus Victrix* – the 'Venus of Victory' – along with *DICT (ator)*

The triumphant Julius Caesar immortalised in marble

QVART (um) – 'Fourth Dictator' – or, more disturbingly, *DICT (ator) PERPETVO* – 'Perpetual Dictator'. A statue with the inscription 'To the unconquerable god' was to be erected in the temple of Quirinus – the third major god, who ranked alongside Jupiter and Mars. Another was to stand inside the Capitol, the temple of Jupiter on the Capitoline hill, among the statues of the kings and Lucius Junius Brutus. This symbolic gesture was particularly offensive to the Republicans, as Brutus was the legendary founder of the Roman Republic. And the month of Quintilus was to be named July after him. Caesar himself seems to have been indifferent to these honours, although of course, he did not refuse them.[122]

'Some actually ventured to suggest permitting him to have intercourse with as many women as he pleased, because even at this time, though 50 years old, he still had numerous mistresses,' said Cassius Dio.[123]

It was said that Caesar began as a king, without actually using the title. He was allowed to wear a purple robe. Purple was a colour extracted from the secretion of a sea snail. Laborious to harvest, it was reserved for the privileged few in Greek times. It also had royal connections as, after defeating the Persian empire, Alexander the Great had swathed himself in the Emperor Darius's purple and gold robes. Caesar was also allowed to wear the red boots of the Etruscan kings – another unpopular move. He sat on a raised couch in the theatre and on a golden throne in the Senate. And when Senators approached him, to propose deifying him, he received them without rising.[124]

Still, Caesar publicly refused to wear a crown and seemed satisfied with a laurel wreath to cover his bald head. At the feast of the Lupercalia in February 44 BC, Mark Antony offered Caesar a 'diadem' – that is, the crown beloved of eastern monarchs. Caesar refused it, but some historians think he staged the incident to counter the rumours he wanted to be king. As Napoleon, who had himself crowned emperor of France, noted: 'If Caesar wanted to be king, he would have got his army to acclaim him as such.'[125]

However, some thought he was testing the water to see whether it would be acceptable for him to make himself king. When two tribunes removed diadems that had been placed on his statues in the Capitol, they were dismissed from office. One of them was tribune of the *plebs* – the ordinary people in whose name Caesar had started the Civil War.

But the Roman ruling class was Republican, averse to the idea of a monarch that would strip it of its traditional powers. Plainly, Caesar had to be stopped and the only way to do that was to kill him. The man best fitted for the task was Marcus Junius Brutus, as he was one of the family of Lucius Junius Brutus, the man who rid Rome of a king once before. However, it is likely that Brutus was Caesar's son, for Brutus's mother, Servilia, was one of Caesar's many mistresses. During the Civil War, Brutus had backed Pompey, but had been pardoned by Caesar after the Battle of Pharsalus. Brutus was appointed governor of Cisalpine Gaul in 46 BC and the praetor of the city of Rome

'Caesar was seated upon the rostra on a golden throne, arrayed in triumphal attire. And Antony was one of the runners in the sacred race; for he was consul. Accordingly, after he had dashed into the forum and the crowd had made way for him, he carried a diadem, round which a wreath of laurel was tied, and held it out to Caesar . . . [W]hen Caesar pushed away the diadem, all the people applauded. When Antony offered him the diadem for a second time . . . and when Caesar declined it again, there was applause from everyone . . . It was then discovered that Caesar's statues had been decorated with royal diadems. So two of the tribunes, Flavius and Marullus, went up and pulled off the diadems . . . This made Caesar angry. He deprived Marullus and Flavius of their office and while denouncing them, he insulted the people at the same time.'

PLUTARCH OF CHAERONEA[126]

in 44 BC. This annoyed Gaius Cassius Longinus who, though his senior, was appointed to the junior post of foreign praetor the same year.

After serving under Crassus in his ill-fated campaign against the Parthians, Cassius had escaped after the Battle of Carrhae and returned to Rome. He organised the defence of Syria, but would have been tried for extortion there if the Civil War had not broken out. He was given command of part of Pompey's fleet. Like Brutus and many of the other conspirators, he had been pardoned by Caesar and appointed praetor.

According to Plutarch, it was Cassius who urged Brutus on.[127] They gathered some 60 conspirators around them, most of whom had been pardoned by Caesar or raised to high office by him. These included Decimus Junius Brutus, who had commanded Caesar's fleet. Another key figure in the conspiracy was Cato's daughter Porcia, who had married Marcus Brutus in 45 BC and convinced him that she would not reveal his secret even under torture.[128] Cicero was excluded because he was considered too timid and could not be trusted to keep the secret.

Cassius convinced Brutus that, at a meeting of the Senate on the Kalends – first day – of March, Caesar intended to have himself proclaimed king in those parts of the Empire outside Italy. That way, the Senators would be forced either to vote for Caesar's kingship or to reveal that they opposed him. Brutus

'Some of them had hopes of becoming leaders themselves in his place if he were put out of the way; others were angered over what had happened to them in the war, embittered over the loss of their relatives, property or offices of state. They concealed the fact that they were angry, and made the pretence of something more seemly, saying that they were displeased at the rule of a single man and that they were striving for a Republican form of government. Different people had different reasons, all brought together by whatever pretext they happened upon.'

NICOLAUS OF DAMASCUS[129]

then claimed he would be forced to 'defend my country and to die for its liberty'.[130] With Brutus committed, the conspirators began planning the assassination of Caesar in earnest.

Caesar himself, frustrated by the politics of Rome, began plotting a new campaign against Parthia. Crassus had yet to be avenged. The Romans also believed that they were the heirs to Alexander the Great and should, at the very least, rule the Hellenistic countries as far east as the Euphrates River. A meeting of the Senate was announced for the Ides – that is, the 15th day – of March in which dispositions for the Parthian campaign. Again, it was thought that the issue of Caesar's kingship would be discussed on the grounds of the prophecy that only a king could defeat the Parthians.[131] Caesar planned to leave Rome on 18 March for Parthia to join his legions in the east, picking up his young relative Octavian, who was completing his schooling and military training in Apollonia. The conspirators decided to kill Caesar at the meeting of the Senate because a large number of them could gather there without inviting suspicion. They also thought it propitious as, with the new Senate house under construction, the Senate was meeting in the Theatre of Pompey, where a statue of the famous general had been erected. It was as if 'some heavenly power was conducting Caesar to Pompey's vengeance'.[132]

Caesar was aware that he was in danger. On the night of 14 March, he was dining at Lepidus's house, when the topic of death came up in conversation. The question 'which death is the best?' came up. Before anyone else had a chance to answer, Caesar said: *An unexpected one.*[133]

Death was often on Caesar's mind. According to Suetonius, in the year before his murder, Caesar said: *It is more important for Rome than for myself that I should survive. I have long been sated with power and glory; but, if anything happened to me, Rome will have no peace. A new Civil War would break out which would be far worse than the last.*[134] It seems that Caesar knew of the conspiracies against him and was preparing to die. According to Cicero, Caesar was reconciled to his fate, saying: *I have lived long enough both in years and in accomplishment.*[135]

There are reasons to believe that Caesar contrived at his own murder. Some time earlier, he had been warned by a seer named Spurinna to 'beware the Ides of March'. His old friend Cornelius Balbus conveyed other portents to him.[136] Caesar was also the most powerful and well-informed man in Rome. It is hard to imagine that he did not suspect a conspiracy against him. His own wife, Calpurnia, feared that he would be killed if he attended the Senate that day. Calming her fears delayed him, but Caesar was finally persuaded to attend by his old comrade-in-arms Decimus Brutus, who gently mocked Calpurnia's concerns – though he was one of the conspirators.[137] Despite all these warnings, Caesar eventually left home without a bodyguard.[138]

That morning, the conspirators had met at the house of Cassius.[140] As praetor, Brutus had to meet clients throughout the morning and judge petitions. Afterwards, he went down the Pompey's Theatre with his adolescent son. Brutus knew there would be some disorder

'Now Caesar's approaching murder was foretold to him by unmistakable signs. A few months before, . . . there was discovered in a tomb, which was said to be that of Capys, the founder of Capua, a bronze tablet, inscribed with Greek words and characters to this purport: 'Whenever the bones of Capys shall be moved, it will come to pass that a son of Ilium shall be slain at the hands of his kindred . . .' [W]hen he was offering sacrifice, the soothsayer Spurinna warned [Caesar] to beware of danger, which would come not later than the Ides of March . . . In fact the very night before his murder he dreamt now that he was flying above the clouds, and . . . clasping the hand of Jupiter; and his wife Calpurnia thought that the pediment of their house fell, and that her husband was stabbed in her arms; and suddenly the door of the room flew open of its own accord.'

SUETONIUS[139]

Pompey's Theatre, the site of Caesar's assassination

after the assassination, so he stationed a party of gladiators near the theatre for crowd control.

Caesar was late and, by all accounts, the conspirators grew jittery. Some, fearing their plans had been discovered, wanted to flee. Brutus, however, remained outwardly calm. Even when word was brought to Brutus that Porcia, in an agony of suspense, had collapsed and appeared to be dead, he was not shaken from his purpose. He remained there waiting for Caesar, who turned up five hours late.

On the steps of Pompey's Theatre, Caesar was met by crowd of people. Artemidoris, a teacher of Greek philosophy from Cnidus in modern Anatolia, thrust a note into his hand warning him of the plot.[141] Spurinna, whom he derided at a false prophet, also met Caesar there.

The Ides of March have come, said Caesar.

'Aye, they have come,' replied Spurinna, 'but they have not yet gone.'[142]

As planned, Trebonius took Mark Antony aside for a chat outside the Senate to keep him out of the way.[143] When Caesar took his seat inside, the other conspirators crowded around him.

Tullius Cimber pretended to submit a petition on behalf of his exiled brother. Suddenly, Cimber grabbed Caesar's purple robe and wrenched it away from his neck.[144]

This is violence, said Caesar[145] – violence of any sort was not allowed in the Senate.

It was the signal for attack. Immediately, Publicius Servilius Casca struck the first blow, just below the throat. But the wound was not deep or life-threatening.

Accursed Casca, what have you done? cried Caesar in Latin,[146] stabbing Casca in the arm with the only weapon he had to hand – the stylus he used for writing on wax tablets.

Casca turned to his brother and said, in Greek: 'Brother, help.'[147]

Caesar tried to get to his feet, but he was stopped by a second blow. The other conspirators surrounding him drew their daggers. Seeing a knife glint in Brutus's hand, Caesar said – not *Et tu, Brute?* (*And you, Brutus?*) in Latin, as Shakespeare would have us believe[148] – but *Kai su, Technon?* (*You too, my child?*) in Greek.[149]

'When he saw that he was beset on every side by drawn daggers, he muffled his head in his robe, and at the same time drew down its lap to his feet with his left hand, in order to fall more decently, with the lower part of his body also covered,' said Suetonius.[150]

Such a flurry of blows followed – directed particularly at his face, eyes and groin – that 'many of the conspirators were wounded by one another, as they struggled to plant all those blows in one body'.[151]

Apart from a groan on the first blow, Caesar said nothing more. Those not part of the plot were too horror-struck to cry out, run away or come to his aid.[152] Caesar was driven 'hither and thither like a wild beast'.[153] Unable to defend himself, he pulled his toga down over his head and sank down, either by chance or because pushed there by his murderers, against the pedestal of Pompey's statue. 'And the pedestal was drenched with his blood, so that one might have thought that Pompey himself was presid-

The murder of Caesar. Wilhelm von Piloty's rendering of the scene in 1889

ing over this vengeance upon his enemy, who now lay prostrate at his feet, quivering from a multitude of wounds,' said Plutarch.[154]

With Caesar dead, Brutus stepped forward as if to say something. But the spell was now broken. The doors of the theatre burst open and the conspirators fled. Mark Antony and Lepidus, Caesar's closest friends, went into hiding, while Brutus and his followers marched up to the Capitol, displaying their knives openly.[155]

For hours, nobody dared approach, until three common slaves put his corpse on a litter and carried him home, 'with one arm hanging down'. A physician named Antistius was then called to conduct what must have been one of the world's first autopsies. He found that Caesar's body had 23 stab wounds. But, in his opinion, none were mortal – 'except the second one in the breast'.[156]

With Caesar now dead, his co-consul Mark Antony became the official head of the state. Mark Antony still assumed that he was Caesar's heir and took possession of his papers and coffers. He seconded Lepidus, the commander of Caesar's troops outside Rome. Having the men and the money, he dictated terms to the

A contemporary forensic study undertaken by Colonel Luciano Garofano, commander of the Italian carabinieri's forensic information centre in Parma, reopened the case of Julius Caesar's murder. He doubted that a shrewd politician like Caesar would walk into such a trap without attempting to protect himself. With the help of a forensic psychiatrist from Harvard, Garofano concluded that Caesar colluded in his own murder. Caesar, 56, was suffering from temporal-lobe epilepsy and blacked out under stress. This affliction made him rash in his actions and caused him to lose control of his bladder and bowels. This embarrassment allegedly stopped Caesar from standing when Senators offered to make him a god. A vain man, he decided to commit suicide in such a way to cement his political gains. By killing him in the Senate, the conspirators had broken Roman law – the very thing they had accused Caesar of doing. They were forced to flee and, within two years, both Brutus and Cassius were dead. By picking Octavian to succeed him, Caesar continued his bloodline and ended the power of the patricians and the Republic forever.[157]

conspirators. They would be given amnesty, provided that Caesar's reforms remained in place and that he was made a god. This ensured that the name of Julius Caesar – like that of Alexander the Great – would be known to this day.

Later that day, Caesar father-in-law Piso opened the will. In it, Caesar had left his gardens to the city of Rome as a public park, and every Roman family were given enough money to embark on a party that would last three months. Several days later, Caesar's funeral was held in the Forum. When the Roman mob saw Caesar's blood-stained cloak and heard of the money that was to be distributed among them, they burst into a frenzy of posthumous adulation. Then, Mark Antony delivered the funeral oration, in which he further inflamed their emotions.

'. . . this father, this high priest, this inviolable being, this hero and god, is dead, alas, dead not by the violence of some disease, nor wasted by old age, nor wounded abroad somewhere in some war, nor caught up inexplicably by some supernatural force, but right here within the walls as the result of a plot – the man who had safely led an army into Britain; ambushed in this city – the man who had enlarged the sacred space beyond its city walls; murdered in the senate-house – the man who had reared another such edifice at his own expense; unarmed – the brave warrior; defenceless – the promoter of peace; the judge – beside the court of justice; the magistrate – beside the seat of government; at the hands of the citizens – he whom none of the enemy had been able to kill even

Mark Anthony delivers Caesar's funeral oration

when he fell into the sea; at the hands of his comrades – he who had often taken pity on them. Of what avail, O Caesar, was your humanity, of what avail your inviolability, of what avail the laws? Nay, though you enacted many laws that men might not be killed by their personal foes, yet how mercilessly you yourself were slain by your friends! And now, the victim of assassination, you lie dead in the Forum through which you often led the triumph crowned; wounded to death, you have been cast down upon the rostra from which you often addressed the people. Woe for the blood-bespattered locks of grey, alas for the rent robe, which you assumed, it seems, only that you might be slain in it!'[158]

When the torch was thrown into the funeral pyre, people tossed chairs and benches into the flames. Actors and musicians stripped off their clothes and flung them into the fire, 'and the veterans of the legions, the arms with which they had adorned themselves for the funeral; many of the women too, offered up the jewels which they wore and the amulets and robes of their children'.[159] Soldiers had to restore order. Even so, the mob attacked the houses of Brutus and Cassius with firebrands. They were repulsed with some difficulty, but the tribune Gaius Helvius Cinna was murdered and his head paraded on a pole. Gaius Helvius Cinna had been a friend of Caesar's, but the mob had mistaken him for Lucius Cornelius Cinna, who was rescued by Lepidus. In the confusion, Cleopatra and her son Caesarion fled the city and returned to Alexandria. Later, a 20-foot statue to Caesar was erected with the inscription 'To the Father of his Country' on the plinth. Sacrifices were made there and disputes were settle by oaths made in the name of Caesar.[160]

'At the time of his death,' Plutarch wrote, 'Caesar was fully 56 years old, but he had survived Pompey not much more than four years, while of the power and dominion which he had sought all his life at so great risks, and barely achieved at last, of this he had reaped no fruit but the name of it only, and a glory which had awakened envy on the part of his fellow citizens. However, the great guardian-genius of the man, whose help he had enjoyed through life, followed upon him even after death as an avenger of his murder, driving and tracking down his slayers over every land and sea until not one of them was left . . . [And] during all that year [the sun's] orb rose pale and without radiance, while the heat that came down from it was slight and ineffectual . . . and the fruits, imperfect and half ripe, withered away and shrivelled up on account of the coldness of the atmosphere. But more than anything else the phantom that appeared to Brutus showed that the murder of Caesar was not pleasing to the gods.'[161]

Although Mark Antony was in charge in Rome, he had a clear rival in Octavian, who arrived from the east with his friend Marcus Vipanius Agrippa (c63–12 BC) and adopted the name Gaius Julius Caesar Octavianus – that is, Caesar from the Octavius family. He was supported by Caesar's veterans, although he could not pay them. Octavian then courted the people's support by raising money to pay Caesar's debts and stage a games.

Decimus Brutus had become governor of Cisalpine Gaul, and Mark Antony marched out of Rome to confront him. While Mark Antony and Decimus Brutus were fighting at Mutina – around modern-day Modena – the Senate convened and Cicero made a speech, in which he warned that Mark Antony would return with an army as Caesar had done. This was the moment, he said, to restore the Republic, and the Senators agreed that the 19-year-old Octavian might be used for the purpose. They gave him a military command. He marched north and defeated Mark Antony, who fled with difficulty across the Alps, where he managed to gain the support of all troops in Spain and Gaul. Octavian marched back to Rome, where he demanded that the Senate confer the vacant consulship on him.

Octavian then declared Mark Antony's amnesty to be illegal and outlawed the murderers of his adopted father. Realising that it was impossible to defeat the man who controlled Spain and Gaul, Octavian reluctantly made peace with Mark Antony. Together, they could destroy the Republic, if they managed to defeat Caesar's murderers, who now rallied their troops on the other side of the Adriatic. In 42 BC Mark Antony and Octavian defeated Brutus and Cassius at Philippi in Macedonia. The conspirators committed suicide – Cassius, Plutarch said, killed himself with the same dagger he had used to stab Caesar.[162]

Mark Antony, Octavian and Lepidus then formed the Second Triumvirate, with Mark Antony taking the east, Lepidus North Africa and Octavian the rest. Unlike the first triumvirate, which was a private contract, this one was official, with the three men given dictatorial powers for five years. Cicero was against the bill enacting this, but was despatched by a murderer. With the passing of the bill, the Roman Republic formally came to an end.

Although Mark Antony was seen as the senior triumvir, Octavian was Caesar's son – which meant he was now, in a sense, the son of a god. Lepidus tried to improve his standing by siding with Sextus Pompeius, who was then defeated by Agrippa. Together Mark Antony and Octavian demoted Lepidus, taking his territory, although leaving him as high priest or *pontifex maximus*.

The empire was then divided between Octavian, who took the west, and Mark Antony, who took the east. To seal the deal, Mark Antony was to marry Octavian's sister Octavia. But Mark Antony had already fallen in love with Cleopatra, who was still unpopular in Rome. It was all too easy to paint her as a manipulative harlot who had tried to take over Rome through Caesar and, when that had failed, through Mark Antony. Octavian declared war on Egypt. In 31 BC Octavian had defeated Mark Antony and Cleopatra at the Battle of Actium, a naval engagement off the Greek coast. The two lovers fled back to Egypt, where Mark

Antony fell on his sword, mortally wounding himself. Cleopatra reputedly committed suicide with the bite of an asp. The latest theory is that Octavian, who wanted her out of the way, murdered her. Her son Caesarion – now Ptolemy XV Caesar – was executed and Octavian used her treasury to pay off his soldiers.

Back in Rome, he established a Praetorian guard to maintain his absolute control and added *Augustus* – 'exalted one' – to his name to become Caesar Augustus. Like Caesar, he had a month named after him. In 27 BC he formally laid down his triumviral powers, saying that he was content with the honour of restoring the Republic. Conscious that the idea of monarchy was still unpopular in Rome, he continued to rule by a succession of consulships, conferred on him by a cowed Senate. He took the power of a tribune – an office formally elected annually – for life and amassed the powers of a number of magistratures without occupying the offices themselves. That way, he managed to run the government behind a Republican facade, backed by a strong army. And when Lepidus died in 13 BC, he took over as *pontifex maximus*.

Caesar Augustus used his unchallenged power to implement many of Julius Caesar's plans. One of these – the granting of Roman citizenship to people who did not live in Italy – turned the Roman Republic into a Mediterranean empire, which bought relative peace and prosperity to some 60 million

Under the rule of Augustus Caesar and his heir Tiberius the Roman Empire reached its high water mark

people. The ascendancy of the Roman empire was secured for the next 500 years in the West and 1,500 years in the East. It transmitted the knowledge and culture of ancient Greece to the modern world and allowed Christianity to spread across the Western world.

When Augustus died in AD 14, he was succeeded by his stepson Tiberius, who, in turn, was succeeded by his adopted son Caligula. When Caligula was murdered in AD 41, his uncle Claudius succeeded him. Although he had no right to the name Caesar, Claudius ruled as Tiberius Claudius Caesar Augustus Germanicus. Thus began the processes that turned 'Caesar' into a title, rather than a family name. Nearly 2,000 years later, monarchs were still being crowned as Kaiser and Czar in Caesar's honour. If Julius Caesar did indeed contrive his own assassination to advance his political vision and to make his name famous for all time, he certainly succeeded.

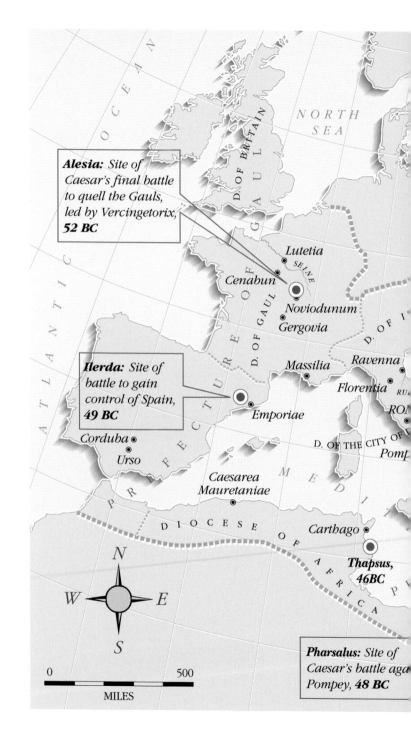

Alesia: Site of Caesar's final battle to quell the Gauls, led by Vercingetorix, **52 BC**

Lutetia

Cenabun

SEINE

Noviodunum

Gergovia

D. OF BRITAIN

D. OF GAUL

NORTH SEA

OCEAN

ATLANTIC

D. OF GAUL

PREFECTURE OF GAUL

D. OF I

Ravenna

Massilia

Florentia

RU

RO

Emporiae

Ilerda: Site of battle to gain control of Spain, **49 BC**

Corduba

Urso

D. OF THE CITY OF

Pomp

Caesarea Mauretaniae

MED

DIOCESE OF AFRICA

Carthago

Thapsus, 46BC

Pharsalus: Site of Caesar's battle aga Pompey, **48 BC**

N
W — E
S

0   500
MILES

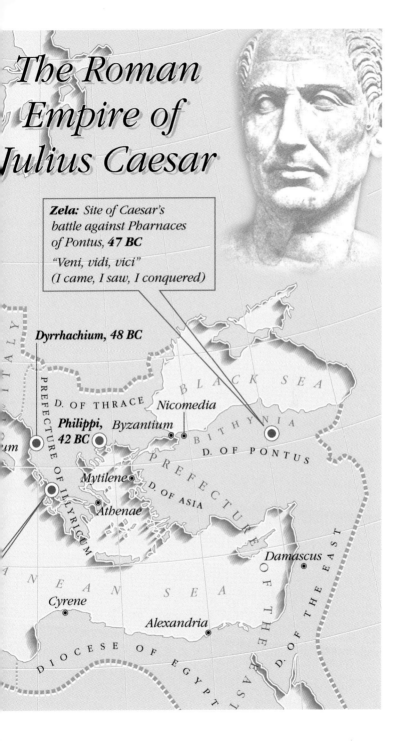

The Roman Empire of Julius Caesar

Zela: Site of Caesar's battle against Pharnaces of Pontus, **47 BC**

"Veni, vidi, vici"
(I came, I saw, I conquered)

Dyrrhachium, 48 BC

ITALY

PREFECTURE

D. OF THRACE

Nicomedia

BLACK SEA

BITHYNIA

Philippi, 42 BC Byzantium

um

D. OF PONTUS

PREFECTURE OF ILLYRICUM

Mytilene

PREFECTURE

D. OF ASIA

Athenae

Damascus

ANEAN SEA

Cyrene

D. OF THE EAST

Alexandria

DIOCESE OF EGYPT

Testimonials

The Road to Power

'Caesar is said to have been tall, fair, and well-built, with a rather broad face and keen, dark-brown eyes. His health was sound, apart from sudden comas and a tendency to nightmares which troubled him during the end of his life; but he twice had epileptic fits while on campaign. He was something of a dandy, always keeping his head carefully trimmed and shaved; and has been accused of having certain other hairy parts of his body depilated with tweezers. His baldness was a disfigurement which his enemies harped upon, much to his exasperation; but he used to comb the thin strands of hair forward from his poll, and of all the honours voted him by the Senate and people, none pleased him so much as the privilege of wearing a laurel wreath on all occasions – he constantly took advantage of it. They say, too, that he was remarkable in his dress; that he wore a senator's tunic with fringed sleeves reaching to the wrist, and always had a girdle over it, though rather a loose one . . . Contemporary literature contains frequent references to his fondness for luxurious living. Having laid the foundations of a country-house on his estate at Nemi and finished it at great cost, he tore it all down because it did not suit him in every particular, although at the time he was still poor and heavily in debt; and that he carried tesselated and mosaic floors about with him on his campaigns. Fresh-water pearls seem to have been the lure that prompted his invasion of Britain; he would sometimes weigh them in the palm of his hand to judge their value, and was also a keen collector of gems, carvings, statues and pictures by early artists; also of slaves of exceptional figure and training at enormous prices, of which he himself was so ashamed that he forbade his entry in his accounts. When he was outside Italy, he would normally use two dining-rooms for his dinner-parties, one for his officers and Greeks. In the other Roman civilians and the more distinguished of the provincials reclined at table. He was so scrupulous and indeed severe in the administration of his household, in matters both small and great, that he had a baker's legs shackled for serving different bread to himself than to his guests; and he executed a freedman whom he liked very much for having committed adultery with the wife of an equestrian, even though there had been no formal complaint.'

Suetonius[163]

Even Caesar's friend, the poet Gaius Valerius Catullus (c54–c84 BC) said that he was a passive pederast and compared him to the notorious pathic – the 'girl' in a gay relationship – Mamurra, Caesar's chief engineer in Gaul.

Well agreed are the abominable sodomites,
the fellators, Mamurra and Caesar.
No wonder, they share the same stain,
one from the city and one from Formiae,
are deeply impressed on each, and will never be washed out.
Diseased alike, very twins,
both on one sofa, dilettante writers both,
one as greedy for lechery as the other,
allied in the rivalry of the girls.
Well agreed are the abominable sodomites.

'On Mamurra and Julius Caesar', *Catullus*[164]

He had love affairs with queens, too, including Eunoe the Moor, wife of Bogudes, on whom, as well as on her husband, he bestowed many splendid presents, as Naso writes; but above all

triumph must remain outside the city, while those who were candidates for the consulship must be present in the city, Caesar was in
a great dilemma, and because he had reached home at the very time
for the consular elections, he sent a request to the senate that he
might be permitted to offer himself for the consulship *in absentia*,
through the agency of his friends. But since Cato began by insist-
ing upon the law in opposition to Caesar's request, and then, when
he saw that many senators had been won over by Caesar's attentions,
staved the matter off by consuming the day in speaking, Caesar
decided to give up the triumph and try for the consulship.'

Plutarch of Chaeronea[167]

The Conquest of Gaul

'Such spirit and ambition Caesar himself created and cultivated in
his men, in the first place, because he showed, by his unsparing
bestowal of rewards and honours, that he was not amassing
wealth from his wars for his own luxury or for any life of ease, but
that he built it up carefully as a common prize for deeds of
valour, and had no greater share in the wealth than he offered to
the deserving among his soldiers; and in the second place, by will-
ingly undergoing every danger and refusing no toil. Now, at his
love of danger his men were not astonished, knowing his ambition; but that he should undergo toils beyond his body's apparent
powers of endurance amazed them, because he was of a spare
habit, had a soft and white skin, suffered from distemper in the
head, and was subject to epileptic fits, a trouble which first
attacked him, we are told, in Corduba. Nevertheless, he did not
make his feeble health an excuse for soft living, but rather his
military service a cure for his feeble health, since by wearisome
journeys, simple diet, continuously sleeping in the open air, and
enduring hardships, he fought off his trouble and kept his body
strong against its attacks. Most of his sleep, at least, he got in cars
or litters, making his rest conduce to action, and in the day-time

he would have himself conveyed to garrisons, cities, or camps, one
slave who was accustomed to write from dictation as he travelled
sitting by his side, and one soldier standing behind him with
a sword. And he drove so rapidly that, on his first journey
from Rome to Gaul, he reached the Rhône in seven days.
Horsemanship, moreover, had been easy for him from boyhood; for
he was wont to put his hands behind his back and, holding them
closely there, to ride his horse at full speed. And in the Gallic campaigns he practised dictating letters on horseback and keeping two
scribes at once busy, or, as Oppius [his financial adviser and
amanuensis] says, even more. We are told, moreover, that Caesar
was the first to devise intercourse with his friends by letter, since
he could not wait for personal interviews on urgent matters owing
to the multitude of his occupations and the great size of the city.'

Plutarch of Chaeronea[168]

The Pacification of Gaul

'This war was begun by the Eburones, under Ambiorix as chief.
They claimed they had been roused to action because they were
annoyed at the presence of the Romans, who were commanded by
Sabinus and Lucius Cotta, lieutenants. The truth was, however,
that they scorned those officers, thinking that they would not
prove competent to defend their men and not expecting that
Caesar would quickly make an expedition against their tribe.
They accordingly came upon the soldiers unawares, expecting to
take the camp without striking a blow, and, when they failed of
this, had recourse to deceit. For Ambiorix, after planting ambus-
cades in the most suitable spots, came to the Romans after sending a herald to arrange for a parley, and represented that he had
taken part in the war against his will and was himself sorry; but
against the others he advised them to be on their guard, for his
countrymen would not obey him and were intending to attack the
garrison at night. Consequently he made the suggestion to them

that they should abandon Eburonia, since they would be in danger if they remained, and should move on as quickly as possible to some of their comrades who were wintering near by. Upon hearing this, the Romans believed him, especially as Ambiorix had received many favours from Caesar and seemed to be repaying his kindness in this way. They hastily packed up their belongings, and setting out just after nightfall, fell into the ambush, where they suffered a terrible reverse. Cotta with many others perished immediately. Sabinus was sent for by Ambiorix under the pretext of saving him, for the Gallic leader was not present at the ambush and at that time was still thought to be trustworthy; on his arrival, however, Ambiorix seized him, stripped him of his arms and clothing, and then struck him down with his javelin, uttering boastful words over him, such as these: 'How can such creatures as you wish to rule us who are so great?' This was the fate that these men suffered. The rest managed to break through to the camp from which they had set out, but when the barbarians assailed that, too, and they could neither repel them nor escape, they killed one another.'

Cassius Dio[169]

Crossing the Rubicon

'Now, Caesar had with him not more than 300 horsemen and 5,000 legionaries; for the rest of his army had been left beyond the Alps, and was to be brought up by those whom he had sent for the purpose. He saw, however, that the beginning of his enterprise and its initial step did not require a large force at present, but must take advantage of the golden moment by showing amazing boldness and speed, since he could strike terror into his enemies by an unexpected blow more easily than he could overwhelm them by an attack in full force. He therefore ordered his centurions and other officers, taking their swords only, and without the rest of their arms, to occupy Ariminum, a large city of Gaul, avoiding commotion and bloodshed as far as possible; and he entrusted this force to Hortensius. He himself spent the day in public, attending and watching the exercises of gladiators; but a little before evening he bathed and dressed and went into the banqueting hall. Here he held brief converse with those who had been invited to supper, and just as it was getting dark and went away, after addressing courteously most of his guests and bidding them await his return. To a few of his friends, however, he had previously given directions to follow him, not all by the same route, but some by one way and some by another. He himself mounted one of his hired carts and drove at first along another road, then turned towards Ariminum. When he came to the river which separates Cisalpine Gaul from the rest of Italy (it is called the Rubicon), and began to reflect, now that he drew nearer to the fearful step and was agitated by the magnitude of his ventures, he checked his speed. Then, halting in his course, he communed with himself a long time in silence as his resolution wavered back and forth, and his purpose then suffered change after change. For a long time, too, he discussed his perplexities with his friends who were present, among whom was Asinius Pollio, estimating the great evils for all mankind which would follow their passage of the river, and the wide fame of it which they would leave to posterity. But finally, with a sort of passion, as if abandoning calculation and casting himself upon the future, and uttering the phrase with which men usually prelude their plunge into desperate and daring fortunes – *Let the die be cast* – he hastened to cross the river; and going at full speed now for the rest of the time, before daybreak he dashed into Ariminum and took possession of it. It is said, moreover, that on the night before he crossed the river he had an unnatural dream; he thought, namely, that he was having incestuous intercourse with his own mother.'

Plutarch of Chaeronea[170]

Notes

1 Tactius, *Dialogue 28*, quoted in 'Women's Life in Greece and Rome', Lefkowitz, Fant, 191
2 Appian, *The Civil War*, 1.2-3
3 Plutarch, *The Life of Julius Caesar*, 1.4
4 Suetonius, *Julius Caesar*, 4
5 Suetonius, *Julius Caesar*, 52
6 Suetonius, *Julius Caesar*, 7
7 Suetonius, *Julius Caesar*, 10
8 Plutarch, *The Life of Julius Caesar*, 10.9
9 Plutarch, *The Life of Julius Caesar*, 13.2-6
10 Plutarch, *The Life of Crassus*, 8.2
11 Caesar, *The Gallic Wars*, 6.13-14
12 Caesar, *The Gallic Wars*, 1.54
13 Herm, G.: *Die Kelten*, Weltbild, Augsburg, 1991.
14 Caesar, *The Gallic Wars*, 2.28
15 Caesar, *The Gallic Wars*, 2.19
16 Caesar, *The Gallic Wars*, 2.25
17 Caesar, *The Gallic Wars*, 2.33
18 Caesar, *The Gallic Wars*, 4.21
19 Plutarch, *The Life of Julius Caesar*, 23.2-4
20 Caesar, *The Gallic Wars*, 4.23
21 Caesar, *The Gallic Wars*, 4.23
22 Caesar, *The Gallic Wars*, 4.25
23 Caesar, *The Gallic Wars*, 4.26
24 Caesar, *The Gallic Wars*, 4.27
25 Caesar, *The Gallic Wars*, 4.30
26 Caesar, *The Gallic Wars*, 4.32
27 Caesar, *The Gallic Wars*, 4.33
28 Caesar, *The Gallic Wars*, 4.35
29 Caesar, *The Gallic Wars*, 4.36
30 Cassius Dio, *Roman History*, 39.53
31 Plutarch, *Life of Caesar*, 23.2-3
32 Circero, *Letters*, XVI to Trebalius Testa in Gaul
33 Caesar, *The Gallic Wars*, 5.1
34 Caesar, *The Gallic Wars*, 5.3-4
35 Caesar, *The Gallic Wars*, 5.9
36 Caesar, *The Gallic Wars*, 5.9
37 Caesar, *The Gallic Wars*, 5.12
38 Caesar, *The Gallic Wars*, 5.13
39 Caesar, *The Gallic Wars*, 5.13
40 Caesar, *The Gallic Wars*, 5.14
41 Caesar, *The Gallic Wars*, 5.18
42 Cassius Dio, *Roman history* 40.5-10
43 Caesar, *The Gallic Wars*, 5.53
44 Caesar, *The Gallic Wars*, 6.35-37
45 Fuller, J.F.C., *A Military History of the Western World*, p145
46 Caesar, *The Gallic Wars*, 7.15
47 Plutarch, *The Life of Julius Caesar*, 27.1-4
48 Caesar, *The Gallic Wars*, 7.71
49 Caesar, *The Gallic Wars*, 7.80
50 Caesar, *The Gallic Wars*, 7.83
51 Plutarch, *The Life of Julius Caesar*, 27.8-10
52 Fuller, J.F.C., *A Military History of the Western World*, p157
53 Plutarch, *The Life of Julius Caesar*, 15.1-5
54 Plutarch, *The Life of Julius Caesar*, 15.5
55 Suetonius, *The Life of Julius Caesar*, 32
56 Suetonius, *The Life of Julius Caesar*, 31
57 Caesar, *The Civil War*, 1.7
58 Cicero, *Selected Letters*, 64
59 Cicero, *Letters to Atticus*, 27 February 49

60 Cicero, quoting Caesar, *Selected Letters*, 68

61 Cicero, *Letters to Atticus*, 67

62 Cicero, *Selected Letters*, 70

63 Cicero, *Letters to Atticus*, 71

64 Suetonius, *The Life of Julius Caesar*, 34

65 Caesar, *The Civil War*, 1.45-46

66 Caesar, *The Civil War*, 3.19

67 Caesar, *The Civil War*, 3.26

68 Appian, *The Civil War*, 2.61

69 Caesar, *The Civil War*, 3.48-49

70 Caesar, *The Civil War*, 3.53

71 Appian, *The Civil War*, 2.60; Cassius Dio, *Roman Histories*, 41.50

72 Plutarch, *The Life of Caesar*, 16.1-9

73 Appian, *The Civil War*, 2.62

74 Plutarch, *The Life of Pompey*, 65-67

75 Appian, *The Civil War*, 2.67

76 Appian, *The Civil War*, 2.76

77 Appian, *The Civil War*, 2.76

78 Appian, *The Civil War*, 2.69

79 Appian, *The Civil War*, 2.80

80 Appian, *The Civil War*, 2.81

81 Caesar, *The Civil War*, 3.96

82 Appian, *The Civil War*, 2.82

83 Suetonius, *The Life of Julius Caesar*, 30.4

84 Lucan, *The Pharsalia*, 7.144-5

85 Velleius Paterculus, *Narratives*, 2.52

86 Appian, *The Civil War*, 2.83

87 Plutarch, *The Life of Pompey*, 77.4

88 Caesar, *The Civil War*, 3.104

89 Plutarch, *The Life of Pompey*, 79.4

90 Plutarch, *The Life of Pompey*, 80.1-3

91 Plutarch, *The Life of Caesar*, 48.4

92 Plutarch, *The Life of Julius Caesar*, 48.5-9

93 Plutarch, *The Life of Caesar*, 49.1-3

94 Plutarch, *The Life of Anthony*, 27.2

95 Plutarch, *The Life of Anthony*, 27.3

96 Plutarch, *The Life of Anthony*, 27.4

97 Plutarch, *The Life of Caesar*, 49.6-8

98 Plutarch, *The Life of Caesar*, 49.10

99 Caesar, *The Alexandrian War*, 69

100 Caesar, *The Alexandrian War*, 70

101 Caesar, *The Alexandrian War*, 75-76

102 Suetonius, *The Life of Caesar*, 35

103 Suetonius, *The Life of Caesar*, 37

104 Suetonius, *The Life of Caesar*, 37

105 Plutarch, *The Life of Caesar*, 52.2-3

106 Plutarch, *The Life of Caesar*, 52.4-5

107 Plutarch, *The Life of Caesar*, 52.6

108 Plutarch, *The Life of Caesar*, 52.7

109 Plutarch, *The Life of Caesar*, 52.8

110 Plutarch, *The Life of Caesar*, 52.9

111 Plutarch, *The Life of Caesar*, 53.4

112 Suetonius, *The Life of Caesar*, 36

113 Plutarch, *The Life of Caesar*, 53.5-6

114 Plutarch, *The Life of Caesar*, 53.7

115 Plutarch, *The Life of Caesar*, 54.2

116 Plutarch, *The Life of Caesar*, 54.3-6

117 Cicero, *Pro Marcello*, 2.7

118 Macrobius, *Saturnalia Conviva*, 3.13

119 Appian, *The Civil War*, 101-102

120 Payne, Robert, *Horizon Ancient Rome*, p121

121 Paterculus, *The Roman History*, 55, 3

122 Suetonius, *The Life of Caesar*, 76

123 Cassius Dio, *Roman History*, 44.7.3

124 Plutarch, *The Life of Caesar*, 60.4

125 Fuller, *Julius Caesar: Man, Soldier and Tyrant*, p302

126 Plutarch, *The Life of Caesar*, 61

127 Plutarch, *The Life of Caesar*, 62.7; Plutarch, *The Life of Brutus*, 8-9

128 Cassius Dio, *Roman History*, 44.13.1-4

129 Nicolaus of Damacus, *Life of Augustus*, 130.19

130 Plutarch, *The Life of Brutus*, 10.4

131 Suetonius, *The Life of Caesar*, 79

132 Plutarch, *The Life of Brutus*, 14.1-3

133 Plutarch, *The Life of Caesar*, 63.7

134 Suetonius, *The Life of Caesar*, 86

135 Cicero, *Pro Marcello*, 8.25

136 Suetonius, *The Life of Caesar*, 81.1-3

137 Plutarch, *The Life of Caesar*, 64.1-5

138 Girling, Richard, *The Sunday Times Magazine*, London, 9 March 2003, pp48-52

139 Suetonius, *The Life of Caesar*, 81.1-3

140 Plutarch, *The Life of Brutus*, 14.4

141 Plutarch, *The Life of Caesar*, 65.1-2

142 Suetonius, *The Life of Caesar*, 81.4

143 Plutarch, *The Life of Brutus*, 17.1

144 Plutarch, *The Life of Caesar*, 66.6

145 Suetonius, *The Life of Caesar*, 81.1

146 Plutarch, *The Life of Caesar*, 66.8

147 Plutarch, *The Life of Caesar*, 66.8

148 Shakespeare, William, *Julius Caesar*, 3,1,77

149 Suetonius, *The Life of Caesar*, 82.2
150 Suetonius, *The Life of Caesar*, 82.2
151 Plutarch, *The Life of Caesar*, 66.14
152 Plutarch, *The Life of Caesar*, 66.9
153 Plutarch, *The Life of Caesar*, 66.10
154 Plutarch, *The Life of Caesar*, 66.13
155 Plutarch, *The Life of Caesar*, 66.2-3
156 Suetonius, *The Life of Caesar*, 82.3
157 Girling, Richard, *The Sunday Times Magazine*, London, 9 March 2003, pp48-52
158 Cassius Dio, *Roman History*, 44.49.1-4
159 Suetonius, *The Life of Caesar*, 84.4
160 Suetonius, *The Life of Caesar*, 85

161 Plutarch, *The Life of Julius Caesar*, 69.1-2
162 Plutarch, *The Life of Caesar*, 69.3
163 Suetonius, *Julius Caesar*, 45-47
164 Catullus, 57
165 Suetonius, *Julius Caesar*, 50-52
166 Plutarch, *The Life of Julius Caesar*, 2.1-7
167 Plutarch, *The Life of Julius Caesar*, 12-13.2
168 Plutarch, *The Life of Julius Caesar*, 17.1-8
169 Cassius Dio, *Roman history* 40.5-6
170 Plutarch, *The Life of Caesar*, 32.1-9

Chronology

Year	Age	Life
102-100		Caesar born in Rome on July 13 to Gaius Caesar and Aurelia.
91	9	Tribunate of Drusus, whose plans to satisfy the Italian allies fails; Drusus assassinated. War breaks out with Italian allies; massacre of Romans at Asculum.
90	10	The 'Social War' begins between Rome and its Italian allies, demanding greater citizenship rights. The rebellion is crushed by Sulla, Marius, and Pompey Strabo, but the allies eventually received enhanced rights. First campaign of young Pompey, Cicero.
88	12	Sulpicius Rufus tribune. Proposal to transfer the Mithridatic command from Sulla to Marius. Sulla marches on Rome with his army; caputres the city; repeals legislation and passes laws strengthening the Senate. Marius escapes. Social War draws to a close. Mithridates overruns Asia Minor, massacres many Romans and Italians; joined by Athens.
87	13	Cinna and Marius occupy Rome; massacre of Sulla's supporters. Sulla lands in Greece and besieges Athens. Carbo consul 87-84. The teenage Caesar is chosen for the lifetime dignity of *flamen dialis* (high priest of Jupiter).
86	14	Marius, elected Consul for the seventh time (with Cinna), dies. Sulla takes Athens, defeats Mithridates' armies. Immediately after election as Consul, Marius dies. Cinna takes control of the Populares against Sulla's faction.
85	15	Sulla negotiates Treaty of Dardanus with Mithridates. Settlement of Asia. Caesar becomes officially a man by assuming the *toga virilis*. His father dies.

Year	Age	Life
84	16	Cinna in power but is later murdered. Caesar weds Cinna's daughter. Carbo remains sole consul.
83	17	Lucius Cornelius Sulla, returning from the eastern Mithridatic War, victorious against the Marian party with the aid of Pompey and Crassus. Massive proscriptions follow. Sulla's legislation returns political power to the Senate; tribunician powers limited. Murena begins Second Mithridatic War.
82	18	Civil War in Italy; Sulla victorious at the battle of the Colline Gate. Massive proscriptions, deaths, property confiscations shake the power structure. Sertorious, last major Marian leader, leaves for Spain. Pompey defeats Sulla's opponents in Sicily; Sulla orders Murena to stop fighting against Mithridates.
81	19	As dictator Sulla reorganised the state and reforms the criminal law. Pompey defeats the Marians in Africa; Sertorius driven from Spain. Sulla hostile against Caesar; Caesar flees Rome. Sulla persuaded to pardon Caesar, who refuses to divorce Cinna's daughter, Cornelia. Sulla impounds Cornelia's dowry and strips Caesar of office of *flamen dialis*. Caesar's only child, daughter Julia, is born.
80	20	Sulla serves as Consul. Sertorius returns to Spain. Caesar leaves Rome for military service with the governor of Asia. At the capture of Mytilene, Caesar wins the *corona civica* (for personal heroism). For the rest of his life he will be awarded public honours (such as being able to wear his laurel crown on all public occasions). He is also permitted to sit in the Senate without age restriction.

Year	Age	Life
79	21	Sulla resigns dictatorship. Sertorious defeats Metellus Pius in Spain.
78	22	Death of Sulla. Lepidus challenges Sulla's constitution. Caesar serves under P. Servilius Isauricus in Cilicia. After Sulla's death, Caesar returns to Rome. He refuses to join Lepidus' insurrection.
77	23	Lepidus defeated by Catulus and Pompey, dies in Sardinia. Pompey appointed against Sertorius in Spain. In Rome, Caesar, as advocate, prosecutes the consular Cn. Cornelius Dolabella for extortion while serving as provincial governor.
76	24	Attempts to restore powers to tribunes. Sertorius successful against Pompey and Metellus.
75	25	Lex Aurelia allows tribunes to hold other offices later. Cicero serves as quaestor in Sicily. Leaving Rome to study rhetoric in Rhodes, Caesar is captured by pirates; his fifty talent ransom takes forty days to raise while he is held captive. Caesar, released, returns and crucifies all the pirates. He then continues on to Rhodes to study under famous rhetorician Apollonius Molon.
74	26	Cyrene made a Roman province. Reinforcements sent to Pompey in Spain. Mithridates invades Bithynia; Lucullus sent against him. On the outbreak of the Mithridatic War, Caesar fights against a royal detachment in Asia province. Returns to Rome. Nicomedes dies, bequeaths Bythinia to Rome.

Year	Age	Life
73	27	Tribune Licius Macer agitates for reform Laws deal with grain distribution. Rising of Spartacus at Capua. Lucullus defeats Mithridates on the Rhyndacus. Caesar joins the Pontifical College.
72	28	Spartacus continues successfully against Roman efforts to destroy revolt. In Spain, Sertorius assassinated; Pompey settles Spain. Lucullus campaigns against Mithridates in Pontus. M. Antonius unsuccessful against Cretan pirates. Caesar serves as military tribune.
71	29	Spartacus defeated by Crassus. Pompey returns from Spain. Lucullus defeats Mithridates who flees to Tigranes.
70	30	Pompey and Crassus elected as consuls; they continue dismantling provisions of Sullan laws.
69	31	Lucullus captures Armenian capital, Tigranocerta. Caesar serves as quaestor under governor of Further Spain. His aunt Julia (wife of Marius) dies; Caesar gives funeral oration, honours Marius and his own descent. Later, Caesar's wife dies.
68	32	Mithridates returns to Pontus.
67	33	Caesar marries Pompeia, granddaughter of Sulla. Votes for Lex Gabinia, to give Pompey total authority to fight piracy in the eastern Mediterranean.

Year	Age	Life
66	34	Pompey destroys piracy in the Mediterranean; his reputation soars. First Catilinarian 'conspiracy'. Cicero, Caesar speaks in favour of the Lex Manilia, giving Pompey unparalleled powers in command of Roman armies against Mithridates.
66-62		Pompey destroys Mithridates, king of Pontus, bringing new territories into the Empire. He completely reorganises the eastern provinces; his reputation is at its height.
65	35	Crassus is censor; works for influence in Spain and Egypt. Pompey campaigns in the Caucasus. Caesar serves as curule aedile with Bibulus. He restores Marius' trophies, formerly removed by Sulla, and gains a reputation for lavish expenditure on games and crowd-pleasing entertainments.
64	36	Pompey victorious in Syria; end of Seleucid monarchy. In the elections, Cataline loses to Cicero for the consulship; some sources suggest Caesar supported Cataline.
63	37	Consulship of Cicero. Caesar triumphs at the polls to win the position of Pontifix Maximus. Birth of Octavian. On 5 December, Caesar's significant speech in the Senate against condemning the Catilinarian conspirators to death without trial. Cato accuses Caesar of foreknowledge of the conspiracy but Cicero supports him. Pompey in Damascus, Jerusalem; end of Hasmonean power. Mithridates dies in the Crimea.
62	38	Defeat and death of Catiline at Pistoia. Caesar elected praetor. Clodius profanes the Bona Dea festival with resulting scandal. Caesar divorces Pompeia for not being 'above suspicion'. Pompey settles the East (including making Syria a province); returns to Italy and dismisses his army in December.

Year	Age	Life
61	39	The Senate opposes Pompey's administrative acts in the East; Pompey holds his Triumph. Trial of Clodius. Caesar proconsul of the province of Further Spain; victorious campaign against the Lusitani which permits him to seek a Triumph in Rome. In Gaul, the Allobroges revolt; the Aedui appeal to Rome for help. Crassus negotiates, unsuccessfully, to reduce tax-farming commitments of the Equites in the east.
60	40	Caesar returns to Rome; Cato filibusters to prevent his standing for the consulship in absentia. Foregoing his Triumph, Caesar enters Rome, stands for office, and wins the Consulship with the support of Caesar and Crassus. The 'First Triumvirate' formed.
59	41	Caesar's turbulent consulship. Land reforms forced through the Senate for Pompey's veterans; Crassus' tax-farming proposals passed. Bibulus retires to 'watch the sky for omens.' Caesar's daughter marries Pompey; Caesar marries Piso's daughter, Calpurnia. Caesar secures Cisalpine Gaul and Illyricum (and, later, further Gaul) as his post-consular province for a five-year term.
58	42	Tribunate of Publius Clodius. Cicero exiled; Cato sent to Cypress which is annexed. Caesar moves against the Helvetii and Ariovistus in the first battles of the Gallic Wars.
57	43	Rioting in Rome between Clodius and Milo. Cicero is recalled in September. Pompey concerned with food supply. Caesar campaigns against the Belgii; all northern Gaul apparently pacified.

Year	Age	Life
56	44	The Triumvirate in disarray; Cicero attacks the land-reform law Caesar passed during his consulship. Caesar meets with Pompey and Crassus at Lucca in April to renew power sharing. Caesar's term in Gaul to be extended. Pompey and Crassus will stand, again, for the Consulship. Caesar campaigns against rebellious tribes in Brittany and Normandy as well as the Aquitani. Cato returns from Cypress.
55	45	Second consulship of Pompey and Crassus; law passed prolonging Caesar's proconsulship for five years with new commands for both Consuls.Caesar campaigns against the Usipetes and Tencteri. First crossing of the Rhine into Germany; first, renconnaissance mission to Britain. Historic thanksgivings voted to Caesar by the Senate.
54	46	Pompey remains near Rome, governing Spain through subordinates. Rioting in Rome. Caesar returns to Britain, spending the winter in Gaul. Ambiorix destroys fifteen cohorts. Winter quarters of the legate Q. Cicero besieged; relieved by Caesar. Labienus campaigns against the Treveri. Death in childbirth of Caesar's daughter, Julia, wife of Pompey; Caesar's mother, Aurelia, also dies. Crassus, in Syria, prepares for Parthian campaign.
53	47	Continued rioting in Rome; no consuls can be elected until July. Caesar undertakes punitive expeditions against the rebellious tribes; second Rhine crossing. The Eburones are exterminated; Ambiorix escapes. On June 9, in Mesopotamia, Crassus loses the battle of Carrhae and his life.

Year	Age	Life

52   48   In January, Publius Clodius murdered by Milo. Disorder in Rome; Pompey elected 'consul without a colleague' on 25 February. Serves alone until order is restored in August. Caesar negotiates from Ravenna and, by the law, of the ten tribunes, is permitted to stand for the consulship in 49 in absentia. The Gallic confederacy formed under Vercingetorix; Gaul breaks into open rebellion. Caesar captures Avaricum, has to abandon the siege of Vergovia, is victorious in the neighborhood of Dijon, surrounds Vercingetorix in Alesia, repels the attempt of the combined Celtic levies to relieve him. Vercingetorix surrenders.

51   49   Optimates attacks on Caesar, who gains support of Curio. Parthia invades Syria; Cicero sent as governor to Cilicia. Death of Ptolemy Auletes; Ptolemy XIII marries Cleopatra; joint rulers in Egypt. Caesar completes pacification of Gaul; surrender of Uxellodunum with multilation of rebellious prisoners. Caesar begins political reorganisation of the province from Nemotocenna (Arras). Probable publication of his Gallic commentaries. In Rome, Marcellus attempts to prematurely recall Caesar from his command.

50   50   In Rome the optimates continue their efforts to recall Caesar and bring him to trial. The tribune, C. Curio, prevents the passing of a decree against Caesar by imposition of the tribunician veto. Curio proposes that both Caesar and Pompey disarm; vetoed. Pompey asked by consul Marcellus to save the State (November). In December, Curio's term expires; Antony takes over as Caesar's leading tribune. Pompey refuses to compromise. Civil War looms. Caesar continues to negotiate to avoid losing his imperium while still running for the Consulship for 48 *in absentia*.

Year	Age	Life
49	51	On 7 January, the Senate decrees that Caesar must dismiss his army by an appointed day and, despite tribunician veto, grants Pompey and the other magistrates state authority. Caesar crosses Rubicon during the night of 10 January and, with one legion, begins moving towards Rome. On 21 February, Corfinium surrenders with little resistance; on 17 March, Pompey abandons Italy and crosses to the Balkan peninsula. On 2 August, Pompey's Army in Nearer Spain surrenders to Caesar following battle of Ilerda; the souther Spanish province follows. Massilia surrenders to Caesar after a six-months' siege. Caesar is elected dictator and, during 11-day term, passes emergency legislation.
48	52	Caesar gives up the dictatorship, elected to second consulship with Publius Servilius Isauricus. Crossing the Adriatic, he surrounds Pompey at Dyrrhachium in April; Pompey breaks through the siege line in July. Caesar withdraws towards Thessaly. On 9 August, Caesar defeats Pompey at Pharsalus. Pompey flees to Egypt, Caesar in pursuit. On 28 September, prior to Caesar's arrival, Pompey is murdered by ministers of the Pharoah in Egypt. Caesar arrives and occupies Alexandria, where his small force is besieged by Ptolemy's hostile forces. Meets and supports Cleopatra in her quest for rule of Egypt.

Year	Age	Life
47	53	Caesar again appointed dictator, this time for one year in absentia. Antony, his Master of the Horse, maintains order in Italy. In March, Caesar's forces relieved by reinforcements from Asia Minor; on 27 March, he is victorious in battle on the Nile. Death of Ptolemy. Caesar installs Cleopatra as Queen and cruises the Nile. Pharnaces of Bosporus defeats Roman army under Domitius Calvinus in Pontus. In early June, Caesar leaves Egypt, moves against the king of Pontus, Pharnaces II (Mithridates' son). On August 1, defeats Pharnaces at Zela, saying: 'I came, I saw, I conquered'. At the beginning of October, Caesar arrives in Rome, further legislative reforms including reorganisation of debt laws. On 28 December, Caesar and his legions return to the coast of Africa to defeat the remaining Pompeian forces. Since 48, the optimates have been collecting armies in the African Province. Cleopatra bears Caesar a son, nicknamed Caesarion.
46	54	Caesar elected Consul for the third time, serving with Lepidus. On 6 April, Caesar victorious at Battle of Thapsus, defeating Scipio and Juba. Suicide of Cato. On 25 July, Caesar returns to Rome where he is appointed to his third dictatorship, this time for a ten-year term. In Spain, the sons of Pompey renew the war. Caesar completes further legislation including reform of the calendar, adding additional days to this year to bring the solar calendar into alignment. Leaves Rome for Spain in the middle of November.

Year	Age	Life

45   55   Caesar serves as his fourth consulship (without a co-consul).
On 17 March, Caesar victorious at Munda; after
administrative reforms, he returns to Rome in October.
The Senate votes extravagant decrees in his honour,
including dictatorship for life and divine worship. Caesar's
images begin to appear on coinage. In the autumn, Caesar
makes preparations for a campaign in Parthia the next year
and makes his will, appointing his great-nephew, Octavian,
as his primary heir, allegedly adopting him as his son.

---

44   On 15 February, Caesar appears at the Lupercalia as
dictator perpetuus (for life), in the dress of the ancient
kings of Rome; refuses the diadem of kingship offered by
new co-consul Mark Antony, along with the title of king.
Announces he will leave Rome for Parthia on 18 March.
Sixty Republicans, led by Brutus and Cassius, join in
conspiracy to murder him. On the Ides of March (15
March), attending the Senate for the last time, Caesar is
stabbed to death. His last words, to Brutus, in Greek, were
'and you too, child?' Octavian returns from Greece.
Antony receives command in Cisalpine and Transalpine
Gaul. Cicero's first Phillipic against Antony.

---

43   Antony's siege of Mutina raised; deaths of consuls Hirtius
and Pansa. D. Brutus killed in Gaul. Octavian declared
consul in August. Triumvirate of Octavian, Antony and
Lepidus (November). Proscriptions; death of Cicero. Brutus
in Macedonia and Cassius in Syria raising armies.

---

42   Julius Caesar deified. Sextus Pompeius controls Sicily.
Brutus and Cassius are defeated at Philippi in October;
both commit suicide.

Sources and Further Reading

There are not a lot of contemporary accounts of the life of Julius Caesar, which leaves the field open for Caesar himself to tell the story in his *The Gallic Wars*, *The Civil Wars* and *The Alexandrian, African and Spanish Wars* all published in the Loeb Classical Library series. Text of these classic translations are now available on the internet. Caesar wrote these works for propaganda purposes, but as none of his failures led to total disasters he did not have to be too economical with the truth. On the other hand, the opportunity for self-advertisement these books provided allowed him to establish himself a reputation as a great general that endures to this day.

The Roman statesmen Marcus Tullius Cicero, an opponent of Caesar during the Civil War, was also around at the time and left a partial account in his letters which run to six volumes in the Loeb Classical Library. But he had little to report during the early years when Caesar was in Spain, or during the year when Cicero was governor of the province of Cilicia in Asia Minor in 51BC. One of his most frequent correspondents was Titus Pomponius Atticus, but when they were both in Rome together, the letters naturally dry up. However, we get from Cicero a first-hand account of what it was like to meet Caesar.

It was more than a century after his death that classical historians got down to work on the life Julius Caesar. In the second century AD, Plutarch wrote his *Life of Caesar* in *Parallel Lives*. Then came Suetonius's biography, written during the reign of the

Emperor Hadrian. This is the source of most of the sensational gossip. Appian wrote an account of the Civil War in his *Roman History* during the reign of Hadrian's successor Antonius Pius. The Roman administrator and historian Cassius Dio wrote *Romaika*, an eighty-volume history of Rome written in Greek, during the reign of Alexander Severus in the third century. Much of it has been lost but the part covering the period of Caesar's life after 69 BC survives, though it has not been established what sources he used. There are, of course, a large number of secondary sources:

Appian, *Roman History*, trans Horace White (Heinemann, London, 1912) – early account of Caesar and the Civil War.

Brunt, P.A., *Social Conflicts in the Roman Republic* (Chatto and Windus, London, 1971) – the standard academic text on the fall of the Roman Republic.

Caesar, Gaius Julius, *The Alexandrian, African and Spanish Wars*, trans A.G. Way (Harvard University Press, Cambridge, Massachusetts, 1955) – Caesar's own account of how he pacified the Roman world.

Caesar, Gaius Julius, *The Civil War*, trans A.G. Peskett (Harvard University Press, Cambridge, Massachusetts, 1951) – Caesar's own account of how he took unrivalled power in the Roman world.

Caesar, Gaius Julius, *The Gallic War*, trans H.J. Edwards (Harvard University Press, Cambridge, Massachusetts, 1986) – Caesar's own account of how he expanded the Roman writ to the north and became a great general into the bargain.

Cicero, Marcus Tullius, *Letters to Atticus*, trans D.R. Shackleton Bailey (Harvard University Press, Cambridge, Massachusetts, 1999) – Cicero's letter to his long-standing friend the Roman knight Titus Pomponius Atticus who spent much of his life in Athens, to escape the Civil War and the troubles in Rome. He later became an historian and wrote an account of Cicero's consulship.

Cicero, Marcus Tullius, *Letters to Friends*, trans D.R. Shackleton Bailey (Harvard University Press, Cambridge, Massachusetts, 1999) – Shackleton Bailey's standard Latin text with an updated version of his earlier Penguin English translation.

Crawford, M and Beard, M, *Rome in the Later Republic: Problems and Interpretations* (Duckworth, London, 1999) – an academic discussion of the problems of discovering what was really happening during the period.

Crook, J.A., Lintott, Andrew and Rawson, Elizabeth (eds) *The Cambridge Ancient History: Volume IX – The Last Age of the Roman Republic*, 146-43 BC (Cambridge University Press, Cambridge, 1994) – the standard account of the period.

Dando-Collins, Stephen, *Caesar's Legions: The Epic Saga of Julius Caesar's Elite Tenth Legion and the Armies of Rome* (John Wiley & Sons, New York, 2002) – the story of the fighting men who carried Julius Caesar to glory.

Dodge, Theodore Ayrault, *Caesar* (Stackpole Books, Mechanicsburg, Pennsylvania, 1995) – a soldier's view of Julius Caesar's military campaigns.

Ellis, Peter Perresford, *Caesar's Invasion of Britain* (Orbis, London, 1978) – a lively and illustrated account of Julius Caesar's sojourn on British soil by an expert on Celtic life.

Fuller, Major General J.F.C., *Julius Caesar: Man, Soldier and Tyrant* (Eyre and Spottiswoode, London, 1965) – Caesar assessed by one of the major military theorists of the twentieth century.

Grant, Michael, Caesar (Weidenfeld and Nicholson, London, 1974) – a definitive account of Caesar's life in Weidenfeld's 'Great Lives . . .' series by the professor of humanity at the University and one of the English languages leading classicists.

Gelzer, Matthias, *Caesar: Politician and Statesman*, trans Peter

Needham (Basil Blackwell, Oxford, 1968) – Caesar assessed from a political point of view by a leading German academic.

Grant, Michael, *Julius Caesar* (M. Evans & Company, New York, 1969) – Short and pithy account of the life of the great man.

Gruen, Erich S., *The Last Generation of the Roman Republic* (University of California Press, Berkeley, 1995) – an exhaustive account of Roman politics and government of the period.

Jiménez, Ramon L. *Caesar Against the Celts* (Spellmount, Staplehurst, Kent, 1996) – how Caesar destroyed the Celtic world.

Jiménez, Ramon L. *Caesar Against Rome – The Great Roman Civil War* (Praeger, Westport, Connecticut, 2000) – how Caesar destroyed the republic.

Kahn, Arthur D., *The Education of Julius Caesar – A Biography, A Reconstruction* (Schocken Books, New York, 1986) – a well sourced account of the development of Julius Caesar.

Meier, Christian, *Caesar*, trans Peter Jones (1995; Folio Society, London, 1998) – an academic assessment of Caesar originally published in German.

McCullough, Colleen, *Caesar's Women* (Century, London, 1996) – how Julius Caesar used women to further his political ambitions.

Parenti, Michael, *The Assassination of Julius Caesar – A People's History of Ancient Rome* (The New Press, New York, 2003) – an attempt to look the death of Caesar from the point of view of the mob.

Plutarch of Chaeronea, *The Lives of Noble Grecians and Romans*, trans John Dryden (Encyclopaedia Britannica, Chicago, 1990) – although written a hundred years after the even, Plutarch is acknowledged as one of the best-read men in the ancient world.

Richard, Carl J., *Twelve Greeks and Romans Who Changed the World* (Rowman & Littlefield, Lanham, Maryland, 2003) – Julius Caesar set among his piers.

Sabben-Clare, J. (ed) *Caesar and Roman Politics 60-50 BC: source material in translation* (Oxford University Press, Oxford, 1971)

– the real deal for academics who want to go back to basics.

Shotter, David C., *The Fall of the Roman Republic* (Routledge, London, 1994) – a short account of the republic's last gasp.

Smith, Richard E., *The Failure of the Roman Republic* (Cambridge University Press, Cambridge, 1955) – although the Roman republic last for nearly five hundred years, how it did, at last, falter.

Southern, Pat, *Julius Caesar* (Tempus, Stroud, Gloucestershire, 2001) – a whistle-stop tour of the life of Julius Caesar.

Suetonis, *The Twelve Caesars*, trans Robert Graves (1957; Penguin, London, 1979) – classical writer and civil servant writing during the reign of Hadrian gives the inside story on the first twelve Caesars with a special emphasis on racy gossip.

Syme, Ronald, *The Roman Revolution* (Oxford University Press, Oxford, 2002) – a reprint of Syme's exhaustive 1939 text on the fall of the Roman republic.

Taylor, Lily Ross, *Party Politics in the Age of Caesar* (University of California Press, Berkeley, 1949) – the classic account of the political manoeuvrings that brought down the Roman republic.

Velleius Paterculus, *The Caesarian and Augustan Narrative* (Cambridge University Press, Cambridge, 1983) – an account of the history of Julius Caesar and Caesar Augustus written by a Roman soldier, statesman and historian during the reign of Tiberius. The text is explained in a detailed commentary by distinguished classicist A.J. Woodman of the University of Leeds.

Welch, Kathryn and Powel, Anton (eds), *Julius Caesar as Artful Reporter: The War Commentaries as Political Instruments* (Duckworth, London, 1998) – nine distinguished classical academics discuss Julius Caesar's Gallic Wars and its value as propaganda.

Yavetz, Zwi, *Julius Caesar and His Public Image* (Thames and Hudson, London, 1983) – re-examining Caesar as the master of spin.

Wedsites

http://penelope.uchicago.edu/Thayer/E/Roman/Texts/ – This site provides public domain translations of Appian, Cassius Dio, Velleius Paterculus, Suetonius's Twelve Caesars and Plutarch's *Parallel Lives* – including the lives of Julius Caesar, Mark Antony, Brutus, Crassus and Pompey.

http://classics.mit.edu/ – MIT's Internet Classics library carries the text of 441 classics from the ancient world, including Julius Caesar's *The Gallic Wars*, *The Civil Wars*, *The Alexandrian Wars*, *The African Wars* and *The Spanish Wars*.

Picture Sources

The author and the publishers wish to express their thanks to the following sources of illustrative material and/or permission to reproduce it. They will make proper acknowledgements in future editions in the even that any omissions have occurred.

The Art Archive: p. 1; akg-images: pp. 11, 16, 22, 43, 45, 47, 103, 105; Getty Images: p. 65; Mary Evans Picture Library: pp. 9, 29, 50, 90; Topham Picturepoint: pp. i, ii, 15, 31, 73, 82, 97, 107, 111.

Index

Alexander the Great
by Nigel Cawthorne
'moves through the career at a brisk,
dependable canter in his pocket
biography for Haus.'
BOYD TONKIN, *The Independent*
ISBN 1-904341-56-X (pb) £9.99

Armstrong
by David Bradbury
'it is a fine and well-researched
introduction'
GEORGE MELLY *Daily Mail*
ISBN 1-904341-46-2 (pb) £8.99

Bach
by Martin Geck
'The production values of the book
are exquisite.' *Guardian*
ISBN 1-904341-16-0 (pb) £8.99
ISBN 1-904341-35-7 (hb) £12.99

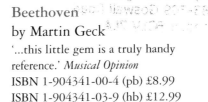

Beethoven
by Martin Geck
'...this little gem is a truly handy reference.' *Musical Opinion*
ISBN 1-904341-00-4 (pb) £8.99
ISBN 1-904341-03-9 (hb) £12.99

Bette Davis
by Laura Moser
'The author compellingly unearths the complex, self-destructive woman that lay beneath the steely persona of one of the best-loved actresses of all time.'
ISBN 1-904341-48-9 (pb) £9.99

Bevan
by Clare Beckett
and Francis Beckett
"Haus, the enterprising new imprint, adds another name to its list of short biographies ... a timely contribution.'
GREG NEALE, *BBC History*
ISBN 1-904341-63-2 (pb) £9.99

Brahms
by Hans A Neunzig
'These handy volumes fill a gap in the market for readable, comprehensive and attractively priced biographies admirably.'
JULIAN HAYLOCK, *Classic fm*
ISBN 1-904341-17-9 (pb) £8.99

Caravaggio
by Patrick Hunt

'a first-class, succinct but comprehensive, introduction to the artist'
BRIAN TOVEY *The Art Newspaper*
ISBN 1-904341-73-X (pb) £9.99
ISBN 1-904341-74-8 (hb) £12.99

Roger Casement
by Angus Mitchell

'hot topic' *The Irish Times*
ISBN 1-904341-41-1 (pb) £8.99

Curie
by Sarah Dry

'... this book could hardly be bettered'
New Scientist
selected as
Outstanding Academic Title by *Choice*
ISBN 1-904341-29-2 (pb) £8.99

Dali
by Linde Salber

'a fascinating view on this flamboyant artist, the central and most excentric figure in Surrealism, seen through the prism of psychological analysis'
ISBN 1-904341-75-6 (pb) £9.99

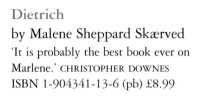

Dietrich
by Malene Sheppard Skærved
'It is probably the best book ever on
Marlene.' CHRISTOPHER DOWNES
ISBN 1-904341-13-6 (pb) £8.99

Dostoevsky
by Richard Freeborn
'wonderful ... a learned guide'
JOHN CAREY *The Sunday Times*
ISBN 1-904341-27-6 (pb) £8.99

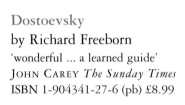

Dvořák
by Kurt Honolka
'This book seems really excellent to me.'
SIR CHARLES MACKERRAS
ISBN 1-904341-52-7 (pb) £9.99

Einstein
by Peter D Smith
'Concise, complete, well-produced and
lively throughout, ... a bargain at the
price.' *New Scientist*
ISBN 1-904341-14-4 (hb) £12.99
ISBN 1-904341-15-2 (pb) £8.99

Gershwin
by Ruth Leon
'Musical theatre aficionados will relish
Ruth Leon's GERSHWIN, a succinct
but substantial account of the great composer's
life'
MICHAEL ARDITTI, *The Independent*
ISBN 1-904341-23-3 (pb) £9.99

Johnson
by Timothy Wilson Smith
'from a prize-winning author a biography
of the famous and perennially fascinating
figure, Samuel Johnson'
ISBN 1-904341-81-0 (pb) £9.99

Joyce
by Ian Pindar
'I enjoyed the book very much, and
much approve of this skilful kind of pop-
ularisation. It reads wonderfully well.'
TERRY EAGLETON
ISBN 1-904341-58-6 (pb) £9.99

Kafka
by Klaus Wagenbach
'one of the most useful books on Kafka
ever published.' New Scientist
ISBN 1-904341-01-2 (hb) £12.99
ISBN 1-904341-02-0 (pb) £8.99